TRUE WEST

TRUE WEST

MYTH AND MENDING
ON THE FAR SIDE OF AMERICA

BETSY GAINES QUAMMEN

TORREY HOUSE PRESS

Salt Lake City • Torrey

First Torrey House Press Edition, October 2023
Copyright © 2023 by Betsy Gaines Quammen

Published by Torrey House Press
Salt Lake City, Utah
www.torreyhouse.org

International Standard Book Number: 978-1-948814-87-4
E-book ISBN: 978-1-948814-88-1
Library of Congress Control Number: 2022951321

Cover design by Kathleen Metcalf and Will Neville-Rehbehn
Interior design by Rachel Buck-Cockayne
Distributed to the trade by Consortium Book Sales and Distribution

Torrey House Press offices in Salt Lake City sit on the homelands of Ute, Goshute, Shoshone, and Paiute nations. Offices in Torrey are on the homelands of Southern Paiute, Ute, and Navajo nations.

To David. Endless thank yous.

Contents

Introduction

THE SUMMER OF 2021 WAS SO DRY THAT PATTY AND Tom Agnew, my rancher friends in Big Timber, Montana, had to send their cows to Nebraska. Couldn't feed them on the dry range of Sweet Grass County. Everything was thirsty. Mornings carried a tang of campfire, smoke from catastrophic fires scorching hundreds of thousands of acres of forest. Things felt wrong—there was a smoldering and parched anxiety in the air. Around town, familiar mountains were held hostage by smog, only faint outlines hinting their existence. Rivers ran well below high-water marks and rocks jutted from ripples like ribcages. Hay was selling at a premium during this stingy season. Little water, little irrigation, little feed, and high prices. Fishing restrictions hamstrung anglers as the warming of streams stressed trout. On summer days that should have been sunny and mild, the hot air was heavy with burning. Extended drought throughout the West was squeezing agricultural and recreational industries, pressuring wildlife habitat, and creating an unshakable sense of foreboding for many of us who call this place home.

I remember an ice-cream truck that summer, winding slowly down the block. A tinny song blasted through a blown speaker as the cheerfully painted Chevrolet, or maybe a Ford, emerged from gauzy haze. No kids came running and the carnival tunes just hung over the empty street like the smoke. Montana summers, sun-dappled and sweet-smelling, the ones we dream of for eight months each year, had curdled. On that stifling afternoon, a creepy ice-cream truck announced the season. Not summer, but fire.

This book began with the drought. A year later things were underwater. Montana saw a thousand-year historic flood come to the Yellowstone River, washing out bridges, roads, and homes. The Gardiner entrance to Yellowstone National Park and the Beartooth Highway were forced to close due to excessive rains, rapid snowmelt, and violent erosion. In the pre-Civil War spiritual "O Mary, Don't You Weep," God promised Noah a new version of apocalypse, not a repetition: *No more water / The fire next time.* But now we are facing both. From fire to flood, the West is wracked by natural phenomena made so much worse in this age of rapid climate change.

On a rare cool evening, my pal Kris Ellingsen remarked on the weird crossroads we stand before. She and her partner, Pete, have lived for years in what was once an old bawdy house, next to a longtime popular steak joint and dance hall, known as Stacey's, a restaurant that at one time called to bronc riders on the rodeo circuit and maybe, on occasion, still might. Now it's mostly filled with tourists coming to eat after a day spent bumper-to-bumper on giant rafts floating the Madison and Gallatin Rivers or cruising ski slopes at the exorbitantly priced Big Sky Resort nearby. Ellingson grew up along the plains and mountains of Montana, and for a long time has seen folks come West with wild expectations—drawn by various booms, from oil to ore, that have pulled at those willing to work hard for good money, before operations inevitably go bust. Those incoming waves include not just the working class, but also monied folk who have come for hobby ranches and fortified retreats, to dabble at cowboying and nibble at nature. Climbers, skiers, kayakers, anglers, mountain bikers, and various other adventurers arrive determined to rip, shred, bag, and slay in various and sundry ways. It's as if the land is prey, butchered and consumed through recreation, extraction, and acquisition. The glories of this landscape, its resources, its stories, and the assorted perceptions of it, have made the West a mythic place, decorated with fictions and burdened with untenable expectations.

The West has changed much in my years of living here, and lately it's hard to keep up. The region has become ever hotter, drier, angrier, and more politically polarized. More people have moved here. COVID-19 refugees flooded western towns, some seeking medical freedoms, others wishing for some rumored palliative effects of desert and mountain air. Wealthy arrivistes grabbed up their corners of mountain paradises nestled next to federal lands, driving up prices and making it impossible for the working class, and even professionals, to buy homes. Christian nationalists bought up religious homeland and real estate agents reaped the spoils of a sudden, steep influx of newcomers lured by dreams of separatism and hyper-freedom. Politics, communities, and neighborly tenor have changed. In my town, trucks and cars now roar by, emblazoned with Gadsden flags—the "DON'T TREAD ON ME" emblem—like a middle finger raised to the community through which they pass. The flag's design is also available on popular Montana license plates. I wonder how many drivers realize that the coiled rattler they paid for, then screwed to the bumper of their Subaru, raises funds for an organization actively supporting the Federalist Society, a group actively working to take away women's rights.

The West is a place of diverse stories, symbols, and signals—and inescapable myths. There is the perception of profuse liberty, copious machismo, untrammeled wilderness, rugged individualism, discovered and "free" lands, cowboy heroics, blank slates, conquered spaces, reliable rain that "follows" tilling into arid lands, and enduring frontier. These myths continue to wind through ways of seeing this place and its peoples, creating hurdles in caring for the environment and communities. Further gumming the works, an onslaught of misinformation has attached itself to western myth in the last few years, leaving outright lies embedded in western legends. People have built their own versions of truth on altars tumbling to pieces, disregarding the limits of land, vulnerable people, unique cultures, and the essentiality of relationships. Right now, there is too much being asked of the West. It sits between history and expectation—a place saddled with hopes that it can't fulfill.

This is a book that ponders the West as a museum of western myths. To explain what I mean by that, let's first consider the meaning of "myth." The word comes from ancient Greek, but traditional stories already existed before the Hellenic empire was established. Such stories are foundational to human communities and their cultures, building a common understanding of gods and divine endeavor, the creation of the world, the meaning of pivotal events, shared sacred values, and the iconography that expresses all those things. Those stories—perpetuated through time as cultural myths—influence ways of understanding and patterns of behavior. The word "museum" also comes from a Greek word, *Mouseion*. In Greek mythology, muses are goddesses that inspired museums—collections of art, literature, and music, enshrining ideas that onlookers come to regard as revelations of truth.

So, let's look at how myths are both understood and entwined into culture. There are sacred stories or origin stories, such as Genesis, Hesiod's *Theogony,* and the Southern Paiute belief that their god Tabuts scattered his people from his torn sack onto the very best western lands. There are supernatural tales and preternatural legends about skinwalkers, zombies, vampires, and ghosts, which can't be verified but persist in popular telling and retelling. There are narratives recognized as historical or semi-historical, involving the Alamo, Christopher Columbus or Jesse James, and neo-scriptural accounts embraced by a corps of believers, such as the account of prophet Joseph Smith being visited by Moroni and later finding the golden plates that members of the Church of Jesus Christ of Latter-Day Saints understand to contain what became the modern *Book of Mormon.* Some myths are built upon defining historical moments, like ideas of American exceptionalism, broadly held, that surrounded the signing of the US Constitution. These proved foundational to other myths, such as Manifest Destiny and the ever-expanding frontier.

Although I will touch upon each of these kinds of myth, what I do in this book is examine what happens when broad and bogus beliefs are affixed to the American West. Myth thus understood as an accepted but deceptive belief, leads us to what I've come to consider a museum of toxic myths—a great cultural hall of follies based on misconceptions. The mythmakers I've focused on, unlike Greek muses, have promoted reckless ideas, bringing the West to a lurching instability, like a Conestoga wagon on a mountain trail, wobbling in dangerous directions. There are tall tales piled atop fabrications, seeping into memory, falsifying history, and turning caricature into grievous miscalculation.

Through a series of conversations and stories, *True West* will take you through this myth museum. Along the way, it will show how such myths distort our relations with one another and with this place. Each chapter takes on a myth, or myths, and highlights how people are either inspired or aggrieved. We'll see how ideas around Manifest Destiny, the frontier, a pursuit of homeland, *terra nullius,* and biblical literalism affect the culture and communities of the West, as they reel from pandemic, polarization, climate change, and distortions that come through AM radio, social media, and Sunday services.

"You have to know the past to understand the present," Carl Sagan once pointed out. In that spirit, I turned to this idea that the West is a museum of myths. I understand, yes, that the idea of a museum is complicated. Some of the world's most famous museums are storehouses for bloody plunder, stolen during slaving raids and other brutal acts of colonization. Human bones and sacred objects lie in basements, or even on display, awaiting repatriation. I cannot and will not defend this. But I do not fully repudiate museums; after all, they are shrines for muses, both good and bad ones. This concept is useful in telling this story of myths. And, to speak personally for a moment, I have a relationship with museums. They played a huge role in my own childhood and helped me better understand the world.

I grew up obsessed with natural history and coveted nothing more than giant collections of pinned beetles, sparkling rows of polished gems, and skeletons of *T. rex* and stegosauruses. As a high school student in the 1980s, I even did taxidermy for my city's natural history museum, cutting open feathered bodies of birds that had died crashing into windows. Carefully I'd work skin from flesh, rubbing cornmeal into the raw parts of blue jays, doves, sparrows, and cardinals to loosen the bonds, stuffing body cavities with cotton, then lacing them with thread. To a dyslexic kid like me, there was something revelatory about such tangible realities. Cabinets of curiosities didn't blur into unreadable words, but instead stood immobile and easier for me to interpret. The lessons from the unmoving moved me.

In addition to stuffing the bodies of familiar animals, I spent many of my most formative moments in the presence of a certain long-dead bird, one individual of a species vanished from this planet. When summer rainstorms pounded the slick, black pavement of the Cincinnati Zoo where I volunteered from ages eight to eighteen, I'd race for a Japanese pagoda. Once an aviary, it is a museum for Martha, the last passenger pigeon. In that pagoda, with hair dripping and clothes sodden, I waited out weather amid memorabilia commemorating Martha's life and death. During her twenty-nine years, she had suffered from a palsy that led to a slight shaking. She never laid a fertile egg. She died in Cincinnati on September 1, 1914, and, decades later, I spent my childhood with her ghost. So many hours I sheltered in this beautiful building, drenched, solitary, and lonely for a bird whose population was once so vast that its flocks, in flight, eclipsed the sun. It was—still is—hard to imagine that this species, once so prolific, has completely disappeared. This museum was a key to understanding something profound—the utter desolation of extinction. Martha's simple monument is a good one. However, things become troublesome when unjustified ideas are institutionalized: when myths beget reality. Some forty years after my time spent with Martha, I am preoccupied with the myth that killed her, that of inexhaustive abundance, justifying relentless plunder, that haunts the West—and the wider world. This myth denies a reality that shakes me to my core: extinction.

—   —   —

MYTHS HAVE BECKONED THROUGHOUT WESTERN HISTORY. Newcomers have wandered Native lands for centuries to find riches, get healthy, chase adrenaline, and grab land—all inspired by myths. This is a place set in the sights of outsiders since Coronado reared his helmeted head in 1540, unsuccessfully searching for gold in the southern realms of the Rocky Mountains. He went back to Mexico emptyhanded, claiming land for God and king.

Other Spaniards came after him, variously motivated, equipped, and armed, with horses, lances, and a Christian deity. The Spanish conquistador Francisco Vázquez de Coronado y Luján sought the fabled Seven Golden Cities of Cibola, coming upon the Colorado River on his journey from Mexico. Fifty years later, Juan de Oñate grabbed what is today New Mexico, taxing, enslaving, and murdering Native people while granting their lands to settlers. Oñate also forced the religious conversion of Indigenous people, repeating the pattern of forced cultural assimilation throughout Mexico and Central and South America. Santa Fe was established in 1610. In 1776, while American founding fathers were busy with revolution and a final ratification of the Declaration of Independence, Spanish friars Escalante and Dominguez sought a route from Santa Fe to a mission in Monterrey. Though unsuccessful, with the help of Ute guides whom the priests named Silvestre and Joaquin, Escalante and Dominguez helped establish what would become known as the Old Spanish Trail, inviting further colonization of lands fiercely defended by Indigenous nations. As the Spanish sought to conquer territory, they brought with them, along with disease, the myth of discovery.

This idea of discovery is completely fraught. No, the West wasn't discovered by white men because it was already inhabited by nations of Indigenous people. Nonetheless, the 1493 Doctrine of Discovery, as codified in a papal bull issued by Pope Alexander VI, declared that any land not occupied by Christians and thus "discovered" by Christians was their land, making conquest over non-Christians legit, at least according to colonizers. The Doctrine gave basis to Thomas Jefferson's Corps of Discovery mission, around 300 years after Europeans arrived in the Americas. Lewis and Clark, like Christopher Columbus, discovered nothing that wasn't already known and already inhabited during their traipse over the lands of the Louisiana Purchase. Still, they laid claim to it. This act was later legalized by the American Supreme Court in 1823 in *Johnson v. M'Intosh*, which held that "on the discovery of this immense continent, the great nations of Europe were eager to appropriate to themselves so much of it as they could respectively acquire. Its vast extent offered an ample field to the ambition and enterprise of all." The justices further contended "the character and religion of its inhabitants afforded an apology for considering them as a people over whom the superior genius of Europe might claim an ascendency." According to the Supreme Court, "ample compensation" was offered to the Native people "by bestowing on them civilization and Christianity, in exchange for unlimited independence." This is the justification for the West's myth of Manifest Destiny: unfettered expansion in exchange for civilizing, missioning, and assimilating. As Don Snow, my droll former professor at University of Montana and later a Senior Lecturer of Environmental Humanities at Whitman College, says of western myths, "I'm fond of pointing out to people on my Lewis and Clark history tours that Jefferson did not purchase land with the famous transaction over 'Louisiana'; what he purchased from France, and knew it, were the discovery rights to that massive territory." It wasn't land that America bought. It was a privilege, a claim, sold from one white Christian dominion to another. Discovery was the idea that Christians were more entitled to resources than others.

Next came the myth of *terra nullius*, land free and yours for the taking. Wrong. In fact, the West has never been an empty place, with land free. It was occupied by peoples for thousands and thousands of years before Europeans began their conquering campaigns. Footprints found in New Mexico's White Sands National Park indicate that Native people have walked out here for twenty-one thousand to twenty-three thousand years, though stories from Indigenous traditions refer to their presence on these lands since time immemorial. For millennia, peoples created various communities, governments, rituals, and patterns of daily life.

As decades wore on, America acquired more land from Mexico in 1857, and a young government funded further scouting missions to map the West and scour it for resources. Their motives stood in grave contrast to those of Native peoples, who typically experienced lands, wildlife, and humans as inextricably linked and most certainly not commodities. So-called mountain men had already swept in to trap and kill beaver to near extinction, carrying with them the same myth that killed Martha's fellow passenger pigeons—the notion of infinite abundance. Gold rushes drew more folks westward, piqued by ideas of God's bounty, vast riches, and easy lucre—also inaccurate. Miners moved into Colorado, Dakota, and Montana territories to claim their fortunes and often lived in misery, eking out an existence in dingy, overcrowded mining towns. Most never laid hands on any viable claims, let alone big money. As more and more people sought livelihoods on these mythic "frontiers," miners in Utah and Nevada territories mixed, not always happily, with members of the Church of Jesus Christ of Latter-day Saints (LDS), who arrived in the Great Basin after their arduous journey along trails west, chasing the dream of a land promised by their founding prophet, Joseph Smith. Seeking religious freedom to practice polygamy and theocracy, the Saints, as they styled themselves, under the leadership of Brigham Young, set their sights on establishing a western empire, Deseret. Though that idea was never fully realized, today's LDS communities throughout the West still embrace Young's myth of Zion, the Mormon homeland.

Beginning in the late 1860s, cattle drives from Texas imported southern ideologies and Confederate sympathies that annealed readily with western frontier individualism. Dust-covered men guided unpredictable and jittery herds across broad plains and introduced the ubiquitous western icon, the cowboy. This myth of a morally upright, range-riding hero, who at his core embodied American values, was a tale spun about men who in actuality were generally young drifters, often short on cash and thirsty for whiskey, serving as the paid hands of cattle barons, many of whom were European.

In the years after the Civil War, skilled veterans moved out to the frontier to fight in the Indian Wars. Black cavalry troops, known as buffalo soldiers, rode with other former Union and Confederate fighters, employing Civil War weaponry to battle Native warriors who fought to beat back an onslaught of buffalo hunters, prospectors, land surveyors, and settlers. As homesteads mushroomed and cattle moved onto bison range, European immigrants, emancipated Black people, and other war vets, plus thousands of Chinese laborers recruited for the purpose, laid track for the Union Pacific and Central Pacific Railroads, building the first transcontinental line, until the operations joined at Promontory, Utah, in 1869. Some Chinese workers who had helped lay the last rails celebrated their role during a commemoration fifty years later. This is all to say that the idea of the West lacking racial diversity is still another myth. Yet people who didn't look like a ten-gallon-hatted buckaroo were often left from the pages of history.

Each incursion—railroads, ranching, mining, and later the designations of national parks—further pushed Indigenous peoples from their homelands. Navajo, Comanche, Apache, Kiowa, Shoshone, Ute, and so many other nations fought to keep their territory from the onslaught of western expansion, spilling the blood of others and shedding their own. When Sioux leader Crazy Horse won the Battle of the Little Bighorn against Custer's cavalry in 1876, it was a victory against the United States government's campaigns of displacement and murder. But by 1890, in the wake of the barbarity of Wounded Knee, the massacre of nearly three hundred people by the US cavalry, the West was firmly in the control of the American government. Native people were required to live on reservations under fraught treaties, amid unscrupulous agents, broken promises, forced marches, and campaigns toward dehumanization and erasure. Yet despite all the effort taken to destroy American Indians economically, culturally, and bodily, Indigenous nations persevered and are a defining component of western culture today, living contradictions of the myth of *terra nullius*. Indeed, ongoing Indigenous resistance, such as the Standing Rock Sioux protest of the Dakota Access pipeline, remains a central hallmark of the true West. The conquered West is yet another myth.

Amid all the myths that color this place, this is one that has become particularly ironic given the aridity of these lands. In 1862, the Homestead Act was passed and the first governor of the Colorado Territory, William Gilpin, beckoned to agrarians, citing Nebraskan Charles Dana

Wilber's malarkey that "rain follows the plow." We know that this isn't true. John Wesley Powell, the indomitable geologist, himself a Civil War vet who lost an arm in battle, told us as much. Powell identified a longitudinal divide on a map of the United States, delineating east from west, defining American geography by rainfall. East of the line is wet, west is dry. He advised members of Congress that, beyond the hundredth meridian (today the ninety-eighth), development should remain constrained within water availability. This view was unpopular to bullish land surveyors and politicians—nothing, including the dearth of water, would stop them from building the West. The year before he resigned from the US Geological Service in 1893, Powell addressed an audience of farmers and ranchers: "I tell you gentlemen you are piling up a heritage of conflict and litigation over water rights, for there is not enough water to supply the land." And here we are, in a thousand-year drought as the Colorado River is squandered to grow alfalfa for China and to keep golf courses green in the desert. The myth of an agrarian West has led to a very scary water crisis.

— — —

IN WRITING THIS BOOK, AND IN EXAMINING THE WEST AS A myth museum, I aspire to serve as both interpreter and iconoclast. We can find versions of truth in museums, but we must continue to ask questions and puzzle together disparate pieces in order to get at answers. Truth is a constellation. I seek to understand how people think, how they see, and how they operate on their ideas. Ideas exist outside of politics, or they used to. No matter where you sit politically, this book is also my appeal to stop looking at this country and each other solely through a political lens.

My exploration takes place throughout collections in the western myth museum. I consider history, culture, and our human story at a time when external issues, from pandemic to land use, climate change to cultural upheaval, misinformation to inequity, bear down on us. In my quest to gauge our situation, I have tried to reconnect with people after months of isolation and to hear their truths while considering reconciliation. *True West* is a book not just on myths, but also on mending fences. I set out to interview myth makers, myth boosters, and myth busters and was reminded over and over again, in spite of the frustrations over misinformation and entrenched belief, how important it is to connect with and listen to people. This is where I found truth among my own misperceptions, strolling down the long halls of a museum of western myths.

CHAPTER 1

BIBLES AND DINOSAURS

T HOUGH THIS STORY COULD BEGIN AMID THE INTER-
mountain West, it started instead as I drove through the tall
blue-green grass of Kentucky on a hot summer day plunged
in a thick midwestern humidity. Back in the days of Daniel Boone,
the very idea of the western frontier, also a myth, had Kentucky at its
forefront. In 2017, I'd come to a state, unfairly famous for god-awful
fast-food chicken, to pick up a puppy awaiting my arrival at a kennel
in the town of Berea. While en route along Interstate 275, I encountered an institution enshrining Genesis as scientific fact, a literal myth
museum.

Here I began to consider what happens when "truth" is offered,
as in this case, within a seventy-five-thousand-square-foot institution
committed to biblical literalism. As its sign came into view—Creation
Museum, Exit 11—my mother, who lives in nearby Cincinnati and
had come with me to meet the new dog, mentioned that she'd always
wanted to see it. I agreed that it might be a lark, like visiting Madame
Tussauds, but at the same time, the idea of its existence felt unsettling.
I asked my mom, "Don't you think it's weird? They built it because
they don't believe in evolution." She replied with something that has
stuck with me: "Who cares what they believe?" We passed the off-
ramp that led to a place swapping faith for science. As we drove, we
moved on to other subjects.

I was six months into a very sad year. We had lost three of our dogs within three months of one another. Nick collapsed at thirteen on the upper landing of our front staircase and fell into convulsions, shaking and foaming at the mouth until my friend and vet, Katie, came to mercifully put him down. Harry, also thirteen, died of what was most likely congestive heart failure at an overnight clinic, after staff had assured us that he was recovering from a very bad day. He didn't. At that same clinic, a month later, our beautiful Stella, blind in one eye, was euthanized at age eight after a couple of months of intermittent seizures, probably due to a brain tumor. This trip to Kentucky, and the long cross-country meander back to Montana, was a needed break from a lonely home. But here I was, shaken by an unexpected distraction: a museum devoted to mythic disinformation.

Who cares what they believe? When Mom asked the question, I'd wanted to respond with something like, "I care, because it's wrong. Facts can't be manufactured by sophists who build a multimillion-dollar waxworks museum just because they're uncomfortable with data." But whatever I grumbled was much less articulate. We were at the beginning of Donald Trump's presidency. Objective truth was suddenly out of fashion, and the decline was getting worse, creating a disabling confusion among that faction of angry citizenry who feel they have a monopoly on patriotism and therefore style themselves as the only "We the People." Trump's team, at every opportunity, trotted out the president's own version of reality—a perspective that senior counselor Kellyanne Conway, on *Meet the Press* just a few months before my trip, called "alternative facts." The Kentucky Creation Museum, and its sister institution, the Ark Encounter—a model of old Noah's ship and its menagerie—fit well with this trend, although these museums fascinated me when I first read of them. Now I was feeling ever more uneasy about slippery slopes, as I watched a country being told to believe in increasingly serious deceptions. Alternative facts were playing out in factional politics, leaving many of us, like Noah, at sea.

I value museums for what they can be when they deal in earnestly presenting fact and abstain from cultural erasure and pilfering. I also adore religious traditions. I've been accused of religious promiscuity on occasion because I am enthralled by the ways humans strive to understand mystery. Various traditions and their sutras, verses, and surahs address the great and enigmatic, and there is beauty and wisdom in these world's sacred texts. But religion isn't science, and to represent it as such is not only disingenuous, it's dangerous. Stephen Jay Gould, the late evolutionary biologist well-known for his popular writings, offered a phrase for the reconciling of religion and science; he called them "non-overlapping magisteria"—that is, fields of culture engaged in different types of exploration. Science empirically derives facts, and religion contemplates both mystery and values. The two can run parallel, as the writer Peter Matthiessen described to me while we sat in my living room several years ago, like arrows rising in the sky. But when religious values are applied to scientific interpretation, as in the observed nature of things, truth trembles, and the arrows clatter to the ground. Of course, science is not without cultural values and religion lives in a real world. It would be great if they were separate, like those two soaring arrows, but the reality is more complicated.

Still, we need both arrows. Scientific empiricism cannot fully explain the world. Philosopher Mircea Eliade believed all human beings, all human societies, have always lived in accordance with myth. It is only a western mind, holding tightly to Enlightenment principles and empiricism, that eliminates the shaping power of myth in culture. But what happens instead is that anti-mythicism of modernity merely repeats the pattern it has attempted to replace: the myth of scientific empiricism is still a myth. In other words, just as religion replacing science shouldn't be the goal, science replacing stories shouldn't be either.

The visionary behind the creation museum is Ken Ham, a Christian fundamentalist from Australia. Opened in 2007, it portrays the earth as roughly six thousand years old and depicts dinosaurs living with humans. By enshrining myths within an "educational institution," as the roadside attraction in Kentucky bills itself, his "science" museum is actually a house of worship. The institution's breathless slogan is "PREPARE TO BELIEVE!," a directive that suggests the goal of grooming visitors to choose faith over fact. The Christian Bible was at one time considered a reliable historical account of human origins, in European culture, but during the Enlightenment this understanding was refuted and largely disregarded. The refutation of biblical literalism still stands in much of the Judeo-Christian world, except for a few places, including parts of the United States. I couldn't foresee, at the time of that drive to Kentucky, how my discussion with my mother would take on such a different meaning a few years later, when wooly ways of seeing, produced by various coalitions and networks, ripped apart our country. Had someone told me of how technology, politics, and pandemic would leave us at such odds, jeopardizing lives and democracy, I'm not sure I would have been prepared to believe. At this moment in history, the idea of truth has grown ever more muddled, and the Creation Museum seems a little like a gateway drug.

I grabbed Manny, the little pup, dropped my mom off, and drove back to Big Sky Country, roughly following the same route as so many settlers took west, along what was once known as the Oregon Trail, across America's high plains. Past farms, billboards, gas stations, roadkill, and badlands, I remained nagged by the idea that falsehoods could be institutionalized, entertaining visitors and empowering contrarians who came to a museum prepared to believe myth packaged as truth. Genesis tells the story of creation as imagined in Judeo-Christian scripture, but it doesn't unveil the natural history of the world.

— — —

GLENDIVE, MONTANA, IS A PLACE KNOWN FOR ITS RUGGED river breaks, paddlefish angling, and a proximity to the largest oil deposit in the United States, the Bakken Formation. It is also home to its own creation museum. It's a conservative community, though it didn't used to be, having grown up around the Northern Pacific and the railroad's union culture. Long after the town's establishment, the Northern Pacific merged with other companies to become the Burlington Northern Santa Fe (BNSF), and that enterprise no longer uses Glendive as a hub. Over the last century, battles have played out nearby as settlers came to the West, perhaps some even hailing from Kentucky. Men hunted and skinned bison, bundling hides to be loaded aboard freight trains at the Glendive Depot, leaving carcasses to rot on a baking prairie. Known as the "gate city," a holdover sobriquet from travelers who caught their first glimpse of Montana Territory from passenger cars hereabouts, its population has ebbed and its prominence has declined. The Bakken fields are now at the bust end of their cycle, a rude awakening from a mythically endless boom, which began about twenty years ago after the introduction of new fracking methods and tools in the 1990s. Farming and ranching again make up a good chunk of the local employment, after Bakken's years of good-paying jobs have dwindled. Downtown, store windows sit empty and the McDonald's, which once bagged up Big Macs and fries for high schoolers and roughnecks, has gone out of business. Perhaps it is this very situation that opens the door to its history—the bust cycle emptiness of Glendive allows for a good look at its past. Light traffic and quiet streets provide uninterrupted views of the grand buildings of Merrill Avenue, the historic Bell Bridge, and the old railroad depot. This is a town built in a bygone era, but Glendive and its environs have a much deeper history. If you dig a little, you'll find evidence of life long before Big Macs, bison, or humans. Buried in crumbling clay and sandstone lie the bones of the ancients. Because it's not just oil and trains that put Glendive on the map. It's dinosaurs as well.

My introduction to this town was by way of the COVID-19 vaccine. In spring of 2021, I heard that a pharmacy out there was throwing away unused doses. My friend Mark Mathis called me with this news, saying he'd heard that Glendive had lots of vaccine appointments available, whereas in my own community an appointment was virtually impossible to book. I was reluctant, because jumping ahead in line to get vaccinated, before some of the state's Native people and elderly had their chances, was something that I did not want to do. I called another friend, involved in helping with vaccine availability for Montana's Native populations, and she told me that the nearby Fort Peck and Northern Cheyenne reservations had far better vaccination rates than the neighboring, predominately white, communities. In fact, Montana reservations began to offer jabs to folks who didn't live there because vaccination rates among tribal members were so high. The Blackfeet reservation and others were therefore providing opportunities for vaccine tourism, though neighboring rural communities remained hesitant, and persistent COVID-19 confusion was part of the reason that Moderna and Pfizer shots got tossed at the end of the day.

So it seemed reasonable to step up, in the face of this waste. Mathis and I drove east to Glendive's Albertsons supermarket and got our first shots. As of late 2022, Dawson County, of which Glendive is the seat, had only vaccinated 39 percent of its population, but that was higher than nearby Prairie and Powder River Counties, at 35 percent and 31 percent respectively. Only one other person, besides Mathis and me, showed up that morning to get poked. I didn't jump a line because a line didn't exist. More than a year later, Idaho, Montana, and Wyoming still remained among the least vaccinated states in the country, although western Indian reservations had the highest vaccination rates nationwide. Indigenous populations had also suffered some of the highest mortality rates in the country during the first year of the pandemic, a misery that evidently left them alert to the value of science-based preventive measures.

A month later, I returned eastward, traveling again past Livingston and the Crazy Mountains, through sprawling Billings, and into the Powder River Basin's eroded country. Across the Yellowstone River from the Albertsons store, downtown Glendive still shows its historical foundations, from the jarring percussion of freight cars to the ghost signs painted on brick buildings, advertising businesses long ago closed. Newer, well-maintained homes stand sublimely above a wide bend of the Yellowstone. Dawson County High School (Go, Red Devils!) boasts an NFL-quality football field and a professional-quality track, courtesy of the Ross and Tara Oakland family and their Bakken oil money. Makoshika State Park's badlands tower east of town, with trails winding through late-Cretaceous Hell Creek Formation sandstone. Known as the Paddlefish and Caviar Capital of Montana, Glendive is a big attraction for anglers that vie for a chance to catch (by snagging, not bait or flies) that prehistoric critter, the paddlefish, a spoon-billed, cartilaginous relative of the sturgeon, a fish that feeds on microscopic organisms and lays yummy eggs. Then there's the attraction in town, right off Interstate 94, known as the Glendive Dinosaur and Fossil Museum.

I've known about the place for years. It's a novelty in the state: a biblically based collection of exhibits that have nothing to do with science, other than subverting it. Montana's current governor, Greg Gianforte, a Christian fundamentalist, even contributed to its founding, to the tune of nearly $300,000. Much like its bigger counterpart in Kentucky, this museum urges visitors to "expect to see facts and evidence you have never seen before." Prepare to believe. Opened in 2009, the small institution tells its story of how the world came into being, eschewing evolution as the source of biological diversity and making the case that it was Noah's flood, not deep time and Huttonian processes, that shaped the geology of earth's surface. On its website, a combative notice—aimed at other natural history museums, those that aren't biblically based—warns of "wide-eyed elementary and preschool children (not to mention their parents and teachers)...funneled into an abyss of scientific deception. No matter whether it's the study of animals, earth science, or astronomy, the wonders of God's creation are prostituted for evolutionism. And the end result is just more confusion, mystification, and cynicism in the lives of our young people and adults."

Why concern ourselves with such tendentious claims? Because this physical museum promotes one of the many myths from which the modern West has been remade. The recent breakdown in trust of science, and the undermining of scientific leaders and agencies, exacerbated during the pandemic, has worked its way into western myths, skewing them all the further to unreality. Biblical literalism encourages disinterest and suspicion, and you'll see in the many stories ahead that such literalism is endemic in our culture.

That said, I am fully aware that science itself is not impervious to taint. It's human of course, and therefore subject to human foibles. We see many examples of this throughout history because part of science is getting things wrong in order to find out what's right. Like biblical literalism, science is a human practice subject to the many shortcomings of our species like bias, carelessness, or ego. And speaking of ego, and of dinosaurs, I'm reminded of one such story that involved both, showing potential pitfalls in scientific endeavor.

The Bone Wars, otherwise known as the Great Dinosaur Rush, concerned two late nineteenth-century scientists, Edward Drinker Cope and Othniel Charles Marsh, who chased remnants of the Jurassic in the dirt of the American West. While digging through beds in Wyoming and Colorado, they flouted both scientific standards and integrity. The two men hated each other so much that in their race to outdo the other's progress, they were rumored to have dynamited their own dig sites, so that the rival couldn't access old excavation opportunities. Their war unfolded during the gold rush in the Black Hills, when Marsh promised Sioux chief Red Cloud payment for the fossils he excavated. In turn the tribe allowed him to dig in peace since he was not after gold. Marsh didn't make good on his promise to pay for the fossils, but he did lobby the Grant administration to provide food and support for the Sioux. During years of ongoing feuds, Cope, whose own reputation had by then grown tarnished, squirreled away evidence implicating Marsh in misappropriation of government funds and other improprieties in his research. Cope ratted out his adversary to a freelance writer who, in 1890, published a piece in the *New York Herald* that effectively ended Marsh's career. Though Cope and Marsh are acknowledged for pioneering the field of paleontology and further proving Charles Darwin's theory of evolution, they died penniless and disgraced. They were more interested in rivalry and glory than they were in objective study. Still, the men's specimens fill museums today, and their work inspired a field to which the Glendive Dinosaur and Fossil Museum owes a debt—the science of paleontology, one the institution actively works to undermine.

On my first visit to the GDFM, not to be confused with the two other museums in town, the Makoshika Dinosaur and Frontier Gateway Museums, I wandered, along with a few families, under an eighteen-foot *Protostega*—that is, the reconstruction of a gigantic, extinct form of sea turtle—not a dinosaur, but this will be the least of the objections. Moving over to a wall, I glimpsed an ichthyosaur, an extinct marine reptile (also not one of the dinosaurs, but an apt addition to the collection), its bones poking from a clay base. A mockup skeleton of *T. rex*, a true dinosaur, native to the American West, towered two floors high in the main gallery on long legs, its stubby arms outstretched. These modeled fauna were impressive and the exhibits seemed like very normal museum fare. But then I went upstairs.

On the second floor, the exhibition *Dinosaurs and Man* was a pretty big departure from the museums I knew. Though paleontologists have mounds of evidence that dinosaurs were extinct sixty-five million years before humans came into being, this museum offers its own "proof" that dinosaurs and humans coexisted. A lovely collection of Asian and European pottery and carvings feature humans fighting dragons and maybe a crocodile. According to museum signage, these works of art absolutely confirm that dinosaurs and humans were once contemporaries. It's the decorated pots that verify their simultaneous existence.

The Alvis Delk track offers further evidence. Named after amateur archaeologist Alvis Delk, it is a model of an eleven-inch human footprint found inside the track of an *Acrocanthosaurus*, a predatory dinosaur that lived in what's now Texas and thereabouts during the early Cretaceous, roughly 110 million years ago. According to Delk and other creationists, the footprint amounts to confirmation that humans strolled with these extinct reptiles. Coincidently, Delk stumbled across the nested prints only a mile from another "young earth" creation museum in Texas—the proximity to his place of work a curious coincidence. For the record, the track has been called "ridiculously fake" by PZ Meyers, an associate professor of biology at the University of Minnesota, Morris. Another professional, the well-known paleontologist Jack Horner, a Montana native, former head curator at Bozeman's Museum of the Rockies, and a consultant to the *Jurassic Park* movies, was also once asked about the GDFM. During an interview with the *Billings Gazette*, he said, "It's not a science museum at all. It's not a pseudoscience museum. It's just not science…There's nothing scientific about it." But that doesn't matter. Glendive's Dinosaur and Fossil Museum is an homage to biblical literalism. If actual paleontologists find the displays to be outrageously false, it's of no consequence. This is a place making its own truth.

Beside the Delk model is a diorama of a man and a woman, clad in caveman wear, poised alongside a *Parasaurolophus*, an herbivorous dinosaur with a head crest, and another *Acrocanthosaurus*. The human couple looks remarkably chill despite giant dinosaurs to both their right and their left. Across the room, a model of Noah's ark—a shrunken version of the three-hundred-by-fifty-by-thirty-cubit original mentioned in Genesis—sits on a stand as little toy dinosaurs await their boarding turn and the impending deluge.

At the rear of the museum is a wall featuring a series of quotes labeled "In Their Own Words." It offers statements meant to discredit scientists and the theory of evolution, including a few from Charles Darwin himself. One quote, drawn out of context, seems to carry Darwin's own lament that his theory is a failure, "a mere rag of a hypothesis." Though no further explanation is given, I later tracked the statement down. It's a phrase from a letter sent to Thomas Henry Huxley, Darwin's colleague, confidant, and faithful supporter, probably on June 2, 1859. Darwin begins the letter, "My dear Huxley, I meant to have added one other word. You speak of finding a flaw in my hypothesis, & this shows you do not understand its nature. It is a mere rag of an hypothesis with as many flaws & holes as sound parts. My question is whether the rag is worth anything?" Spoiler alert: his answer is a confident, *oh yeah.* "I think by careful treatment I can carry in it my fruit to market for a short distance over a gentle road." In other words, Darwin tells his friend, "I'm onto something, dear Huxley, I just need more evidence." Signing off, he says, "Ever yours | Most truly | C. Darwin." This rag-borne fruit was a central tenet in the theory of evolution—natural selection.

This letter exchange, and the "mere rag" phrase, reflects the fact that, while writing his book *On the Origin of Species*, Darwin didn't understand the phenomenon of reversion—traits not seen in parents could appear in offspring. Neither Huxley nor Darwin understood hereditary traits, and though they were contemporaries with Gregor Mendel, they weren't privy to his obscure paper on the subject. Mendel's theory, developed from his pea plant experiments, brought him closer to understanding genes, but Darwin was still clueless. Yet natural selection, the idea that organisms well-adapted to their habitats have a higher likelihood of surviving and having little ones, was right all the same. Though the quote in Glendive's dinosaur museum is meant to show that Darwin doubted the validity of his theory, the letter, in its totality, shows him believing in his "rag." Natural selection would be explained in *On the Origin of Species*, a masterful start, not a final declaration. Population genetics came later, long after Darwin and Mendel. Which is to say, science can take time to arrive at conclusions, leaving some, in the meantime, exasperated and skeptical of advancement. Even the theory of evolution needed to evolve. And that is the nature of science.

—   —   —

I HAD THE OPPORTUNITY, ONE INCREDIBLY HOT AFTERnoon—the car thermometer read 112 degrees—to interview the creation museum's director, Robert Canen. We sat in his small office that opened onto a gift shop. Visitors wandered aisles chocked with books, such as *Big Plans for Henry*, "a biblical understanding of dinosaurs," for children—in this case Henry the Hadrosaur, a duck-billed dinosaur. There were also cloth-bag keepsakes filled with pieces of dinosaur bone, chunks of ancient turtle shell, and slivers of petrified wood. Volunteers occasionally popped their heads in to touch base. A young man in fatigues, visiting with his family from Texas, came by to ask if he could give Canen an oil change. With an enthusiastic yes, Canen handed the fellow his keys.

The museum director is a kind man with a friendly, unassuming manner, a whitening beard, and Benjamin Franklin glasses. He moved to Glasgow, Montana, from California when he was in eighth grade and was raised in a devout Christian household on the Hi-Line, the state's northernmost latitudinal highway. His father drove a bus. After graduation, he married his high school sweetheart, moved out of state to study at Trinity Bible College in North Dakota and the University of Minnesota, and later returned to eastern Montana as a pastor. After a career at the Glendive Evangelical Church, and years of coaching baseball while raising his kids, he took over the management of this museum from its founder, Otis Klein. Canen continues to minister to a small congregation in nearby Bloomfield, Montana, but he is mainly focused on curating the museum as well as serving as the president of the Foundation Advancing Creation Truth (FACT), an affiliate organization supporting the museum. FACT warns on their website about the "abyss of scientific deception" into which the unsuspecting but faithful might fall, when touring non-creationist-oriented natural history museums.

A biblical literalist who sees the Bible as a historical account of the world, Canen considers planet earth to be around six thousand years old and the Great Flood to be responsible for its geology. Though there is abundant evidence of vast age, such as deposits of the mineral zircon found in Australia's Nuvvuagittuq greenstone belt, dated radiometrically at over four billion years old—the oldest mineral ever assessed—four billion years doesn't fit into Canen's worldview. "We think that in order for scripture to fit together…" He paused and started again. "We think it's a stumbling block for many people when they try to bring, what we would say, millions of years into the Bible." Let alone billions. "It has problems. You have to do what we would call theological gymnastics to try to make it work." He referenced Occam's razor, a concept that the simplest explanation is generally the best explanation. "There's virtually no one who could read Genesis," explained Canen, discussing the age of the universe, who "would arrive at anything other than that God created it in six days. The flood really happened. That's the way it's written." But the thing is, the Bible is not science and sometimes truth requires a bit of a mental workout. Though Darwin's theory requires time and attention to understand natural selection, Genesis is not a reliable source on the origin of species.

The reputation of science took a hit during COVID, as did the very notion of truth. Many Americans came to view science—that is, consensus-based knowledge built upon data-driven and peer-reviewed study—as unreliable. The pandemic left some folks scratching their heads about what science is and how it works. Meanwhile, scientists were stepping up, buckling in, and working tirelessly to understand the virus and conceive effective safety measures against it. As a result, vaccines were developed in record time. There are lots of researchers still at work on SARS-CoV-2, and they may well be at it for a while. There are still unknowns. The country where the virus originated is loath to be transparent and Darwinian evolution is ever at play.

There is also an aversion right now, not just toward science but toward concepts that require nuance and teasing out. And then there are unknowns. People are weary of ambiguity, and they've grown distrustful of experts who take too long to deliver, or who seem to change their minds. The Bible, or some cynical modern-day prophet, can fill such uncomfortable fissures between certainty and uncertainty with absolutism. When I later talked Canen's ideas over with a friend, Rebecca Watters, a whip-smart wolverine biologist who grew up with evangelical cousins intent on converting her, she explained how difficult it is to have a conversation between sides with such different ground rules. "Science accepts or even extols uncertainty," she explained, because a hypothesis, to be of any value, has got to be falsifiable—this according to science philosopher Karl Popper. Within the scientific process, uncertainty moves one closer to truth, but biblical literalists, or those who walk lockstep with a particular ideology, view uncertainty as an unsatisfactory, discomfiting limbo compared to "higher truth"—an irrefutable absolutism issued by a revered authority. To a scientist, explained Watters, uncertainty is an "affirmation that the scientific process is working," but to a creationist, it's proof that science is tenuous and unreliable.

On that broiling day in Glendive, Canen went on to tell me about a time during college when he was involved in a debate over evolution, defending creationism while an opponent championed Darwin's theory. Canen, who defended intelligent design, the act of a creator wisely cobbling together the universe, took a stance that because there are some uncertainties in the theory of evolution, "you can't know for sure." Like quicksand, this position effectively traps and sinks any counterpoint, no matter how valid. To say "you can't know for sure" shuts down discussion. Uncertainty is what keeps fields of science moving forward, but in certain religious circles, it becomes an excuse for condemnation of any idea that seems frightening or challenges orthodoxy.

Sitting in his museum, I realized that this is where we are right now with so many issues. Without empirical science, which takes time and attention, "truth" can be backfilled with a mere whisper of potentials. Saying something *could be true* places the burden of proof on the wrong person. Science may be imperfect, but it has brought us everything from penicillin, to batteries, to CRISPR. And that is the truth. In 2009, Jack Horner was asked to weigh in on the ongoing debate between evolution and creation. He replied, "You can't have a debate about science and opinion. It's not apples and oranges. It's more like apples and sewing machines." There is no way forward in logical dialogue with "you can't know for sure." It's a retreat into epistemological nihilism.

Canen holds his beliefs firmly, even when scientific data confront

his worldview. "The beginning of death, disease, and violence is sin...
The fossil record is a record of death. It has disease in it and there's
violence in it. So, if the Bible is right," he told me, "then dinosaurs *had*
to be around while people were around." Dinosaurs such as *Acrocan-
thorsaurs* were red in tooth and claw, though docile herbivores such
as the *Parasaurolophus* group more likely had spinach between their
teeth. Still, they roamed together according to Canen's line of thinking, and violent carnivores ravaging the earth were a consequence of
Eve's sin in the pursuit of knowledge. In Genesis, that fateful apple
brought God's wrath to the world. To look at things any other way
doesn't make sense to a biblical literalist, so the Glendive Dinosaur
and Fossil Museum acts as an elaborate production of biblical confirmation.

This literalist construal of the Bible has come to have serious
implications in the West. Interpretations of various passages enable
people to believe and act upon Christian primacy over Indigenous
populations; to embrace myths of infinite resources in spite of scarcity;
to claim dominion over land, air, and waters, as well as the animals
that depend on these; and to accept the inevitability of end-times, as
foreseen by preppers and evangelical Christians, replete with violence,
disasters, and death. From Genesis to Revelation, proof-texters find
support for the notion of Christian mastery over all living things, and
for a future compounded of broken seals, war, pestilence, pale horses,
and the Lamb of the Lord. We've seen these themes again and again as
literalists have come west to build communities in expectation of this
ominous chapter in God's plan.

America, of course, is never mentioned in the Bible, which means
neither is the West. Nonetheless, this place has become a place of biblical literalism and a holy frontline for religious battles. It might not be
in the Bible, but it has been sacralized by folks bringing their biblical
interpretations to build homelands.

I asked Canen why he took this job as director of a museum. Was the creationist dogma something about which he had always felt passionate? "One, I believe it. Two, I think it's important to show people that they can have confidence," he said. "I want to let them know that they can trust it." Canen, who I really enjoyed and was grateful to for his generous time, voiced a rationale that sounded eerily familiar: an all-or-nothing way of framing things dominates political thinking these days. Worldviews shape realities even when there is enormous evidence to the contrary; they can fuel the rise of movements like Christian nationalism, another phenomenon taking over parts of the West. Not to say that Canen's particular beliefs are dangerous, but his logic is. A conviction or a culture that insists on absolute fealty to an idea or a series of ideas, whether it's biblical literalism or an inherent evil in people who think differently, wreaks havoc. People should be able to question issues, faiths, political party positions, and even science, but in Canen's reasoning, facts that confront his worldview are best disregarded as mental acrobatics—a misguided variant of Occam's razor. Geology, paleontology, and evolution seem too byzantine to consider when Genesis offers everything a person needs to know. Someone who is convinced that dinosaurs lived with people isn't a direct threat to anyone's safety, but the implications of Canen's paradigm are. And they become especially toxic when mixed uncritically with other myths.

Chapter 2

Luciferase

B ESIDES CHECKING OUT DINOSAURS DURING MY time in Glendive, I drank iced tea on patios, ate sandwiches at the Beer Jug, and shared coffee at kitchen tables, listening to folks talk on everything from oil pipelines to politics. I picked potatoes, kayaked the Yellowstone, and hiked in badlands, all the while considering the intersect between myth, misinformation, and polarization. My own perceptions were sometimes confirmed and sometimes challenged. Before I left his office, Robert Canen surprised me with his take on vaccines. He and his wife had been inoculated. He'd caught the virus early on in the pandemic, after some time spent with his one-year-old grandson. After the baby tested positive, Canen began to feel sick. "I was a little bit concerned about [the vaccine], until I listened to a guy from Creation Ministries International. Dr. Robert Carter, he's a microbiologist," Canen said. "He did a really good job of explaining the kind of vaccine." Canen had been concerned that the vaccine had been rushed, but he got the shot and encouraged his congregants to do the same. The fact that the vaccine topic became so politicized chagrined him, and even the news that the shots were highly effective had been off-putting, he told me, because it was "so in your face." But he listened to someone he trusted, and was convinced, despite his skepticism, to get immunized.

In late spring of 2021, a tall, loose-limbed man walked over to greet me as I slowed my car in his driveway. Throwing out a hand, Derrick Weber (I changed his and his family's name at his request) cheerfully announced himself as one of the only people in Glendive to vote for Joe Biden. I'd been introduced to Weber through a mutual friend in Billings who thought I'd enjoy interviewing him. Retired from the Burlington Northern Santa Fe Railway, he now farms a lovely piece of land a few minutes drive from town. Weber loves lively banter, is an avid reader, and has an endless admiration for the broad Yellowstone River that winds past his property. He has a way of dragging out "Well…" far longer than the little word deserves, and tells mildly raunchy jokes, laughing loudly with each punchline. To be fair, I do too. He maintains great relationships with many of his old colleagues, several of whom I've now met. Devoted to his family—a son and his wife live on the property with their kids—he has pulled them into the operations of his farm. But as friendly as he is with former coworkers, relations closer to home were somewhat strained in 2020 and 2021. Unlike Robert Canen, Weber's daughter-in-law has been influenced by people who eschew the COVID-19 vaccine, and she has gone down bewildering and distorted alleys on social media on that topic and others. This caused an initial unease in the family, but the Webers have since agreed to disagree.

With the issue put aside, the Weber family farm seems a peaceable kingdom—a place of joyful commotion. Tom turkeys strut over scurrying piglets, all bumping by corrals full of sheep. Cows and calves amble over dirt, peeking between wooden slats for pitched hay. Pumpkins and melons ripen in a field along the east side of the property, and a greenhouse with peppers and herbs sits to the west. The Yellowstone River makes up the eastern boundary, running wide and muddy below steep, crumbling banks filled with ancient mollusks called ammonites. Weber and his family butcher their own animals, smoke their own bacon, and brine and can their own vegetables. Cars, farm equipment, and assorted bits and pieces lie scattered throughout acreage crisscrossed by irrigation pivots above bright green patches of hay, while various sizes of muck boots dangle from a stand of iron rods on the porch of the old farmhouse. A large shipping container holds the possessions of Weber's son, Sam, and his wife, Debra, while they await completion of a manufactured house on the property. The Weber grandkids, Abe and Lilia, help with chores, tending to quail and watching over tomato plants, cavorting in happy mayhem, often tailed by a black-and-white herding dog named Dora. It's idyllic, a modern approximation of the romantic myth of the western agrarian life, as was endlessly marketed in the late nineteenth century by land spectators and the railroads. For the Webers it's real, but achieving and retaining any such idyll has been difficult and rare. Many settlers to this area during the early and later homesteading periods, lured by promise, left after failure, realizing that farming in the arid West ain't easy. Still, rural life has been idealized, packaged, and promoted as an antidote to urban ills, and during COVID, this myth was once again recycled.

Since my first visit, I've now called on the Webers several times. With each trip Derrick and his wife, Sarah, load me up with the bounty of their farm—melon, squash, quail eggs, potatoes, bacon, sausage, homemade wine, or whatever is on hand at any particular time in the season. He sends further bounties my way, some five hours west, by intermediary. Just the other day, I found a bag of sweet corn on my porch, courtesy of the Weber farm. He later texted me a recipe for fritters, adding, "Good every time, sure to impress. Bon appetit."

One evening as sunset pinked the sky above the Yellowstone River, Weber and I discussed the town's dinosaur museum, which he has not visited, put off by his Catholic school upbringing and his early career as a biology teacher. With a fine view of the river from his small hunting cabin about a quarter mile from the main house, we stood on the porch looking out on open land. When the cool night sent us inside, we continued our conversation, rambling from one subject to another. He recommended a book I would later read, *A Hard Won Life: A Boy on His Own on the Montana Frontier*, a rather extraordinary work based on interviews with one Fred Van Blaricom, an orphan fending for himself in Glendive in the 1880s at the age of seven. *A Boy* is full of western tall tales as well as myth-shattering stories about drunken and decidedly unheroic cowboys; strict gun laws in frontier towns; and brutal acts of on-going violence, by whites, against the Sioux people. Interviewed much later in life, on the other side of Montana in the Bitteroot Valley, Van Blaricom discussed his experience with inoculation against smallpox in the 1870s, which he believed had saved his life during an 1883 outbreak in Dawson County. After reading me a bit of the book, Weber put the volume down and shared his concern over his family's experience with vaccines. His daughter-in-law, Debra, not only refused COVID vaccines, she has stopped inoculating her children against infectious diseases altogether.

I later met Debra, a warm and engaging woman in her late forties, who over the years has worked as a hair stylist in Maine and a therapeutic riding instructor in Wyoming. She currently is a representative of a Texas-based company that researches the "effects of food and food constituents on gene expression, and how genetic variations affect the nutritional environment." She comes across as a bit of a free spirit, having married Sam Weber in 2007 at Burning Man, an annual gathering of seventy thousand artists, partiers, hedonists, and spiritual seekers who revel together every year in Nevada's Great Basin. She and Sam moved to Glendive, where he grew up. The farm life suits her—quiet days along the river, homegrown beans and chickens, field-ripened fruit, an Edenic place to live a small-town dream in a state with more relaxed vaccine protocols than elsewhere. Resistance settling atop the agrarian western myth.

Over the last years, Debra Weber has become a determined anti-vaxxer, thanks to some initial skepticism that led to full-blown indoctrination. It happened to so many people. The internet gives "information" a la carte, suiting tastes and proclivities and pushing folks ever deeper into silos. When exploring vaccinces, small misgivings will take "researchers" into algorithms that fling them to the scariest of places—soon jabs aren't just suspect because of rare side effects, they are instruments of Satan. The internet is a much more efficient and far-reaching vehicle for confusion and biblical literalism than the Glendive Dinosaur and Fossil Museum. And because the Web is rife with a jetsam and flotsam of fiction and fabrication, there is enormous disparity in American understanding of events, viruses, and nearly everything.

Becoming ever more adamant about medical liberty during the pandemic, Weber, a one-time liberal, changed parties over this issue. Republican states are less likely to adopt stringent vaccine protocols, a topic about which she has become increasingly ardent. Before coming to Glendive, she and her family had lived for a while in Kennebunkport, Maine, where she first felt misgivings about her children's health as handled by Maine's public school system. A teacher had told her that her son, Abe, had ADHD. Weber didn't buy it. Another teacher expressed concerns that her daughter, a straight-A student, was having trouble finishing assignments. This didn't sit well either—nothing was wrong with her children, she believed. In addition to what she considered inappropriate feedback from school personnel, she also grew concerned over the state of Maine's vaccination protocols, which on a national scale of comparison are strict. Religious and philosophical exemptions cannot be used as an excuse not to vaccinate children, though that rule applies only to the basic childhood immunizations, not to COVID-19 or flu shots. Maine is "very draconian," she said.

In her move west, she and her family came to Montana, a state with a rightwing legislature focused on loosening vaccine requirements. Only 62 percent of Montana children receive the complete vaccine series. It was childhood vaccines, Weber believed, that had adversely affected her children's health. Abe struggled with vision issues, but not ADHD, and vaccines, she said, set him back after his several sessions of vision therapy, and now she was done with the whole business. Neither Abe nor Lilia have completed the recommended course of childhood vaccines, nor will they ever get the COVID vaccine, if Weber has anything to do with it.

My family and I have all been vaccinated, but I didn't want to dismiss Weber's concerns. Rather, I wanted to listen to her story of life on a farm as rural refuge and Montana as libertarian safe haven, free from what she feels are overbearing vaccine laws. Maybe I was missing something in Weber's apprehension.

I spoke with Dr. Kellyn Milani, a naturopathic doctor in Bozeman, Montana, who also has some misgivings over CDC vaccine protocols for children. Milani is not anti-vax, but I hoped that she, as a practitioner of alternative medicine, could help me understand the misgivings of vaccine skeptics. She told me that she would be getting her own new baby, born during the pandemic, vaccinated, but doing it on a schedule different from federal recommendations. In the state of Montana, inoculantions for children include diphtheria, tetanus, pertussis, measles, mumps, rubella, polio (IPV), Hib (*Haemophilus influenzae*), hepatitis B, varicella, hepatitis A, pneumococcal, influenza, and rotavirus, many of which are combined in vaccines. Religious and medical exemptions are allowed.

Milani, like Weber, had apprehensions about corporate medicine, from children's vaccines and aluminum levels (a much-discussed health issue in alternative health circles), to unethical practices in Big Pharma, to a concern that natural health advocates get vilified by the press and others when they don't walk in lockstep with conventional medical experts. But as I further discussed Weber's contentions, both Milani and I became struck by the idea that vaccine hesitancy was linked to something much bigger and more troubling.

— — —

DEBRA WEBER JOINED MILLIONS OF PEOPLE DURING THE pandemic in "doing their own research." According to Karen Douglas, who studies the psychology of conspiracy theories at the University of Kent, in England, when "people are scared and uncertain about the pandemic and are looking for ways to cope with the uncertainty, insecurity, and loss of social contact," they turn to conspiracy theories, which "seem to thrive in times of crisis." After hours and hours of googling the fields of vaccines, epigenetics, and disease, Weber told me, she now feels she is in a position to advise others. When we last talked, she did not see the virus as that big of a deal. To be sure, some of Weber's skepticism had to do with her geographical location. Glendive residents didn't experience the horrors of COVID-19 as did people living in Seattle, New York City, or Bergamo, Italy. They didn't hear sirens blaring night and day at the beginning of the pandemic, or see military vehicles full of dead bodies lining the streets, which my husband and I heard about from our anguished Italian friends. Some people living in densely populated areas barely left their apartments for months whereas many westerners, particularly in rural communities, continued to enjoy the outdoors. It's no wonder that some of those who could escape from big coastal cities moved to smaller, less regulated places in the West. So I can almost understand how Weber, given her social isolation and sources of information, arrived at her views on COVID-19. Still, the rural West kept her well-positioned to consume misinformation without confirmation or challenge, since she saw none of the pandemic's carnage.

Weber's online sleuthing has taken her into dodgy anti-science corners and full-blown Christian apocalyptic narratives and biblical literalism. As she found "evidence" that suited her increasing suspicions, she got further and further into self-deception. She told me that Bill Gates developed an mRNA vaccine called Luciferase with a patent number of 060606. "Sounds like a sick joke," she said, referring to the sixes, which she and others have identified as the mark of the devil as per the book of Revelation. When I later tracked this story down, it turned out that an entity known as World Intellectual Property Organization by Microsoft Technology Licensing, LLC, filed a patent application for an enzyme called Luciferase (named after bioluminescence markers found in lightning bugs and jellyfish, among other glowy critters). The patent number is WO2020060606. By the way, there is no Luciferase in COVID-19 vaccines, but this devilish tale has still gained traction in conspiracy theory circles. A White House correspondent for the right-wing news outlet Newsmax, Emerald Robinson, got fired in November of 2021 when she tweeted: "Dear Christians, the vaccines contain a bioluminescent marker called LUCIFERASE so that you can be tracked. Read the last book of the New Testament to see how this ends." If that notion was too cockeyed for Newsmax, it had to be cockeyed indeed.

As Weber and I talked, the conversation grew ever more odd. In addition to Lucifer's vaccine additive, she told me, thousands of microchips are being inserted into each human body with each vaccine syringe. She added that Bill Gates had a plan both to control humans and then, in a curiously converse turn, to eradicate them. Over nearly three hours, our discussion lurched from her children's health concerns to QAnon. When I asked her about these wild conspiracy theorists who believe that Donald Trump and someone named Q are secretly fighting a deep state and the Hollywood elite, who drink the blood of children, she laughed. No, she's not into that stuff, she assured me.

But she had definitely sampled the fare. Hillary Clinton and Barack Obama, she said, were also involved in all sorts of corrupt and vile undertakings, as were Chief Justice John Roberts and Mike Pence. "I've seen terrible stuff about Mike Pence," she said. This stuff, proliferated by online trolls, helped inspire the construction of a gallows on January 6, 2021. Some suggested that Pence deserved hanging for his "terrible" deeds—among these were his agreeing to certify the 2020 electoral ballots in the Senate.

As the pandemic provided space for disinformation on vaccinations, these ideas became braided with stories about child trafficking, Christian ideology, Trump's Stop the Steal campaign, body doubles, blood bathing, and the end of the world. Initial uncertainty and fears over childhood vaccines took Weber into a maw of lies, schemes, and imaginings of the Apocalypse. "I've never seen so many doctors and scientists talk about this," she said. "THIS is why they say this is Biblical. They say 'This IS the End Times and Revelations.'" The vaccine itself, she told me, is "the mark of the beast."

Weber's ideas aren't new. The conspiracy theory of injecting microchips has been around since the 1990s when fringe thinkers connected them with the "mark of the beast." In 2000, when the FDA approved the VeriChip, a bit that could be implanted under people's skin to store and scan information, conspiracy theorists floated the idea that the Antichrist will one day demand all humans be implanted with said devices. Still, the connection between chips and Mephistopheles was rather peripheral until the early 2020s when it went mainstream along with other QAnon bugaboos. How a vaccine skeptic like Weber, who wasn't religious, though perhaps vaguely new-agey, espoused these ideas is a reflection on the dark, engulfing, indoctrinating power of social media.

Weber once voted for Hillary Clinton and Barack Obama, who have been major targets of QAnon. "I voted for a lot of these people.

But I pray to God they are not true," she said of the stories of eating babies and global cabals, recycled from anti-Semitic tropes around pedophilia and blood that date back to the Middle Ages. Then she offered a bit of stunning illogic. "There is so much out there," she said, "some of it must be true." This brought to mind Robert Canen's position on evolution during his college debate—"you just can't know for sure." For both Weber and Canen, uncertainty not only rules out rationality; it weirdly becomes a smoking gun.

— — —

SCIENCE IS CIRCUITOUS, AS I'VE NOTED, WHEREAS BIBLICAL literalism, simple memes, and even gossip can seem an easier route to "enlightenment" for the impatient, fearful, and confused. Science is a hard process. It's methodical. It lacks the cheap thrill of conspiracy theory. It's human, which means it's fallible. Yet, over the last few years conscientious people have worked their asses off to arrive at better understandings of what we are facing with the pandemic. Finding truth in virology or, for that matter, in climate change, depends on confirmation and reconfirmation—that is, many research studies adding evidentiary support to one another, toward an eventual consensus of best scientific knowledge. This takes time. Science philosopher Thomas S. Kuhn pointed out in his 1962 book *The Structure of Scientific Revolutions*: "Because scientists are reasonable men one or another argument will ultimately persuade many of them." Not to mention—as Kuhn didn't but should have—the scientists who are women. "But there is no single argument that can or should persuade them all." Among experts, there will be errors, botches, reassessments, and disagreements, but reasonable men and women build consensus, while opportunists pedal nonsense. Science is provisional; it changes, it evolves. The picture it paints of reality is always a work in progress.

But to some, that feels scary. Falsehoods twisted in myth can be more reassuring than the ever-unfinished but ever-improving frieze offered by science. What we know today can change tomorrow, but the empirical process is our scaffolding for advancement.

This is hardly the first time we've seen anger during pandemic and misunderstanding over medical advancements. In eighteenth-century Boston, the Puritan minister Cotton Mather challenged religious and medical orthodoxy in seeking ways to fight smallpox. Mather was more inclined to believe that God helped those who helped themselves, and he felt that the pervading pious fatalism—the belief that death and disease were God's will—was leading to preventable deaths. Famous for his role condemning witches during the Salem trials, Mather had lost eleven of his fifteen children, some to the smallpox outbreak of 1721. In his anguish and desperation, he decided to wrest the fate of his surviving children from God's hands, instead choosing a controversial therapeutic. A man who had formerly been enslaved, Onesimus, described to the minister a technique, practiced in his village in Africa, that came to be known as variolation. This involved wounding a healthy person and applying, to that small wound, pus collected from the blister of a smallpox victim. The idea was that those inoculated with the ooze would experience a much milder version of the pox— mostly this worked, but sometimes it didn't. Though people did die from variolation, about one in forty, one in seven died from smallpox itself. Many who survived without being inoculated were left severely scarred.

Mather was condemned for his position and one angry detractor even lobbed a bomb into his home. The projectile would have killed him if it hadn't been a dud. This near miss led the minister to rage in his journal, "The Town is become almost an [*sic*] Hell upon Earth, a City full of Lies, and Murders, and Blaphemies [*sic*]…Satan seems to take a strange Posession [*sic*] of it, in the epidemic Rage, against that notable and powerful and successful way of saving the Lives of People from the Dangers of the Small-Pox." Three hundred years later, blasphemies still proliferate and suspicion still abounds.

—   —   —

DURING THE EARLY PHASE OF THE COVID PANDEMIC, WEBER told me, she began to watch an online program called *The HighWire*, an offering of anti-vax conspiracy theory, every week for two to three hours at a time. During this period of great unease, the program offered fertile ground for Del Bigtree, impresario extraordinaire and a former field producer for *Dr. Phil*, to promote medical mendacities. Bigtree also led an anti-vax nonprofit organization, the Informed Consent Action Network. With zero medical training, he has been kicked off platform after platform for spreading misinformation, but even now is a presence on Rumble, a site with no community standards.

In the course of "researching" her concerns, Weber enmeshed herself in a cultural phenomenon that preceded COVID-19 but exploded during the pandemic: conspirituality. That is, a hot mess of conspiracy thinking and spirituality. As a former liberal and as a natural health practitioner, Weber might have been particularly susceptible to this potpourri, as were yoga moms, alternative healers, and a whole lot of Instagram influencers. The word *conspirituality* was coined in 2011 by two sociologists, Charlotte Ward and David Voas, in an article for the *Journal of Contemporary Religion*, where they explored a nexus between New Age spirituality and conspiracy theory. Conspiritualists, they wrote, are engaged in a campaign to defy sinister forces controlling "politics and social order" while society awaits a "paradigm shift." Conspirituality, as amplified by raucous social media influencers, has the appeal of a religious movement in which adherents are part of an "awakening" in their crusade against the elite, the deep state, and doctors.

Social historians Richard Kahn and Tyson Lewis published an article in *Utopian Studies* that traced the intersect of conspiracy theory and "utopian longings of the masses." That combination, they wrote, appealed to "right-wing fanatics, leftist conspiracy buffs, New Agers, college students, and an increasingly dissatisfied and questioning" group of people who are seeking "something deeply provocative." People inclined towards these ideas are looking for something special, according to Kahn and Lewis, a sort of secret knowledge that distinguishes them and makes them feel superior to the unenlightened public. COVID-19 and all the confusion that transpired around it—we are still trying to understand the pandemic and put it in perspective—gave conspirituality an even bigger following than it had when these writers identified it.

COVID skepticism mixed with partisan politics, election distrust, and anger aimed at the CDC, all of which fueled conspirituality culture. This played out on a national scale when Del Bigtree participated in the January 6, 2021, MAGA Freedom Rally just prior to the breach of the US Capitol building. He told the audience that day, "I wish I could tell you I believed in the CDC...I wish I could tell you that this pandemic really is dangerous...I wish I could believe that voting machines worked...but none of this is happening."

During this turbulent period, many people relied on politics in addition to various media to determine truths, becoming entrenched in partisan ways of seeing—whether in their understanding of disease or their doubts over election integrity. The media fed on viewers' preferred narratives. What's unconscionable is that lies about vaccines and ineffective COVID treatments led to hundreds of thousands of deaths. Further, known falsehoods led to the insurrection that followed Bigtree's January 6th speech. In early 2023, Dominion Voting Systems, the company behind those voting machines, issued a legal filing in their $1.6 billion suit, that included texts from News Corp owner

Rupert Murdoch and Fox News personalities Laura Ingram, Tucker Carlson, and Sean Hannity, who all privately denied election fraud, as they publicly peddled it for ratings. This resulted in a bunch of hoodwinked protesters forcing their way into the United States Capitol. Though some were simply stirred up, others were violent.

— — —

SINCE 2020, WHEN THE PANDEMIC HIT, THE FLOODGATES OF controversies and conspiracies have opened. News, speculation, and accusations come out every day about disease origins, efficacy of masks or boosters, and nefarious links among US agencies and Chinese labs. It's enough to give anyone whiplash. This bombardment from Internet, print, and television news media is overwhelming and creates further confusion and mistrust. As one news item seems to verify a position one day, another refutes it the next. This keeps us anxious, angry, and evermore wedded to presumptions. It keeps us mad at one another for being "too stupid," to "get it."

And there is good reason we are fed up. Like Weber, and so many of us, I too spent endless hours on my computer during the early pandemic, trying to understand what was happening virologically, politically, and culturally. To be candid, I sought diversion as well as enlightenment. You can only take so much focused research. Then comes time for a break, for, in my case, videos of orphaned elephants sucking on big milk bottles or dogs doing whatever. One of my favorite distractions before COVID had been JP Sears, a comedian who posted satirical shorts for years, gibing gluten-free diets, political correctness, and the Burning Man culture. This person was entertaining, lighthearted, and funny. And then he wasn't. At the beginning of the pandemic, Sears appeared with Mikki Willis, director of two wildly inaccurate "documentary" videos, both titled *Plandemic*. Both feature a controversial one-time virologist named Judy Mikovits making dark and unsupported claims about sinister forces behind COVID-19. *Plandemic: The Hidden Agenda behind Covid-19* was the first big social media splash related to the pandemic.

Willis introduces Mikovits in his film as "one of the most accomplished scientists of her generation," claiming that her 1991 doctoral thesis revolutionized the treatment of HIV/AIDS, and that she had published a blockbuster article in the journal *Science*. In fact, not only is she most certainly *not* one of the most accomplished scientists of her generation, her article in *Science* was retracted due to inaccuracies.

On camera, Mikovits says that masks make people sick and that medicines such as hydroxychloroquine are being intentionally disparaged in order for people like Anthony Fauci to make profits. "The game is to prevent the therapies until everyone is infected and push the vaccine," she says. She also claims that "flu vaccines increase the odds by 36 percent of getting COVID-19." Thoroughly discredited by her peers, Mikovits became a darling in certain pseudoscience circles because she told conspiritualists just what they wanted to hear, and *Plandemic* was viewed millions of times. Though YouTube yanked the film from its platform for spreading misinformation, her book *Plague of Corruption*, also widely panned, became a bestseller in 2020. Condemned by many professionals in her field, Mikovits nonetheless amplified misunderstanding widely, and left people vulnerable to both deceits and disease.

I had been following JP Sears on social media when he joined with filmmaker Mikki Willis in spreading rabid COVID-19 conspiracy theories. In May of 2020, I expressed disappointment over his support of *Plandemic*. Another follower, Anthony (I'll omit his last name), writing from Texas, responded to my post: "No contagion exists. The testing method doesn't even prove that someone has viable transmissible virus you ignorant fucktarded cunt." Hmm, I thought. I'd never been called that before.

The exchange with Texas Anthony happened in advance of

COVID vaccines and before the 2020 elections, but it showed how vicious, albeit jejune, people became while defending their beliefs. People like Sears, Bigtree, and Mikovits made Anthony, and people like him, feel justified in their bile and smug in their smarts. They laid wait on social media to pounce, equating their own opinions with expertise and eviscerating those who dickered.

Sears's videos continued to get edgier and edgier, attracting attention from very unlikely corners—at least it seemed so at the time. When I saw that he had partnered with the gun-glorifying Black Rifle Coffee Company, a politically committed caffeine emporium, it seemed jarringly discordant. As the former gun-company executive and later critic of gun commerce, Ryan Busse explained in his book, *Gunfight: My Battle Against the Industry that Radicalized America*, Black Rifle Coffee is "a multi-million-dollar company inspired by military guns" that is "a rollicking combination of war zone and frat party." One of the company's founders, Mat Best, according to Busse, "helped normalize an edgy brand of tactical bravado that celebrated the AR-15 as a necessary component of manhood and militaristic patriotism." In 2021, Black Rifle Coffee's website featured Sears modeling company merchandise, now a poster boy for a brand that was everywhere during the January 6th insurrection. Many proudly wore the Black Rifle Coffee logo gear, including a man who carried zip ties through the Senate chamber, as he sought out members of Congress. Sears, a goofy-looking redhead, muscularly jacked, and clad in yoga clothing, once poked good fun at diets and virtue signaling. Now he shills gun culture, cryptocurrency, and even pathetic, QAnon-laced content. In the last video I watched, he characterized liberals as "evil, tyrannical people controlled by Satan," while wearing a Fetal Lives Matter T-shirt, an example of merchandise that he sells, by the way. It left me depressed. Clearly, Sears had found a new audience.

During the pandemic, while JP Sears turned militant, Mikki Willis became famous, and anti-vaxxers Del Bigtree and Robert F. Kennedy Jr. pulled in millions of dollars for their non-profits, Debra Weber of Glendive, Montana, just wanted to keep her family safe. But under their influence she made the situation less safe, particularly for her older in-laws. Efforts to research and justify her concerns over vaccines led her into deep dark holes. This was not done from ignorance, nor from idleness, but from an inclination to reaffirm personal views, plus the enticement of mad algorithms that pulled her into conspiracy theory. Months and months of pandemic created a culture fueled by fury and mistrust, social disruption, political upheaval, and fevered dreams of End Times. Like Weber, some sought refuge in states where libertarianism fed resistance to health recommendations from federal agencies. Three years along and counting, Idaho and Montana remain two of the least-vaccinated states in the country, and Wyoming is dead last. Seeking lax protocols and sanctuary in country living, newcomers moved into the mountain West, though infection and death rates eventually reached both rural and urban populations—bucolic places are not safer for their scenery.

Weber chased the myth of a wholesome, healthful life, in a quiet corner of Montana where a small population could insulate her ideas while the internet fed them. She saw the farm as a safe haven from the welter of imposed imperatives, intrusions, and mandates. And yet, she continues to live amid such realities. No matter how idyllic, secluded, and self-driven life feels on rural lands, there are still regulations to abide by. All of the animals mooing, oinking, barking, and bleating on the Weber farm have been inoculated with scientifically developed vaccines.

Chapter 3

Winning the West

A S WE WERE WINDING DOWN OUR THREE-HOUR chat, Debra Weber asked me, "Did you ever watch *The Matrix* with Keanu Reeves?" Of course, I replied. Did I remember the part when he was asked if he wanted to take the red pill or the blue pill? I said yes. She was referring to the scene when Laurence Fishburne's character, Morpheus, gives Reeves's, Neo, an opportunity to stay in a fantasy world by swallowing the blue pill, or to take the red pill and enter reality. This scene is commonly referred to in conspiracy theory circles as an exemplum of the idea of waking to the authentic state of things. JP Sears even made a video, "Blue Pill People," ridiculing those taking COVID-19 precautions as sniveling scaredy-cats. Covered in blue paint, he mutters in front of the camera, "It's not safe out there. It's only safe in here," while looking pathetically through the window. The message: only delusional people follow COVID-19 protocols and pop blue pills. Actually, I tell Weber, "I've been to both the Red Pill Expo and the Red Pill Festival," the latter being a western version of the former. "Then you know what I mean," she said. I did.

In October of 2020, the annual Red Pill Expo was held on Jekyll Island, Georgia. The Expo is the brainchild of G. Edward Griffin, a ninety-year-old longtime member of the ultra-conservative John Birch

Society, an organization founded in the 1940s by eleven men who saw the specter of communism everywhere. A year after the Georgia event, the Red Pill Festival, a regional offshoot inspired by the national event, came to St. Regis, Montana. Both attracted anti-government activists, snake oil vendors, manipulators, chumps, and me.

Griffin has been ballyhooed by the former Fox News personality Glenn Beck and by the Infowars impresario Alex Jones, who once introduced him as "a writer and film producer, with many titles to his credit…listed in Who's Who in America…a living icon." And Jones would know a star huckster when he sees one. In 2022, the Infowars star was ordered by courts to pay over a billion dollars to the families of the Sandy Hook victims for broadcasting that the murder of twenty children at that elementary school was a staged hoax.

Through a long career, Griffin, like his admirer Jones, has peddled lies under the guise of revelation, giving rise to the idea of the red pill. He claims that 9/11 was an inside job, that AIDS isn't real, that vapor trails from jet engines are actually chemical streams controlling the climate, and that vitamin B-17 cures cancer. He also asserts that FEMA is not out to help people during disasters but scheming to control them under emergency conditions.

Of all Griffin's anti-government animosities, his hatred of the Federal Reserve System is the most intense. He calls it "an instrument of totalitarianism…in which the world's money cabal deliberately encourages war as a means of stimulating the profitable production of armaments and of keeping nations perpetually in debt." He refers to the machinations of the Fed as the "Rothschild Formula," an anti-Semitic term referring to a wealthy family of European Jewish financiers who gained prominence during the Napoleonic Wars. In the circles Griffin runs in, the Rothschild family in particular and Jewish people in general are often blamed for the many wrongs in the world—conspiracy theory larded with hate.

The 2020 Red Pill Expo was jammed with Federal Reserve protesters, Trumpers, QAnon adherents, religious crusaders, and that year's latest crop of dissidents, the COVID-19 skeptics. Presenters ranged from *Plandemic* director Mikki Willis to Del Bigtree, Debra Weber's central source on vaccines, to David Icke, a Brit who claims that reptiles disguised as humans control planet Earth. On the first day of the conference, Patrea Patrick's documentary *The Titanic Never Sank!* aired over lunch break. But this wasn't just a lineup of your typical tinfoil-hat-wearing folks. Assault-rifle-toting dissenters were on the schedule as well. Stewart Rhodes, founder of the militia group the Oath Keepers, took to the stage and talked about civil war. Richard Mack, founder of the Constitutional Sheriffs and Peace Officers Association, boosted the idea that law enforcement should stand up to the government as the central power in this country. Both these men hail from the West and both had been at the game of rebellion for a while. Streaming the event at my dining room table, I watched the varied and strange assortment and realized that extremists from disparate bases were joining together.

I remember that stomach-churning moment when it became apparent, at least to me, that American anger and delusion were being corralled by certain western insurgents, all bumping together in befuddled distortions, rage, and an embrace of authoritarianism. Rhodes had already been talking about the possibility of an illegitimate government if Joe Biden won in the then-upcoming election, and he continued to do so that day on the stage. The seeds of insurrection at the US Capitol building were planted well in advance of voters going to the polls. After Trump's loss, Rhodes told Infowars host Alex Jones, "Just as Americans across the country stormed the Bundy ranch to stand up for a rancher's family, we need to go to Washington with the same conviction." Rhodes and Mack had long been at odds with the government, but it was the Bundy ranch, the site of an armed uprising, that gave them their first taste of insurrection. At the expo in Georgia, they worked to rally the disgruntled and the deceived, serving revolt with a side of red pills and the febrile dreams of patriotic duty.

— — —

DURING THE SUMMER OF 2022, JASON VAN TATENHOVE, AN ex–Oath Keeper from Colorado who once worked for Stewart Rhodes, appeared before the House Select Committee to Investigate the January 6th Attack on the United States Capitol. During his testimony, he confirmed that Rhodes had indeed been involved in the coup attempt and had entreated Trump to invoke the 1807 Insurrection Act, which would have permitted the then-president to engage militias to subdue a rebellion that took the form of a "stolen election." Van Tatenhove said that the Capitol breach "was going to be an armed revolution," which "could have been the spark that started a new civil war." Where did his own involvement with the Oath Keepers start? he was asked. "My time with the Oath Keepers began back at Bundy Ranch, with that first standoff," he answered. The first standoff.

That took place in 2014, when federal officers came to Nevada to confiscate rancher Cliven Bundy's cattle, which were trespassing on public lands, and militia members took up arms to stop the government efforts. A confrontation ensued. Glorified as the "Battle of Bunkerville," it was not in fact a battle—not a shot was fired—despite the way it has later been portrayed by the Bundys and their supporters. As with other western myths, like the Alamo (a fight to defend owners of enslaved people, not freedom) or the gunfight at the OK Corral (thirty seconds of mayhem that took place in a vacant lot, not a corral), the Battle of Bunkerville is a misrepresentation. Cliven Bundy, the patriarch of a large Mormon family, had racked up over $1 million of court-ordered fines and unpaid grazing fees after he lost his permit to graze cows on a parcel of public Bureau of Land Management land.

The story unfolded like this: In the 1990s, amid federal efforts to protect the desert tortoise under the Endangered Species Act, the Department of the Interior set up a compensation package for ranchers throughout Clark County, Nevada, to retire their public lands grazing permits, essentially paying them to stop using lands that weren't even theirs. Bundy did not take the deal. These federal protection efforts were part of a deal the government struck with Las Vegas developers, allowing construction to go full steam ahead into the reptile's habitat, in exchange for contributions to a fund to buy out the ranchers. Though it's true that developers would use less land than livestock operators, it rankled many that casinos, hotels, golf courses, and condos could still sully the desert, but not cows. After refusing the federal offer, Bundy continued to graze and enlarge his herds, even letting them drift onto the long-retired allotments of his neighbors. His flagrant disregard for the law and the land finally spurred the Feds to action. After years of such trespassing, a confiscation order intended to impound his "unauthorized" cattle was issued by a court. In April of 2014, federal officials came to Gold Butte, Nevada, to enforce the law.

But the old rancher would not go down without a fight. Bundy issued a made-up edict, dubbing it the "Range War Emergency Notice and Demand for Protection," and called on his county's sheriff and others to come to his rescue and fight the government. Bundy's pleas, amplified over the internet, attracted vigilante militia forces from all over, including Rhodes' Oath Keepers and Mack's Constitutional Sheriffs and Peace Officers Association. Coming together with Gadsden flags, assault rifles, pocket copies of the US Constitution, and folding chairs, a mob of about seven hundred people engaged in a standoff with law enforcement, bringing north- and southbound traffic to a halt on Interstate 15 along the Utah-Nevada border. With guns aimed between the two sides, it could have ended in a hail of bullets had there been as much as a backfire from one of the hundreds of idling vehicles awaiting the stalemate's end. But after two long hours, the Feds turned tail, leaving the Bundys and their supporters to claim victory. Bundy's cows continue to illegally graze to this day. In the aftermath, Bundy's son Ryan, flushed with adrenaline and exultation, stood before the crowd as the federal officers and the Las Vegas police drove away. He hollered a phrase expressing another myth of this region, one fraught with horrors but central to the place. "The West has now been won!"

—   —   —

THE WEST IS A STORIED LAND OF LAST STANDS AND shootouts. Ryan Bundy was echoing the age-old victory cry, one that came out of the Indian Wars, made famous by Teddy Roosevelt's *The Winning of the West*. Roosevelt published four volumes of *The Winning of the West*, between 1889 and 1896, amid his varied political and financial defeats, with the oft-repeated themes: righteous revolution, the love of liberty, and the sacrifices and hard work that come in campaigns of settlement to build a nation. His work took an ugly satisfaction in the slaughter of Indigenous people in colonizing the land, and his ideas continued to influence how American culture imagined the West.

They also laid a framework for understanding other western myths, like free land, Manifest Destiny, and notions of wilderness. One misconception, of course, was empty territory free for the taking because land used for millennia by millions of America's first people was not "owned" in the way white people construed ownership. Just as the Bundys think they are more entitled to public lands than others, early settlers, as white Christians, felt that they were a more suitable culture to live in the West than the non-Christian Native peoples. This idea was rooted in the 1493 papal bull's Doctrine of Discovery, which developed an American angle in Manifest Destiny, a phrase coined in 1845 by journalist John O'Sullivan, in a column about annexing Oregon Country and Texas. He wrote that it was the "manifest destiny to overspread the continent allotted by Providence for the free development of our yearly multiplying millions." By this, he meant the white millions who had moved to North America. It became the rallying cry for continued campaigns of "Indian Removal" and undergirded the push to make the West, despite its aridity, into an idyllic, God-given garden like the lush lands of the East and South. It was used as a kind of motto by boosters of expansionism, and came to be a slogan for American exceptionalism, divine fortune, and superiority. It was a malleable concept and one with staying power.

Some seventy years after Roosevelt's work, a 1962 movie, *How the West Was Won*, adapted from a series in *Life* magazine, provided perspective on how the West was imagined—and how, by many people, it still is. The movie's narrator, Spencer Tracy, regales the audience with the following treacle:

> The West that was won by its pioneers, settlers, adventurers is long gone now. Yet it is theirs forever, for they left tracks in history that will never be eroded by wind or rain—never plowed under by tractors, never buried in a compost of events...From soil enriched by their blood, out of their fever to explore and build, came lakes where once there were burning deserts—came the goods of the earth; mine and wheat fields, orchards and great lumber mills. All the sinews of a growing country...a people free to dream, free to act, free to mold their own destiny.

But this never was the truth of the West. Hubris and biblical notions of both dominion and earth's "subdual" sent some West with fantasies that couldn't withstand the realities of the place. Tractors plowed through sod, resulting in the Dust Bowl. Artificial desert lakes

have become shrunken puddles. Good paying jobs in the timber industry supported families, until the inevitable bust left sawmills closed,
communities suffering, and lands denuded and eroded from clear cutting. Most recently, the idea of unfettered freedom fomented violent
mobs, some inspired by Ryan Bundy's proclamation. The real fantasy
of winning the West is that it was available to be "won" (or lost) in the
first place.

—   —   —

THE BUNDYS' FIGHT HAS BEEN UNIQUELY SUCCESSFUL IN
garnering public attention, in part because it is fixed in the West and
draws on myths such as wide-open ranges and unrestrained freedoms.
Some supporters have come to see their fight through the lenses of
David and Goliath, black hats and white hats, cows and cowboys.
Those perspectives certainly guide the Bundys themselves. But their
story is also a western version of the American Dream. According to
historian David Hamilton Murdoch, "The idea of the West has always
been involved in a special relationship with the American Dream—
that belief in the good society, in a special mission, and in a destiny
unique among nations." But the American Dream is our country's
most hopeless myth. The Bundy's dream, their special mission, has
been to claim land they don't own, while flouting federal law and the
Constitution. They have inspired armed conflict and ongoing defiance.
In the West, they became folk heroes, and many others, like Stewart
Rhodes, aspired to their mythic status.

Rhodes, with his Oath Keepers, stood alongside the Bundy family
at the Battle of Bunkerville in 2014. Jowly, grizzled, balding, wearing
an eye patch behind glasses after accidently shooting himself in the
face years earlier, he was drawn to the January 6th coup attempt by
his own sense of a special mission. It was clear, from his words at the

Red Pill Expo, that he would not take a Trump election defeat lying down. So he went to DC and declared war on the government, working on a transition of power. For his actions, Rhodes was found guilty of seditious conspiracy, tampering with documents, and obstructing an official. The initial indictment declared that Rhodes and other militia members

> organized teams prepared and willing to use force and to transport firearms and ammunition into Washington, DC; recruited members and affiliates to participate in the conspiracy; organized trainings to teach and learn paramilitary combat tactics; brought paramilitary gear, weapons and supplies—including knives, batons, camouflaged combat uniforms, tactical vests with plates, helmets, eye protection and radio equipment—to the Capitol grounds; breached and attempted to take control of the Capitol grounds and building on Jan. 6, 2021, in an effort to prevent, hinder and delay the certification of the electoral college vote; used force against law enforcement officers while inside the Capitol on Jan. 6, 2021; continued to plot, after Jan. 6, 2021, to oppose by force the lawful transfer of presidential power, and using websites, social media, text messaging and encrypted messaging applications to communicate with co-conspirators and others.

As Rhodes' former associate Jason Van Tatenhove later testified before Congress to the January 6th Committee, the Bundy Standoff was a seminal event in the imagining of and network behind ongoing revolt. But the family patriarch was unimpressed with the insurrection he helped inspire. Cliven Bundy posted on Facebook after the Capitol breach, "100,000 should have spent the night in the halls and 100,000 should have protected them." Congress should never have certified the election, in his view, just as feds should never have messed with his cows.

Tasha Adams, Stewart Rhodes' estranged wife, hopes that she's coming close to finalizing her divorce. It has been five years since she filed her paperwork, and the process has been expensive and draining. She is cheered that she finally knows the address of her estranged husband, who is currently incarcerated, so she can finally serve him papers. Ready to shake off her old identity as the wife of Rhodes and cofounder of the Oath Keepers, she is telling journalists and those who are interested in her story that she's an open book.

In the fall of 2022, after a couple of long phone calls with Adams, I drove upstate to visit her in Eureka, Montana, an old logging town eight miles from the Canadian border. It's a little place of around 1,500 residents, carved into thick timber that surrounds the community like soaring coniferous buttresses. It's remote in a way that would appeal to a paranoid, anti-government agitator. But it's also charming—the old brick buildings on Main Street, the nearby Lake Koocanusa, a riverwalk path for walkers and bikers, and gracious locals. While there, I was complimented three times on my shoes.

I met Adams at Café Jax, where we talked over big plates of eggs heaped atop English muffins, while our cups of coffee were endlessly refilled. Liberty, Tasha's sixteen-year-old daughter, was set to perform in the musical *Ride the Cyclone* at Lincoln County High School. Her son Dakota and his sister Sequoia attend college in Kalispell while working construction a couple of days a week. Adams had recently joined a gym, eager to be more active and social after so much isolation and stress.

Our meeting occurred during the first week of Rhodes' trial and Adams, having herself been in the limelight lately, appearing in many outlets from CNN to the *Los Angeles Times*, confessed that she was both adrenalized and exhausted. So much had happened to her in the last few years. She'd spent two years planning her escape from the growing abuse of Rhodes, and the divorce had been prolonged, with failed restraining orders and virtually no access to joint finances. In her early fifties, with platinum blonde hair, porcelain skin, and a quick sense of humor, she's steely and determined even through her world weariness. At times Adams came across as charmingly girlish, but it's clear she's got bark.

Rhodes and Adams married in 1994, three years after they met in Las Vegas, where she had been his dancing instructor for "general ballroom, rhumba, foxtrot, cha-cha, swing," she explained, adding, "He wasn't very good." Still, she fell for him, or rather for a version of him—one he aspired to, a hero with a glorious destiny. Early in their marriage, he had talked her into gigs cocktail waitressing topless and later stripping, making her feel, she told me, like an ATM machine. She would work and he would take the money. As the couple had children, she stopped with adult entertainment, turning instead to selling clothes on eBay. The growing family struggled as Rhodes lost multiple jobs, moving the family from place to place, searching for that special mission, his American Dream. Still, like so many other women in abusive relationships, she thought she could help him find his elusive direction, which would make everything better. That's what she kept telling herself, as the abuse increased.

There are reasons why Adams felt Rhodes had potential to become something great. He'd been a paratrooper in the army for three years, until he broke his back. Then, graduating summa cum laude in 1998 from the University of Nevada, Rhodes looked toward pursuing a law degree at an Ivy League university. He studied, Adams explained, how to make himself a competitive candidate among the monied and recently graduated. Being a nontraditional student in his thirties from the West, with Hispanic heritage, a stint in the army, and a sweeping résumé (from concealed-carry instructor to sculptor of bosomy females in bronze for MGM's now-closed Grand Adventures Theme Park), Rhodes thought his profile would set him apart from other applicants. He was right. Yale, the University of Chicago, and Harvard all accepted him, Adams recalled. "He knew he wanted to get into a top school and that they wanted diversity," so he wrote in his submission essay about everything from "his migrant farmer family" to details on "his sister's brain injury."

From Yale Law School, he went to work for libertarian Ron Paul, in whose ambit he became convinced of the Y2K doomsday theory, which held that computers wouldn't be able to process the millennial year change and all hell would break loose on January 1, 2000. For the family, the year 1999 was spent getting ready for an end-times scenario, prepping weapons, fuel, and other supplies back in Las Vegas, where they lived in an apartment on the brink of eviction. They were almost out of food. Adams told me she fed the children dried apple chips and oatmeal from the Mormon cannery, a storage center run by the Church of Jesus Christ of Latter-day Saints, which offered prepackaged foods to families in need. She had grown up in an LDS household, and Rhodes claimed he had converted.

Though he had gone to one of the finest law schools in the country, Adams's soon-to-be ex-husband couldn't get a practice going. After almost getting kicked out of their Las Vegas residence, the family moved to Polson, Montana. In ongoing attempts to find meaning and make money, Rhodes, along with Adams, created the Oath Keepers in 2009—an organization, according to Adams, meant to be "an ACLU for libertarians." She feels that initially Rhodes wanted an organization that was noble and upstanding and remembered some of his promotional material as embarrassingly caricatured. "He had a video set to the soundtrack of *The Last of the Mohicans*." His message—essentially pro-gun, pro-Constitution, and anti-government—was meant to appeal to the Ron Paul crowd. Adams recalls that, on the morning after

Rhodes' Oath Keepers website went live (with a link to her PayPal account), the couple woke up to $70,000 in donations. "He told me I could pay the electric bill," she said, then he took the rest of the money, leaving the family stranded for weeks at a time. She couldn't break from her husband when she had six little ones, dogs, no car, and no money. "The kids had holes in their shoes and he had $300 boots." She laughed, seeing bitter humor in his outrageous self-involvement and western fantasy.

In 2010, Adams had a miscarriage. She remembers her midwives looking at a sonogram of the baby while Rhodes walked the halls of the clinic yelling at members of the Oath Keepers board over the phone. He stalked and screamed, while the women shared the awful weight of the image. He finally paused when he noticed the pall in the room. Looking at the ultrasound, Rhodes switched his phone to speaker and announced to his directors, "Our baby is dead." In the minutes after his wife learned of this unbearable loss, Rhodes used the miscarriage to end an argument with his board. He never comforted her, not even later that night when she began to hemorrhage. When she told me this story, we were both in tears.

Still, she stuck with him, even accompanying him once to the Marble Community God and Country Celebration in eastern Washington, where he had been a featured speaker several times over the years. You'll hear more about this place in a bit, but suffice to say for now, it figures prominently in the cultural geography of militia maneuvering in the West. At the Marble annual gathering, according to Donna Capurso for *Redoubt News*, "like-minded folks can participate in activities giving glory to God and sharing the resurgence of dedication to the principles of liberty and freedom of our founding fathers." The celebration is "so refreshing," Capurso continued, because it gives folks a chance "to visit with others that are passionate about preserving our republic for their children and grandchildren and were not hesitant to speak their minds about the condition of our country and the multitude of liberals that are trying to destroy our country and the foundations it was built upon."

The year Rhodes took his family to Marble, 2013, organizers put them up in a lovely home and gave them a stack of vouchers to use at the event's food trucks. Adams told me that the kids were beside themselves, gorging on all of the offerings, and completely missed their father's speech. "They called it Cheesecake Camp," Adams told me, giggling at the memory of her kids carrying around heaping plates of the dessert piled on graham cracker crust. She told me that they all thought the Marble people were crazy, but they left with bellies full of something other than apples and oatmeal.

Rhodes then moved the family to Trego, Montana, a town of about 850 people—so isolated, Adams said, that cops can't be found for miles in any direction. Here he built a series of partially finished tunnels in the yard of their rental property in case he had to bug out if the Feds came calling. The couple's young daughters used it as a sort of subterranean dollhouse. After his arrest for his role at the January 6 insurrection, Adams tweeted, "Folks, if you ever feel tempted to rent a backhoe and dig escape tunnels in the backyard of your rental house, keep in mind it may come back to haunt you if you later attempt to overthrow the US government." In other words, although Oath Keepers was founded to mint warrior heroes, Rhodes had known that at some point, the Feds would come after him for his pursuit of a calling.

Two years after her miscarriage, Adams delivered a stillborn child, at which point she began to withdraw from her husband. Despite the isolation of northwestern Montana, Adams was relieved when he left her, in 2014, to join the rogue cowboys and militia gathered for action at the Bundy ranch. Now considered a hotshot in militia circles, Rhodes expected to throw his weight around at the standoff and further establish himself as a leader in the patriot movement. But he made some missteps that eroded his credibility among other patriots. Adams had tried to warn him about the politics involved in LDS patriarchy and that the Bundys, themselves LDS, wouldn't easily turn over the reins to Rhodes during their rebellion no matter his military experience. There was tension and territorialism among the various militia members and Rhodes passed along misinformation that the Feds were planning a drone strike, withdrawing his Oath Keepers from what he feared would be a kill zone. No drones were launched and Rhodes was ostracized for his bad intelligence and cowardice. Although he did raise tens of thousands of dollars for his organization on the strength of his involvement with the Bundys, he came back to Montana with his tail between his legs.

The Oath Keepers organization, at the start, was comprised primarily of ex-military, cops, and folks discontented with Obama's America and the ongoing impacts of recession. According to a 2022 report from the Anti-Defamation League, the group by then had thirty-eight thousand members in its database, including people in elected positions, law enforcement, and armed forces. Adams described the people Rhodes targeted in his recruitment efforts as "those who felt out of place in the modern world." They were prone to a "hyper-masculinity," Adams told me. "The only value they see is providing and protecting." In that spirit, Rhodes puffed himself up as the traditional family man, a paterfamilias and guardian, strutting around in fancy cowboy boots while leaving his own family wanting.

Like Rhodes, many of his recruits struggled to find purpose, seeking manly pursuits to fill unrealized dreams. When "you can't cowboy your life," Adams observed wryly, you're apt to be enticed by the myths Rhodes offered. Lots of the folks he enlisted, she said, seemed to suffer mentally. "He was predatory. Someone working at Home Depot, who needs a real duty," would see the Oath Keepers as a ticket out of feelings of insignificance and traumatic stress. He once told her,

"I wish I was living in another time. I'd be a traveling preacher." But in this time, in a sense, he was. During a hearing over fellow Oath Keeper David Moerschel's role in the January 6 breach of the Capitol building, Moerschel's defense attorney, Scott Weinberg, referred to the influence of Rhodes over his client. "I feel Mr. Rhodes is a right-wing televangelist…a faulty leader" who "lives off other people's dues and manipulates them." He added, "But we're also going to learn he's incompetent."

As with his law school applications, Rhodes was tactical in the way he ran Oath Keepers, following trends in the ever-growing patriot culture that would keep money flowing. Initially the organization was inspired by libertarianism, but as his culture became increasingly engaged in alt-right conservatism and insurgency, he took some real one-eightys, according to Adams and her oldest son, Dakota. Both mother and son were especially surprised by Rhodes' reversal on Black Lives Matter because at one point, according to Adams, he seemed sympathetic to the movement. In 2014, during the protests in Ferguson, Missouri, Rhodes considered staging an armed Oath Keepers march there with Black militia members, not in counterprotest but in support. This revelation surprised me, but Adams explained that Rhodes hated racism. Still, he canceled the march after backlash from his supporters. Instead, Rhodes joined counterprotests, with his Oath Keepers standing armed on the roofs of buildings, claiming to protect private property during the protests as the militia would do again in 2020.

Adams also told me that Rhodes was initially concerned about COVID, until members, including the group's national chaplain, Chuck Baldwin of Kalispell, Montana, turned on him for taking precautions. He then "stopped wearing a mask," she said. Later, having fully reversed his COVID stance, Rhodes would share a stage at the Red Pill Expo with *Plandemic* film director Mikki Willis, trading conspiracy theories and falsehoods threaded into myths of machismo and exceptionalism.

As he made his speech at the Red Pill Expo, six years after his involvement at the Bundy ranch and not long before the 2020 election, Rhodes was again crafting a plan, one that would make him a central player in the coup attempt months later. The Bundys would not join him. Stoking the fires of an uprising to an ever-widening audience coalesced around delusion and distrust, he told the crowd in Georgia, "You are your own self-defense. You must organize yourselves in the next thirty days in your towns and counties…We will have our men deployed outside the polling stations to make sure you are protected, especially in swing states." He predicted a civil war on the horizon, promising that "we have members [Oath Keepers] in every state in the union and we are standing them up right now." Stand back and stand by, as Donald Trump had told another militia group, the Proud Boys, one month before during a September 29 presidential debate. Inspired by Trump and the "first standoff" at the Bundy ranch, Rhodes was laying groundwork, no longer to stand by but to make his move, by bringing the Battle of Bunkerville to the US Capitol.

Adams explains Rhodes as a paradox. "He believes that he is sort of a chosen person," she told one interviewer, and "believes he almost has magical powers." She describes Rhodes as seeing himself as an LDS hero, a figure destined, as in the controversial Mormon White Horse Prophecy, to save the American Constitution. This idea he shares with Ammon Bundy, another of Cliven's sons, who, one year after Bunkerville, led the takeover of the Malheur National Wildlife Refuge in Oregon. The White Horse Prophecy foretells of a Latter-day Saint hero protecting the Constitution and saving the republic from corruption. Still, for all Rhodes' delusions of grandeur, his deep inse-curities make him something of a chameleon. He didn't just pivot from racial justice to counter-demonstrating, and from COVID precautions to COVID denial. His very personality changed. He would become "obsessed with people and start to talk like them, dress like them," said Adams. She watched him buy a leather vest, get tattoos, and start wearing a cowboy hat, imitating others.

Following the 2014 Nevada standoff, Rhodes swaggered, fundraised, and looked for the next fight. But by then he was unraveling. Money remained tight and he became ever angrier and more abusive. At one point, he put the barrel of a gun to the head of the family dog. He later choked the couple's then thirteen-year-old daughter, until her brother, Dakota, whom Rhodes had started viewing as a rival male, stepped in to save her. This was the final straw for Adams. She began to plan how to leave her husband and keep custody of her six children.

To understand how Rhodes was central to the insurrection after the 2020 election, we must look at his many inspirations. His kids call him the King of the Apocalypse, Adams said, so there's the book of Revelation. There's the White Horse Prophecy of an LDS hero. There's the mirage of patriarchal provider and protector. There's the strutting cowboy who protected Bundy's cows. And finally, there's his own illusory American Dream.

Notions of the American Dream often get passed on by older generations. Think of Willy Loman and Biff. Or Cliven Bundy and his boys. With Rhodes, it came from the maternal side of the family. His mother, improbably named Dusty Buckle, was a bit of a restless soul who married several times, moving the kids from situation to situation, while working as a minister, a pyramid schemer, a public speaker, "and a grifter," as Adams put it. Buckle spent her life seeking and scamming throughout various jobs and relationships. She also "changed religions every week," Adams said, and as for her son, she "was obsessed with him."

The daughter of Mexican farmworkers, Buckle claimed that her grandfather once rode with Poncho Villa. More recently they picked fruit, and the family had a favored expression: after the grapes. This meant winning the brass ring. Reaping the harvest. It meant the moment of culmination and bounty, when bunches of grapes, warm, round, and heavy with juice, got sheared from vines and boxed, bound for ice boxes and fine wines. It represented an exquisite moment—a time of success, a job well done, a paycheck that made possible food-laden tables, a happy family, and the satisfaction of a mission accomplished. It was a time of glory. Of self-realization. For Rhodes, this was always the goal, but always just out of reach. Out of reach for him, for his grandparents, for his mother. From a struggling childhood, to Yale Law, to the Bundy ranch, to the Ellipse, Rhodes longed for something that eluded him—purpose, respect, admiration, victory.

This desperate hunger for success, his erratic striving for the American Dream, brought him in tactical gear to Washington, DC, on January 6, 2021. Embracing still another whopper—the Big Lie of Trump, requiring followers to "stop the steal"—Stewart Rhodes played his part in trying to overthrow American democracy. He'd stockpiled weapons in a nearby hotel, then waited outside the US Capitol for Trump to invoke the Insurrection Act. This, he hoped, would be his moment—thwarting the peaceful transfer of power and insuring Trump's continued reign. But it was a miserable shitshow. A year and a half later, he was found guilty of seditious conspiracy and now faces up to sixty years in prison. Rhodes did not win the West, nor the coup. He failed in his mission to be a folk hero and remains estranged from many of his former associates, from a wife, and from every one of his children. The stories and myths that sent Rhodes lurching through life, from one direction to another, failed him. The fruit he picked, in desperation, incompetence, and delusions of grandeur, proved a very bitter harvest.

— — —

YUVAL NOAH HARARI'S BOOK *SAPIENS: A BRIEF HISTORY OF Humankind* explores how *Homo sapiens* evolved with big brains and sophisticated ways to communicate. Harari also explains how we are members of a myth-making species—we invent iconic narratives in order to unify groups and create common cultures. He points out that telling effective stories is not easy: "The difficulty lies not in telling the story, but in convincing everyone else to believe it. Much of history revolves around this question: how does one convince millions of people to believe particular stories...?" A gripping story wields enormous authority. In listening to such a narrative, brainwaves synchronize, bonding interlocutor with beholder. Rapport is built over shared understanding. This phenomenon gives humans immense power because it enables strangers to cooperate and work towards common goals. Shared stories build cohesion and galvanize actions, whether they are literal interpretations of the Bible, QAnon conspiracy theory, or the heroics of rebellion. The Battle of Bunkerville helped inspire a movement of people who want to fight a tyrannical government and win.

At play as well in this movement is the process of schismogenesis, a creation of division. Coined by Margaret Mead's much less famous husband, anthropologist Gregory Bateson, the idea holds that human groups identify themselves and define others through difference. It's a way of separating ourselves from the other, whether in politics, religion, or race. Instead of coming together through shared values, schismogenesis creates opposition and establishes polarized groups who don't merely disapprove of the other, but actively oppose them. We are living in a culture driven by myth, as well as sets of contrarian views that often pit us against those who think differently. It's not only militia and QAnon who are schismogenic, but the many Americans who have entrenched in unmoving dogmas, unwilling to examine their own intransigence. Though most of us do not let this stubbornness turn into armed standoffs.

After the Battle of Bunkerville, aspiring paladins Ammon and Ryan brought the White Horse Prophecy, and their mission to win the West, into Oregon. For forty-one days in 2016, Cliven's sons, along with dozens of armed militia members, held the Malheur National Wildlife Refuge hostage, in a confused and confusing protest against public land management and the incarceration of Steven and Dwight Hammond. This father and son had served time for arson on federal land, but later were ordered back to prison to finish mandatory sentences. Both Bundy brothers were eventually locked up and charged with crimes, but later acquitted, for their role in the armed takeover. Additional charges against Ammon, Ryan, and Cliven for their Nevada standoff were still later dropped, after the judge declared a mistrial. Stewart Rhodes, who did not participate in the Malheur occupation, was never arrested or tried for his involvement in Bunkerville. The Hammonds were pardoned by Donald Trump, and there is currently an ongoing investigation to determine if the former president was bribed to do so.

The takeover of Malheur seemed downright clownish at the time, but with the shooting death of protester Robert "LaVoy" Finicum, the protest had a martyr to add credibility to the rebellion in Oregon. Finicum died weeks into the refuge takeover, as law enforcement officers attempted to arrest him on January 26, 2016. He'd been on his way to meet a "constitutional sheriff," a man friendly to the occupation of the refuge.

The idea of constitutional sheriffs has a relatively short but feverish history, traceable back to the posse comitatus movement, a virulent far-right brainstorm of the 1960s, 1970s, and 1980s. The idea is an old legal concept, dating back to the 1870s, that purportedly gives a county sheriff the authority to recruit any citizen in helping keep the peace. It has influenced sovereign citizens, tax protesters, and white and Christian nationalist movements and was formalized under the newer label in 2011, with the founding of a Constitutional Sheriffs and Peace Officers Association by the former Arizona sheriff Richard Mack. At the Red Pill Expo of 2020, after Stewart Rhodes talked of impending civil war, Mack discussed this idea of constitutional sheriffs. His organization, the CSPOA, is a militia-backing, posse-comitatus-supporting group of elected officials who have sworn to take on federal government forces if they feel the Constitution is being violated. In other words, Mack encourages law enforcement all over the country to arbitrarily enforce (or not enforce) laws they personally determine to be just (or unjust). On that day Finicum was shot, some of the participants in the Oregon takeover were on their way to meet Sheriff Glenn Palmer of Grant County, who they hoped could be helpful to their cause.

Finicum was driving the first vehicle of a convoy when it was intercepted by law enforcement. When the cops commanded that he surrender, he flatly refused, shouting, "Back down or you kill me now. Go ahead. Put the bullet through me. I don't care. I'm going to go meet the sheriff. You do as you damned well please." He then gunned the Dodge Ram he was driving, before nearly hitting an FBI agent and crashing the pickup into a snowbank. When Finicum exited the vehicle, he first held his hands up, but then reached into his pocket, where he kept a 9mm Ruger SR9 handgun. He was yelling at the police and federal agents, "Just shoot me!" and that's what happened. This death eclipsed, insofar as members of the patriot movement were concerned, the ineptitude of the Malheur occupation. The shooting gave an otherwise little-supported uprising—in which neither Rhodes nor Mack participated—its central story.

Ammon Bundy, with his fifteen minutes of fame during the occupation, might have faded into history had it not been for one other factor, far more broadly inflammatory than the death of LaVoy Finicum—the pandemic. In state-imposed safety mandates during the first year of COVID, Bundy had found his next Malheur. He told me by phone, in March 2020, that state, county, and federal protective measures were affronts to his sense of liberty, just another example of officials grasping power, like the Feds who'd tried to grab Dad's cattle. Bundy's idea of liberty is grounded in another version of the American western ethos, a claim—no, rather a right—to boundless personal freedom unencumbered by federal regulation.

Bundy moseyed from the cause of public lands to a new shtick. At the beginning of the pandemic, he began recruiting disgruntled people who needed a sense of purpose, some form of duty—just as his old buddy Rhodes had done with the Oath Keepers. Bundy's new organization, People's Rights Network, which some call a neighborhood watch, and others call a vigilante group, quickly enlisted fifty thousand members, according to its website. These enlistees, nicknamed "Ammon's Army" by the Institute for Research and Education on Human Rights, unleashed their rage upon county health departments, school boards, state officials, and even police. They came armed with disinformation, a rabid sense of duty, and, in some cases, with guns. Bundy channeled the passions of such foot soldiers from what was once a war over public lands into a broader network. They aimed their fury at health-care providers and law enforcement officers calling for protection orders, masks, and vaccines.

I reached Bundy by phone at his home in Emmett, Idaho, in March 2020, at a time when the state's Republican governor, Brad Little, had issued a stay-at-home order. During our conversation, Bundy told me that, unlike others he ran with, he did not believe COVID was a hoax, though he contended the whole thing was exaggerated. Death rates were inflated, he claimed, and though the stay-at-home order allowed him time with his family, which he said he was enjoying, Bundy felt it was tyrannical overreach. During disruptive events—in this case, pandemic—he argued, the government takes opportunities to control people and consolidate power. On that much we agreed. William Barr had recently approached Congress to ask permission to arrest people without habeas corpus during Black Lives Matter protests. As Bundy had done in the past while engaged at Bunkerville and Malheur, he was ready again now to take a stand and fight the government, this time against safety protocols. A few weeks after our exchange, Bundy defied Governor Little's stay-at-home order by holding an Easter service, along with a pastor named Diego Rodriguez, a Christian Dominionist, in a warehouse with capacity for one thousand people. Maybe sixty showed up. But Bundy and People's Rights were just getting started.

Twelve days after Easter, he was involved in another act of defiance when a mom in a Boise suburb decided to take her children to a public park, despite its being closed due to COVID concerns. Police officers arrived to find Sarah Walton Brady and a handful of other women disobeying the closure order while their children played on swings. They were asked to go. The mothers did not. Yet the cops were quite patient with these white women. In a video of the event, the arresting officer says, "Please, you're not allowed to use this area right now. We really ask that you leave." Brady flat refused. After forty-five minutes of cajoling, the police finally arrested her, though they clearly did not want to. As she was taken away, she urged the other mothers to "call the Idaho Freedom Foundation," a hardcore right-wing advocacy group that uses every hot-button issue—from medical freedom to critical race theory to LGBTQ grooming—to rile their base, further their power, and raise money. They are effectively reshaping Idaho politics, and their efforts could provide a roadmap for taking over other western states, and the country. We'll see a lot more of this group—stay tuned.

The night of Brady's park protest, Bundy doxed the arresting officer, making public the man's personal information from private documents, and led a rally at the man's house. This now COVID cowboy continued his intimidation tactics, inspiring others to join him. For the last two years, his protests at the state capitol have seen Bundy booked on charges of trespassing, resisting arrest, refusing to wear a face mask, and obstruction. On the first occasion, police hauled him out of the state capitol building, handcuffed to a swivel chair. On the second occasion, he was bound to a wheelchair. After being sentenced for his offenses, Bundy failed to carry out the forty hours of community service, then spent ten days in jail for contempt of court.

Bundy was later taken into custody for trespassing again. He and his followers had been protesting the hospitalization of a severely malnourished child, the grandchild of Diego Rodriguez, the Dominionist pastor who cohosted the Easter service. The infant was placed in the care of St. Luke's Meridian Medical Center by Idaho's Department of Health and Welfare, at the request of his family doctor. After the baby was treated, he was released to his parents, Marissa and Levi Anderson, but the parents failed to return for necessary follow-up care in spite of multiple attempts to reach them. For three days, Ammon's Army mobbed the hospital, endangering staff and others who needed care. The protesters accused personnel of illegally vaccinating the child, poisoning him, and, according a lawsuit filed by the hospital, being part of a "kidnapping and child trafficking ring and then inciting followers by stating that countless children, like the infant, would be kidnapped, trafficked, and potentially killed unless immediate action was taken to destroy the Saint Luke's Parties and others." All the while, People's Rights protestors waved signs outside the medical facility, livestreaming and raising money, cashing in on libel. Things grew so tense that, at one point, the facility implemented a "lockdown," diverting ambulances to other medical facilities, further jeopardizing the health of people who needed care. St. Luke's suit against Bundy and Rodriguez states, "Defendants also organized a campaign of technological disruption. They encouraged their followers to flood

St. Luke's phone lines and email inboxes in an effort to shut down St. Luke's operations." Hospital lawyers note that Rodriguez openly boasted "employees would be shunned by their families and lose their careers while Saint Luke's itself would be run out of business." Currently the pastor is rumored to be in Florida hiding from Idaho courts.

Just before year's end in 2022, Bundy told David Pettinger of the Idaho Freedom Foundation-linked outlet, *Idaho Dispatch*, "They're [St. Luke's] suing me for defamation. They're probably going to try to get judgments of over a million dollars and take everything they have from me," Bundy explained. He and Rodriguez spread QAnon-laced lies during social media campaigns as a hospital and its personnel were trying to save a desperately undernourished baby. As far as any consequences that he may face for his smear campaign and dangerous interference, he also said in the video, "if I have to meet 'em on the front door with my, you know, friends and a shotgun, I'll do that. They're not going to take my property."

In addition to the suit, Bundy pled guilty to a misdemeanor for trespassing and was given 90 days in jail (with 78 days suspended and credited with 12 days of time already served), probation for a year, and a fine of $1,157. He said several supporters have already offered to pay his fine. Of this plea, Bundy told the court, "This is an effort to extend a peace offering...To say, 'Hey look, I don't really want to fight anymore over this.'" But given that the hospital lawsuit is a whole different animal, and that St. Luke was reportedly upset with these plea terms, we'll see how this "olive branch" plays out. At the time of writing, St. Luke's Health System has asked the Ada County judge to again hold Bundy in contempt of court as they pursue at least $7.5 million in damages over Bundy's and Rodriguez's smear campaign. "St. Luke's suffered significant economic damages in addition to the damages suffered by the individuals," the medical center's lawyer told the *Idaho Statesman* in February 2023. This is an ongoing story and given Ammon's threats about friends with shotguns, and his family's track record, it might not play out well, or he might finally face consequences.

In neighboring Montana, Ammon's Army organized a weeks-long campaign outside the home of Matt Kelley, the Gallatin County health officer. Among Kelley's many duties, he was in charge of COVID safety measures. In front of his home, two men, from out of town, ranted and raved against the county's COVID protocols (mask requirements and shortened business hours for bars) and Kelley himself. Sometimes they were joined by others with signs and shared beliefs. Kelley's neighbors, a few of whom initially confronted the demonstrators—much to the men's delight, angry discourse being their métier—abandoned the idea and decided to withdraw. They disappeared from the street, taking alternate ways home so as not to drive down their own block, depriving the demonstrators of reactions and satisfaction.

Folks left large RVs all down the street to tie up parking, leaving the protesters to scramble. From one motor home, fart sounds and an erectile dysfunctional commercial looped continuously, turned up to the highest volume. Reacting to a particularly disgusting noise, at one point a protester exclaimed, while livestreaming and trying to fundraise, "Well, that's rude!"

The larger community of Bozeman also pushed back. There was a rally for Kelley downtown on Main Street, with people cheering and holding signs celebrating him, his staff, and health-care providers. Moms and kids, including my sister and nieces, tied balloons to neighborhood mailboxes in solidarity. Other supporters chipped in for restaurant gift certificates and cleaning services for the Kelley family. The People's Rights protesters eventually lost interest, showing up for shorter and shorter stints, and then disappeared.

The ordeal was extremely unnerving to the Kelley family and those in the neighborhood. Kids were scared to play outside. Especially upsetting was an occasion around Thanksgiving when the protesters, including Roger Roots, the attorney for Proud Boy Dominic Pezzola during his January 6th seditious conspiracy trial, had a turkey on a leash. Some worried they were going to butcher the tom in the street. Of course, this was the point for the People's Rights Network—their confrontational tactics were meant to wear folks down. Despite its name and professed mission, People's Rights is in the business of taking rights *from* people who don't walk in lockstep with their ideology.

— — —

IN THE SUMMER OF 2021, I WAS CONTACTED BY A TENACIOUS organizer from Idaho, a man named Gregory Graf, who was going toe to toe with some of the most truculent right-wing agitators in his state. A Republican himself, Graf has been infuriated by the radicalization of his party. Ammon Bundy had just announced his bid for governor, running as a Republican (though he would later declare himself an Independent). Graf was the first to tell me about the Idaho Freedom Foundation (IFF), the group Sarah Walton Brady asked her friends to ring after she was arrested at Kleiner Park in Meridian. This organization serves to amplify the influence of the far right in the state, such as former lieutenant governor Janice McGeachin, famous, or infamous, depending on your point of view, for deputizing militia when Governor Brad Little left the state on business. McGeachin made her views on Christian nationalism abundantly clear when she told one interviewer, "God calls us to pick up the sword and fight, and Christ will reign in the state of Idaho." IFF has also successfully promoted Dorothy Moon, an ultra-right Republican who beat incumbent Tom Luna to become the new chairwoman of her party. Moon, in her acceptance speech, said, "We have to make sure with the Democrats coming at us with full force that we have our barriers up, our guns loaded and ready to keep us safe." Ironically, this chilling rhetoric has less to do with the Democrats than with other Republicans who do not march in unison with the IFF hard-right points of view.

Graf is a fast-talking, effusive man who makes his living as an online reputation manager. If your company has a public relations mishap, he's your guy. On a summer afternoon in 2021, I shared a meal in Idaho Falls with him and his wife, Andrea, a curly-headed strawberry blonde woman who is every bit as invested in their fight as her husband. The temperature soared to one hundred degrees, but we'd chosen a restaurant that was blessedly cool, amid the din of customer chatter and Motown music. Plates clattered. Kids fussed. Marvin Gaye sang about grapevines. And Graf deluged me with stories.

He cofounded an online group called the Idaho Conservatives, which describes their role and mission as "Real Conservative Republicans fighting extremism." The Grafs represent a group of folks who want to blow the lid off of corruption and bad actors, determined to resist their party's headlong dive into militia-loving and other Red Pill–style radicalism.

Had I heard the term "confrontational politics"? Graf asked me. He went on to explain that it's a concept taken from California's now deceased Republican state senator Hubert Leon ("Bill") Richardson's 1998 book of the same title, *Confrontational Politics*. The book describes how a minority—specifically, of hard-right Republicans—can win through aggressive, assaultive tactics. "Being 'right' is not enough," Richardson writes. "Politics is the art of leverage, knowing how to move the fulcrum. How? By comprehending that a minority of people can control the direction of government by controlling a minority of voters." Richardson rails against socialists, and brags, "I'm the giver of ulcers." He advocates hostility, conflict, and endless pressure to wear the other side down. This philosophy, which has become a blueprint for Idaho's radical right, encourages intimidation and outrage at meetings, hearings, gatherings, and proceedings, rather than decorum. The thinking goes, politicians, public servants, and administrators should feel frightened of their constituents; that will keep them in line. Richardson's techniques and philosophy have been taken up by Idaho's extremists to secure election and, once elected, to arrogate more power. Although Ammon Bundy is relatively new to Idaho, his People's Rights organization, like IFF, has embraced Richardson's techniques. It's not all armed standoffs, but it's still about victory.

IFF networks with organizations working to replace traditional conservative Idaho Republican elected officials, whom they label RINOs (Republicans in Name Only), with extremists. Its mission is "to make Idaho into a Laboratory of Liberty by exposing, defeating, and replacing the state's socialist public policies." But what socialists? Where? This is already a staunchly conservative state with a constitution mandating that the legislature pass a balanced budget. In 2020, Trump and Pence won over 63 percent of the vote. There are only three left-leaning Idaho counties among forty-four. Suggestions of sliding into socialism are absurd in one of the reddest states in the nation. The Democratic Party has been considerably diminished since the days of Senator Frank Church, which is one reason why arch conservatives are moving to Idaho, pushing the state ever further right, and making newcomers like Ammon Bundy feel right at home.

In his efforts to keep Idaho from becoming irreparably extreme, Graf has had several brushes with both hard-right politicians and members of the militia. Online trolls affiliated with IFF have called him "Greasy Greg," a slur in reference to his Latino heritage. Eric Parker, a Republican senate candidate from Hailey, a member of the militia group the Real Three Percenters Idaho, and a participant in the Bundys' Nevada standoff, has threatened Graf and his family. According to a legal filing by Graf's lawyer, "The hostility toward Graf following his support of successful Republican candidates in primary races has resulted in extreme attacks against Graf including death threats; threats to the safety of his family, specifically including his children, by posting photographs on the social media pages of extremist groups including The Real Three Percenters of Idaho, an Idaho offshoot of the far right national militia movement and paramilitary group known as the Three Percenters."

Currently Graf is being sued for defamation by an IFF-endorsed former state representative, Chad Christensen, who is also a Three Percenter and a member of the Oath Keepers. In 2020, Graf was approached by a woman from Idaho Falls who claimed to be vetting Christensen as a job candidate. Unbeknownst to Graf, this woman was colluding with Christensen by asking questions about the former state rep on a secretly recorded call. Christensen intended to use the recording to embarrass Graf and get him fired. He had looked into Christensen's background in the course of helping a more moderate Republican candidate, and discovered accusations of several alleged improprieties in the then-candidate's history. Graf shared some of this information with the woman. Unbeknownst to him, her recording became evidence in Christensen's defamation suit against him. Graf is now counter-suing Christensen and other hardliners connected to the IFF network.

I have been struck, while researching for this book, by the urgency that so many people feel about telling their stories—there is a sense of obligation in standing up for truth. The Grafs have dug into their savings and Greg has risked his job security in his determination to speak out about what has happened to his Republican Party. He left a position at the wellness firm Melaleuca, to become independent in his current field because right-wing operatives had tried to get him fired and he didn't want to cause his company, and its leadership, trouble.

To continue his activism, he struck out on his own. The Grafs have made expensive enemies, and their battles have torn them from their spiritual life. The family stopped attending the Church of Jesus Christ of Latter-day Saints because two of the local congregants serve on the board of IFF and are engaged in legal actions targeting Graf. Andrea told me that her choice to leave the Church left her bearing no ill will, but the move did cause friction in their social network. Yet, in spite of all of the pressures put on them, they continue to fight for decent governance, rational discourse, and civil communities.

This fight is not confined to Idaho. Tasha Adams, Stewart Rhodes' estranged wife, is also battle-ready. She left her husband and a very tight-knit culture of extreme patriots and has been fearless in telling her story and protecting her family from the toxicity of rampant and violent extremism. Adams, the Grafs, Matt Kelley's neighbors, and others whom you will meet in the next chapters are embodiments of an ongoing struggle throughout the West—a struggle to answer the questions: Who defines the region, who runs it, and who controls it? Divisive politics are happening all over the country, to be sure, but there are western communities being co-opted, destabilized, and renovated by outsiders intent on gaining ground. As we'll see, Nevada's Battle of Bunkerville, the occupation of Oregon's Malheur, and the rush of anti-government folks moving into states such as Idaho, Washington, Colorado, and Montana to establish like-minded communities built for confrontation, have turned the edges of the far side of America into a sort of Western Front.

CHAPTER 4

THE ANTHILL

←————   — — — — —   ————→

THERE'S A ROAD THAT CONNECTS WELL-APPOINTED
mansions with run-down compounds in Stevens County,
Washington, a sparsely populated chunk of rural landscape
in the state's northeastern corner. It's a place where there is as much
friendliness as there is caution—a kind of a mind-your-own-business
spot with a no-trespassing vibe. People have a healthy respect for
the privacy and convictions of their neighbors, whether they stand in
agreement or not. Along with its retirees, artists, and weekend warriors, Stevens County is also known for its armed militia, religious
zealots, and separatists.

"Let's face facts," urges an article from a 2019 edition of the
Chewelah Independent, the newspaper that takes its name from the
second largest town in Stevens County. "We're a bunch of hippies. We
have a cute redneck side. There is a sprinkling of hipster in here, there
is a logger side and then there's the North Face jacket-wearing crowd."
Among this hippie, redneck, hipster crew is another demographic sector—extremists who have moved to this region over recent decades,
seeking to build community with like-minded others. They have set up
networks in Stevens County as well as in the nearby Idaho Panhandle
and western Montana. There are many factors and influences bringing
them here, including the American Redoubt—a campaign encourag-

ing people to come west and await the inevitable breakdown of the republic and its economic collapse. Though not everyone moving to Stevens County does so to join the Redoubt, its ideology is a defining one.

Redoubt: a temporary or supplemental fortification, says the dictionary. This embodiment of the concept, American Redoubt, is just the latest in a long history of zealous enterprises that brought religious ideologues to the West with intent to establish their own fortified cultures. These include Richard Butler's Aryan Nations in Bonner County, Idaho; Bo Gritz's Almost Heaven in Clearwater County, Idaho; Elizabeth Clare Prophet's Church Universal and Triumphant in Park County, Montana; Barry and Anne Byrd's Marble Fellowship in Stevens County, Washington; and, though they broke away from a religious tradition already settled in the Great Basin, the Fundamentalist Church of Jesus Christ of Latter-day Saints, in Washington County, Utah, and Mojave County, Arizona. American Redoubt was envisioned by a fiction writer and libertarian who styles himself "James Wesley, Rawles." The comma in the name is intentional. According to journalist David Neiwert, who has written about radicalism in the West for decades, the weird punctuation "is a sovereign-citizen thing." Travis McAdam of the Montana Human Rights Network further explained the "strange punctuation" is a way to signify that the name belongs to a "true flesh-and-blood person, the sovereign self, as opposed to the corporate shell controlled by the government." It's a silly belief maintaining that the government uses birth certificates of newborns to establish corporate trusts, in essence making that person a shell account for the US Treasury. Bizarre punctuation and syntax are supposed somehow to disrupt the legal system if the sovereign citizens pursue legal actions to access funds in their nonexistent treasury account.

Mr. Wesley, Rawles describes himself on his survival blog as a former US Army intelligence officer and a Christian Libertarian—a

Judeo-Christian worldview is a defining aspect of his separatist movement. In examining religious perspectives within the American Redoubt, one finds several takes on Christian fundamentalism that are designed to overlap notions of patriotism. Many versions fall under New Apostolic Reformation (NAR), a take on Christianity that regularly defers to ongoing extrabiblical revelation over canonized doctrine, say a message from God with a specific time for a war to restore His kingdom. NAR also calls for community takeovers. According to researcher Frederick Clarkson and investigative journalist Cloee Cooper of *Religious Dispatches*, NAR entails a set of beliefs calling for adherents to "control the seven leading aspects of society: family, government, religion, education, media, arts and entertainment, and business." This is exactly what is happening in communities throughout the Redoubt. Here NAR blends with Christian nationalism, the erroneous belief that the founding fathers were essentially evangelical Christians; Dominionism, the drive to unite church and state, thereby flouting the first clause of the First Amendment of the US Constitution; and Christian reformationism, a type of Dominionism that seeks to supersede the secular government and rewrite the US Constitution using Mosaic law.

All of these understandings create cohesion among survivalists, militia, and religious zealots, allowing them the opportunity to hold both God and country as a single priority, without favoring one over the other. Patriotism becomes devotional without breaking the commandment, "Ye shall make you no idols nor graven image." Many of the people building homeland in the American Redoubt buy into a national "founding myth," which holds that this country was God's promised land stewarded into nationhood by devout Christian founding fathers. In order to preserve this ideal, religious war ever hovers on the horizon. It's useful to remember that, notwithstanding all of the hyper-patriotism and calls for theocracy, America is in no way, shape, or form mentioned or foreshadowed in the Bible, and the founding fathers, influenced by Enlightenment principles, the deist Thomas Paine, and rational Christianity, were not Christian nationalists. While the contemporary concept of "homeland" has strong roots in Judaism, this NAR-influenced movement is attracting many antisemites who blame the Jewish people for the world's ills. In the Hebrew Bible, a promised land is given by God to Abraham and his descendants. It's the motivation behind Zionism and the Jewish nationalist movement, and it inspired the revelations of prophet Joseph Smith in conceiving Mormon Zion, an idea taken West with Brigham Young. Now antisemites are flowing West, lured by a Judaistic myth.

Rawles tries to distance his enterprise from the legacy of hate left by other notorious settlements in the West, though Redoubt is being established in a place with an ongoing history of fanaticism and supremacism. "I am a separatist," he has written, "but on religious lines, not racial ones. I have made it abundantly clear throughout the course of my writings that I am an anti-racist. Christians of all races are welcome to be my neighbors. I also welcome Orthodox Jews and Messianic Jews because we share the same moral framework. In calamitous times, with a few exceptions, it will only be the God-fearing that will continue to be law-abiding. Choose your locale wisely." In other words, come west.

Rawles seeks a refuge for those who share his particular taste in politics and his faithful expectation of the impending collapse of America. He has written that he was "now urging that folks Get Out of Dodge for political reasons—not just for the family preparedness issues that I've previously documented. There comes a time, after a chain of abuses when good men must take action. We've reached that point, folks!" In its claims of sovereignty, American Redoubt echoes other secessionist efforts in the West, such as the State of Jefferson in northern California and southern Oregon; the State of Liberty in eastern Washington, and Greater Idaho; and those eastern Oregon counties who've voted to glom onto the Gem State. His campaign is not unique. Like the Bundys, Rawles sees the West as a place for the last stand in the battle against the federal government. Just as Brigham Young tried to do with the establishment of Zion, Rawles wants to carve a homeland into western flanks. This is their myth—the West as a promised land. As the Redoubt project spreads across the Northern Rockies and into the Pacific Northwest, Rawles and his followers imagine its concretization in communities like Marble, just up the road from Chewelah.

Marble was an old ghost town when Barry and Anne Byrd took it over in the early 1990s. Podcaster and writer Leah Sottile gives a terrific overview of its history in the second season of her podcast, *Bundyville*. The Byrds began calling it Marble Country, which, according to an article in *Redoubt News*, "is a small community of Christian Patriots which was founded in 1991." They and their followers became the Marble Fellowship. Their page is a flutter of news about the exploits of the Bundy family, the comings and goings of Ron Paul, and updates on the Marble Fellowship's annual gathering, the God and Country Celebration. A social mixer for extremism, the God and Country Celebration was the event Tasha Adams and Stewart Rhodes once took their kids to, leaving them to roam amid faithful patriots and cheesecake.

Over the years, the God and Country Celebration has also hosted Matt Shea, a Washington state representative who lost his seat, and now is a militant pastor; Jeanette Finicum, whose deceased husband, LaVoy, is viewed as a martyr for the patriot cause; Redoubt's Jack Robinson (also known as John Jacob Schmidt); Marble's own Pastor Barry Byrd; and Nevada Republican Michele Fiore, a Bundy supporter who after losing her bid to become state treasurer in 2022, became a justice of the peace in Nye County, Nevada, in spite of her lack of law degree or judicial experience.

The spiritual foundations of Marble come from Christian Identity ideology, as conceived by a Colorado minister by the name of Pete Peters. According to an investigation by the Southern Poverty Law Center, "Peters propounded his white supremacist views, claiming to have Biblical proof that whites are God's 'chosen people' and people of color are inferior and soulless. He also denounced Jews and gays, saying at one point that homosexuals should be executed." In 1992, two months after Randy Weaver's standoff at Ruby Ridge in nearby Boundary County, Idaho, Peters organized a pivotal gathering in Colorado that forged the modern militia-and-patriot movement. Weaver's wife, Vicki, and his fourteen-year-old son, Sammy, and even his dog, a yellow Lab named Striker, had been shot dead during a standoff with US marshals and FBI agents, an eleven-day siege in late summer of that year. Those killings ignited anti-government sentiment across the country, especially among edgy resisters living at the Aryan Nations compound in Kootenai County, Idaho, about an hour from the Weaver's home at Ruby Ridge. In attendance at Peters' gathering in Colorado were Richard Butler, the head of the Aryan Nations, and Louis Beam of the Ku Klux Klan. It is said that Beam once remarked, "Where ballots fail, bullets will prevail." This a chilling position that more and more radicals seem to entertain these days, like Republican Solomon Peña in New Mexico, who was arrested in 2023 after allegedly paying four men to shoot at the homes of four elected Democrats. The far side of confrontation politics.

Before Peters died in 2011, he spoke at events in Marble and nearby Colville, also in Stevens County. Although the Byrds and the Marble Fellowship have denounced Christian Identity, the couple still continues to build a vision atop histories of anti-Semitic, homophobic, and white supremacist culture that crisscross the West. Marble is but one example, and there are plenty of like-minded others scattered across Washington, Idaho, and Montana, etching this ideology into multiple communities and states—attempting to recreate this region as a religious bastion. That's the hope and intent of American Redoubt, making alarming progress in many ways, shapes, and forms.

Terry Sayles has been familiar with Marble for years, having lived both in Colville, thirty miles to the south, and in Northport, eleven miles north. His mother, a member of the Church of Jesus Christ of Latter-day Saints, visited Marble while working on the Bo Gritz presidential campaign in 1994. Sayles, who now lives in Arizona, has watched the spread of right-wing agitation across the West, from the Grand Canyon State to the Evergreen State. He has seen militia groups and anti-government, anti-immigrant, anti-vaccine conspiracy theorists stretch their tendrils from Stevens County, Washington, to Idaho's Panhandle, to Arizona's southern border.

A former teacher and tire salesman, Sayles now tracks extremist networks, noting, among other things, how relationships play out across geographies. For example, he told me over a few phone conversations about a man named Michael Lewis Arthur Meyer, who goes by Lewis Arthur, though some call him Screwy Louie. Lewis holds the distinction of having been booted out of both Malheur in Oregon, during the occupation led by the Bundy brothers, and from the standoff in Nevada. He now heads an anti-immigration and vigilante group in Arizona called Veterans on Patrol (VOP), though Arthur is not a veteran himself. In 2018, Arthur claimed to have discovered a "sex camp" near Tucson, where, so he said, Mexican cartels, or maybe it was rich elites, held trafficked children. Pedophilia, trafficking, and organ harvesting loom large in QAnon circles, and adherents such as Arthur see evidence of these activities everywhere. His angry posts and videos about the purported sex camp garnered broad attention, including from members of a motorcycle gang in North Idaho, Panhandle Patriots. The head of the club, Mike "Viper" Birdsong, went down to the border to patrol with Arthur and other members of VOP, presumably hunting for "pedos" (pedophiles) and illegal immigrants. It turned out that Arthur's discovery was actually an abandoned camp for transient people. Facts (such as his absence of veteran status, and the absence of a sex camp) didn't stop Arthur from earning modest fame and tens of thousands of followers on social media. He also raised funds for VOP to support his various operations, such as ripping open water tanks used by immigrants crossing the desert. Most recently, he has claimed responsibility for hiding a woman and her baby in Idaho after she lost custody of the child to his father. Arthur explained his position in a social media post: "We obey God...not the Globalist Government. So many of you are fed up right now...GOOD. Now let's start assembling in numbers they cannot control and take over all Government/Law Enforcement responsibilities ourselves." Inspired by the Bundy family's tactics and the rantings of QAnon, Arthur is doing what other conspiracy-theory-fueled "patriots" are doing across the Rockies. With no confidence in the government or "the system," they lurch from cause to cause across western states, building networks and engaging in vigilantism while calling themselves heroes.

Jay Pounder is a Washington man in his early forties, who, like Terry Sayles (now in Arizona) and Greg Graf (in eastern Idaho) follows the strands of this reticular movement, the links among Pastor Matt Shea, Marble Fellowship, IFF, the Bundys, the national Three Percenters, the Oath Keepers, the Panhandle Patriots, the anti-immigration groups, the extreme politicians, the crackpots, and the grandstanders. Pounder lives in Spokane, where Stevens County people—the North-Face-wearing hipsters, the rednecks, the loggers—go to shop, see doctors and dentists, or maybe catch a movie. Sporting a baseball cap, rectangular framed glasses, and a wiry beard, Pounder met me in a downtown coffee shop and lost no time in picking up where Graf and Sayles had left off. He teased out the spider's web that connects these groups and the work he has done to thwart their effectiveness. Malheur, he said, offered a blueprint for future takeovers of federal property and campaigns to win the West. It also better connected the Bundys with Pacific Northwest networks. Together Pounder and Graf have worked to trace and expose toxic political beliefs that now proliferate across the region.

Like Graf, Pounder is concerned about radicalization within the Republican Party and within his faith. "It's hard because, as a conservative, I want to be very careful how I address that." People, he worries, may think that conservatism is being represented by "guys like [Ammon] Bundy and Matt Shea or Caleb Collier, but it really isn't." (Collier is the former western executive field coordinator for the John Birch Society.)

Pounder was "brought up with the conservative Christian faith and learned to be a servant of the community." As he got older he found it harder, due to a little too much partying, to get up on Sundays, so he fell away from the church. That changed when his girlfriend, Kinslee, now his wife, dragged him out of bed one morning and hauled him back to the house of God. Pounder's faith once again became a central pillar of his life.

In 2008, he was supporting a young family as a banker for Washington Mutual. Then the financial crisis hit. Despite assurances from bank leadership that all was well, the Pounders lost their retirement savings, leaving him furious and searching. He tried to make sense of the recession, and his bank's betrayal, which led him to grave concerns about our economic system, specifically the Federal Reserve. "The banking industry, the instability of it, and the amount of money we produced" were the things that troubled him. "I still believe, from an economic standpoint, Americans are not in good shape." So Pounder decided to research and write "the book myself. It's called *The Red Pill.*"

His book tackles the idea of the Federal Reserve, which is also the nemesis of Red Pill Expo's founder, G. Edward Griffin. "The Federal

Reserve System," Pounder writes, is made "of fraud and lies," and readers must "take the red pill and wake up to the world around you and begin to realize that we cannot sustain our current way of life." He predicts economic ruin and civil meltdown, and offers tips to prepare for this inevitability. His book made him a star among militant alt-right networks. "I kind of brought" the notion of the red pill, he told me, "to the mainstream of the Patriot Front."

According to journalist James Pogue, the red pill reference from *The Matrix* was first adapted to current politics by far-right gamer Curtis Yarvin in 2007, eight years after the movie appeared. Yarvin has since been very influential in advancing Trumpism to a younger crowd, as well as related political indoctrination, playing that role along with natty Peter Thiel and disheveled Steve Bannon. But Pounder appealed to a different crowd, those involved in Redoubt circles. It would be Trump who brought them all under the same tent. As Pogue pointed out in another piece in *Vanity Fair*, some members who run in Yarvin's circle, the so-called new right, are also coming to settle in the West. Lured by the same myths foundational to Pounder's former mates, they are coming to prepare for some type of collapse.

After the publication of his book, Marble Fellowship folks, Redoubt organizers, and other extreme figures looked to Pounder. Matt Shea, when running for state legislator, even asked Pounder to help with security at campaign events. Shea, having trained as a lawyer (the pastor business came later), began his political career in 2008, advocating for tax limits and gun rights, and enjoyed broad support in Spokane Valley, a municipality outside of the city of Spokane. Pounder wholeheartedly backed him. Even as Shea's strident Christian nationalism, agitating, and ambitions became more troubling, Pounder told me, he stuck with the man. Then two incidents made him turn away from the now disgraced politician/pastor and his circle: a Donald Trump election victory party and Shea's "Biblical Basis for War."

Newly reelected state representative Shea hosted an election party, on November 8, 2016, which Pounder and his wife attended. When it became clear that Trump had won the presidency, "there was this kind of rumbling below the surface," he said. People started chanting, "We will have our time! We'll have our time! We'll have our time!" Then "somebody blew the shofar"—a sort of bugle made from a ram's horn, used as an instrument for religious ceremonies since Old Testament times. It was blown also at Malheur and is a tip of the hat to the biblical siege of Jericho, when the walls came tumbling down. "I remember my wife looking at me, giving a look that meant, 'What is *that*?'" The Pounders witnessed as the celebratory mood warped into expressions of outrage. Jay thought he even saw people in attendance giving the Nazi salute, though he still can't quite believe that. "Shea got onstage and started chanting, 'It's our turn now! Our turn now!' And with that the room turned on a dime, from a joyous occasion…to a 'let's go destroy something.'" With the election of Donald Trump, Shea, Marble Fellowship, and the Redoubt, along with Curtis Yarvin's red-pill-eating alt-right, had found their champion. It was their time and their chance—with a fine line between their unbridled joy and their rampant fury.

"Trump got elected," Pounder told me, "and all of a sudden everyone who felt abused and pushed around said, 'Finally we got our man! He's going to kick the door open and we're going to go charge in behind him, take the Democrats out.' And so that visceral anger Trump fed for years, it got worse and worse and worse." Trump knows "exactly what he's doing," Pounder continued. "He feeds people—he whips them up into a frenzy. It's like peeing on an anthill." Pounder laughed, then conceded, "I know girls don't do this. We as boys did." When one pees on an anthill, he explained, "all of a sudden the ants go really, really, really fast… They don't have the direction, but they know something is going on." For a moment Pounder channeled the excited ant: "We got to stop it, we got to fight it!" He paused. "But in the end, it's just piss. And that's what Trump did, he peed on the anthill of America, got everyone whipped into a frenzy, and when January 6th rolled around, all these groups felt angry. They knew they weren't going to win anymore because Biden had been elected, so what did they do? They stormed the anthill." Their politics are not electoral but authoritarian; not governmental but anarchist.

The second incident that pushed Pounder away from Matt Shea was Shea's four-page manifesto, titled "Biblical Basis for War," distributed privately before the 2016 election and eventually leaked online in October 2018. "I had it in my possession…and it was November 2016." Pounder explained Shea's and his supporters' vision in terms of religious fundamentalism, biblical literalism, and vengeance. "They want a *Handmaid's Tale* or something," he said. "It's a religious theocracy. Other minorities are bad. They are 'less than.' Women are less than—they can be servants of the man. It can be argued from a biblical basis depending on what version of the Bible you read." Shea's plan called on people to "surrender" to his regime if they supported same-sex marriage, "idolatry" (the practice of other faiths besides Christianity), and communism—the ever-present alt-right and John Birch boogeyman. "If they do not yield," Shea's document states, "kill all males." This "Biblical Basis for War" was part of the plan to establish the kingdom of God on earth, rule it as a theocracy, and demand an absolute adherence to biblical laws as set forth in the document. Pounder said that, with Trump in charge, Shea and others believed they were finally going to be able to implement their vision—a Christian nationalist homeland. Toward that end, Shea and the Marble Fellowship courted LDS members such as the Bundys and others, though they perceived them as outside their particular worldview. Both Pounder and Graf feel that if this group ever made their vision manifest, they would turn on those outsiders, even LDS people, as failing to qualify under their idea of "real Christians." But in the meantime, the Bundys, and others, make good bedfellows.

After years of working with Shea, Pounder took the manifesto and other documents to the FBI. In addition to the "Biblical Basis for War," he gathered up materials outlining militia maneuvering, military field instructions, ham radio operations, setup of mess units, and implementation of constitutional sheriff posses. Shea and his followers "had called for 'constitutional changes' to 'sanctify to Jesus Christ' in the new government," Pounder said. He now regrets his involvement and has since distanced himself from Shea, telling a *New York Times* reporter, "I'm deeply sorry for moving this stuff along. I thought I was doing God's will by being involved and helping Matt [Shea]. This is not Christianity. This is not what liberty is."

After Pounder spilled the beans, he told me, he received one or two death threats a week. "Had to change the phone number three or four times," he said. "There were people who would fire shots at our house. We think we had two intentional fires set on our land. My kids were threatened at school." When I interviewed him, his kids were seventeen, fifteen, and fourteen. I asked if they had been scared, and he said, "My boys are very obstinate, like me. They weren't going to take it. We had some school discipline issues" when one of his sons acted out at school in defiance. But nonetheless, they persevered. "We don't live in fear. It was hard on my wife, there was a lot of sleepless nights. A lot of, 'What's that outside?' From the standpoint of doing the right thing, it was the right thing to do." His experience is sadly not uncommon in today's America, when we see Christian nationalists become ever more convinced that those who think differently are the enemy. And these folks have established themselves across a connected swath of eastern Washington, North Idaho, and western Montana.

When news hit about Shea's "Biblical Basis for War," the Washington state legislature commissioned an independent investigation.

Their findings were published in what is known as the Rampart Report, which detailed Shea's plan to replace "US democracy with a theocracy and the killing of all males who do not agree." The report alerted people that Shea was determined to present "a significant threat of political violence against employees of the federal government." It also provided more details on the Malheur Refuge takeover, a "meticulously" planned act "by conspirators that included Rep. Shea," who "led covert strategic pre-planning in advance of the conflict." This conflict was an exercise in insurrection that tested institutions, methods, and laws. As extremists battle to secure territory across the promised land of milk and honey, in the West we are seeing its curdle.

—   —   —

AFTER A DAY OF INTERVIEWS AND COFFEE WITH JAY Pounder, I drove to the Red Pill Fest, the Georgia counterpart in Montana, to see the cast of characters I'd spent the last few days getting briefed on: Matt Shea, Redoubt's John Jacob Schmidt, Joey Gibson, the leader of the Patriot Prayer militia, and various extreme state legislators. Leaving Spokane, a blue spot on a very red map, and motoring onward into the rural West takes one across unceded Indigenous land, which was crisscrossed by French and British mountain men in the nineteenth century. The region became a trading hub, frequented by fur trappers, until the hide trade gave way to timber and silver operations. In 1881, the Northern Pacific Railroad promised to unite the area with the rest of the world. Boxcar-riding laborers looking for jobs moved from Washington to Idaho to Montana and back again. In his novel *The Cold Millions*, Jess Walter depicts the clash between workers and barons in 1909, and Spokane itself is one of the book's most compelling characters.

There was no place like it then, Spokane—such hell and

hair on that town. A full day's ride from anywhere isolated between mountain ranges on the stair-step deck of water-falls...basalt cliffs jutting like teeth from pine-covered hills, train bridges latching the valley and in the center that big river, which carved a steep, tree-lined canyon from the silver mines to the forested mountains of Idaho to the rich Washington farmland...Spokane felt like the intersection of Frontier and Civilized, the final gasp of a thing before it turned into something else.

The drive across eastern Washington, the Idaho Panhandle, and western Montana provides a study in how the modern West is configured, marked by expansionism, extraction, and the ebb and flow of labor and money.

Spokane and Coeur d'Alene give way to outlying communities, urban and rural bound together by commerce, though often culturally worlds apart. Spokane would not be Spokane without the resources, or the communities, that surround the city of 217,000 people. Its very existence can be attributed to railroad, timber, gold and silver interests, and the dispossession of lands. To the southeast of Spokane lies the Coeur d'Alene Reservation, established in 1873 for the Coeur d'Alene Tribe, the Schitsu'umsh people. Beyond the reservation boundaries, the road over Fourth of July Pass brings you into the heart of silver country, where a billion dollars' worth of the precious metal has been hauled out of the Gem of the Mountains, Hecla, Sunshine, Hercules, Bunker, and other mines. These operations began with the rushes of the nineteenth century but slowed to a crawl with the bust of the 1980s. The Hecla's Lucky Friday Mine is still open and there is currently an effort to restart operations in the Bunker Mine, shuttered since 1991.

The gold and silver hauls helped fund the majestic buildings of Spokane, but the working people of the Silver Valley, whose parents and grandparents labored to build wealth for those few who benefitted most, are burdened with a history of inequity and a residuum of toxic tailings—the same bitter legacy that burdens many western mining towns, from Montana's Butte, to Colorado's Idaho Springs, to Arizona's Bisbee. While the barons drank champagne, residents of mining communities fought for better wages, confronted murderous Pinkertons, and worked in dangerous conditions. This is the truth behind the myth of the motherlode.

Some mines in the area are still operational, but for the most part, economic opportunities aren't what they used to be. Kellogg, Murray, and Mullan, once bustling towns, now struggle. At the end of the Silver Valley sits the town of Wallace, Idaho, the very picture of old western mining culture. Its last brothel closed in 1989. A friend of mine, who raised her kids in Spokane, told me that she's heard plenty of tales about dads who took their sons there as a rite of passage. Just another Wild West story binding Spokane to the Silver Valley.

Wallace has had brushes with federal agents that left sour impressions. In 1991, 150 federal agents swarmed through it and other nearby towns. They targeted fifty-eight bars, in some cases smashing windows to confiscate cash and video poker machines, along with the quarters inside. Locals saw this as excessive and harsh for towns struggling to stay afloat. It certainly furthered mistrust among a population that already harbored suspicion of their government, as rural Americans are apt to do. According to journalist Tim Egan of the *New York Times*, the 1991 action "was the biggest single federal law-enforcement raid ever in the Rocky Mountain region…Not since the late nineteenth century, when federal troops were sent here to battle union organizers, have so many government agents moved so heavily against one community in the region." The Feds left the valley with $500,000 and two hundred video poker machines. Weirdly, though the machines were legal in Idaho, gambling was not.

The raid was viewed by many as ham-handed and unfair. Said one local, "What we have in these saloons is no more harmful than bowling on Sundays…It's petty, insignificant, victimless entertainment. We're talking quarter games. We might be hicks in the sticks, but we know what overkill is." A year later, after the Silver Valley raid, US marshals and the FBI would kill Sammy Weaver and Vicki Weaver in Ruby Ridge, North Idaho. There *are reasons why* rural westerners distrust the government, join militias, and talk about red pills. Extremists coming to the West take advantage of communities already traumatized by economic hardship or experiences of federal harassment, and they launch recruiting efforts.

Like the towns of the Silver Valley, St. Regis, Montana, just east of Wallace, has had its booms and its busts with the prices of ore and lumber. Recently, the Coeur d'Alene-based Idaho Forest Group told their ninety-nine employees in St. Regis that the company was closing its mill there—ninety-nine jobs suddenly gone, a bad hit for a population of three hundred people. One former resident of St. Regis told me that there wasn't much to do growing up there except play sports, drink, get pregnant, or do the impregnating. It's a small town, vulnerable to anti-government organizers who can take advantage of resentments. That's one of the reasons it was the site of the Red Pill Festival in 2021 and one of the things that make me worry about extremism impacting western rural communities.

The gathering took place in the heat of late July, a month that gets hotter every summer. Amid folding chairs and at picnic tables, an audience of roughly two hundred people sat to hear the day's lineup. Attendees, mainly in their sixties, seventies, and eighties, cheered the master of ceremonies, Montana state representative Derek Skees, who is originally from Florida. He spent the day heckling Democrats, RINOs, and journalists in attendance, specifically those from the *Washington Post* and *Vice*. Skees ranted about members of the media being "card-carrying Marxists" and "useful idiots." Film them, Skees instructed the audience, so they can't trap you. Shove those cameras back in their faces. "There are reporters and repeaters," he said, later adding, "Liberals love to frame the debate. You need to debate the frame." Amid laughs and applause, he spoke in sometimes nonsensical idioms, wearing a big, wild, unsettling grin.

Finally, after a lineup of interchangeable speakers talking stop the steal, communism, gender, abortion, and threats to guns, the festival's headliner and Jay Pounder's old boss, Matt Shea jumped on stage shrieking "Freedom! Freedom!" At last the audience was getting what it came for: the fire and brimstone of an old-time revival from the preacher that journalist Shawn Vestal in the *Spokesman Review* called the "Redoubt rock star."

"What is the truth?" Shea, a pale, strident man in his late forties, asked the elderly crowd. "When Pontius Pilate asked that question, he crucified truth! But he asked the question to the foremost authority in the universe, he just didn't want to hear the answer." Shea's voice became ever more shrill. "The truth is found in the Bible!" he hollered. "Truth is reality as God sees it!" A biblical literalist, he told the crowd of his plans to build the kingdom of God and usher in a Christian nationalist government. "We are gaining ground for liberty. We are taking ground for liberty. We are advancing the kingdom of Jesus Christ."

He's been in the trenches for years in this holy war, collaborating with rebels over seizing public lands, politicking as a state representative, and amening from his pulpit. His fight is ongoing and he's actively recruiting. "I don't care if the tyranny comes from London…I don't care if the tyranny comes from Washington, DC. Americans will not lose the fight for liberty. That's what makes us Americans!" he yelled. Stand up and fight for Christ's sake! Don't sit on your hands or mill idly by, "just following the plan."

"I'm going to let you in on a secret, you guys. We are the plan! We are the plan! We are the plan! I want you to say it out loud! I am the plan!" The audience echoed him. He continued. "God-fearing self-reliant freedom-loving Americans fighting on their own soil for their own families for their own communities. That's the plan!"

This isn't the first time Shea has screamed his rallying cry. Back in 2013, at the Marble Community's God and Country gathering, sharing the same stage as Stewart Rhodes, he'd urged his audience of Christian patriots: "Arm yourselves. Arm your families. Arm the church...We've got to prepare ourselves mentally. And part of that, too, is we've got to realize that every generation—blood is required of every generation. In some way, shape, or form, blood is required of every generation." That's the plan.

In 2021, shortly after the January 6 insurrection, he told people attending another rally in North Idaho, "We have to fight back in every single sphere we possibly can, and if they come to take our guns we will stand and look them in the eye and say, you are not taking one step further. This is the line in the sand. And our country will remain free for our kids and our grandkids, amen, hallelujah, in the name of Jesus Christ."

Now, eight years after his "kill all males" directive in the "Biblical Basis for War" document, and his investigation by the FBI, his removal from the Washington legislature's Republican caucus, and a paltry $4,700 fine for defacing the Washington state capitol, Shea repeated the same themes in St. Regis, conflating hate with patriotism and patriotism with Christianity.

"Freedom! Freedom!" he screamed again in that quavering high alto, a finale to his Red Pill sermon. "When you leave here tonight answer the question yourself—what will you do for liberty? What will you sacrifice for liberty? What will you give for liberty?" The answer is fight. Shea and many of his fellow firebrands see blank maps where people live, western battlefields in peaceable rural communities, and

American Redoubt supplanting local politics. Having helped seize a federal wildlife refuge during the Malheur takeover with the Bundys, Shea now aspires to a different sort of takeover—of whole communities, by attrition (driving some people out), migration (welcoming fellow zealots in), political organizing, and intimidation. He makes one thing clear: Christian nationalism, as imposed on the Wild West, is not a loving faith but a vicious one.

— — —

IN RECENT DECADES, NEW RESIDENTS HAVE TAKEN OVER IN North Idaho, building aggregations of the like-minded to grind away at city councils, school boards, and party committees. This is a culture of the extreme right. The Panhandle, that thin band of territory extending toward Canada, spans narrowly across right-wing religious networks from eastern Washington and into the state of Montana. Its story nowadays is a case study of how the alt-right is building power, but it also offers lessons for those trying to fight these takeovers.

The influx of arch-conservatives predates James Wesley, Rawles and his comma. In the 1990s, politics began to change in the state as newcomers, largely from California, poured into the Pacific Northwest and the northern Rockies. They included conservative Republicans, evangelicals, preppers, and white supremacists, many of whom wanted to live among the ideologically unified and light complected. Quite a few California police officers have retired here, including one dubious fugitive, Mark Fuhrman, famous for his role in the O. J. Simpson murder case and infamous for his racist remarks. North Idaho is frequently referred to as North LAPD.

States in the Intermountain West have been seen as frontiers for people fleeing urban areas and progressive politics, escaping to live among green mountains and sparkling rivers. They see the region as a safe haven for those troubled by civil unrest, taxes, and big government. With a history of being a conservative state, Idaho once nonetheless elected moderate Democrats to high office—Fred Dubois, Moses Alexander, Frank Church, Cecil Andrus, Walter Minnick—until things began shifting in the seventies and eighties when unions lost power and LDS members left the party over issues such as abortion. In 1980, outside money from the Virginia-based National Conservative Political Action Committee and various operatives went after then-Senator Church. Buddy Hoffman, an evangelical pastor who moved from Georgia to Idaho, founded the Treasure Valley Baptist Church and became politically active. He coerced churchgoers who had been apolitical to register to vote, maintaining that Church was far too liberal, and from that point began his fight against the state's bipartisan culture. Quoted in the *Washington Post* in 1980, speaking of politicians he considered insufficiently conservative, Hoffman said, "You've got to make them a little afraid of you. If they aren't they won't pay attention to you," adding, "They've pushed us and pushed us and pushed us in different areas. People are beginning to stir. We are reflecting what a great percentage of Idaho is." But this was the voice, and accent, of a newly arrived Atlantan. Similarly minded refugees were not yet a sizable faction in the Gem State. Though Frank Church was defeated that year by his Republican opponent, Steve Symms, it was by less than a percentage point. Cecil Andrus, the four-term Democratic governor, didn't seek a further term in 1994, though his popularity remained high, and the last Idaho Democrat to hold a national office was Representative Walter Minnick, who served one term and lost his seat to Raúl Labrador in 2011. After that, members of the right (with more notable newcomers) began in earnest to consolidate their power.

The Sagebrush Rebellion also pushed the state further right, as Democrats involved in forestry and mining industries shifted parties, disgruntled by public land regulations and environmental protection laws. In the same year that Frank Church lost, Dorian Duffin, a self-described conservative, lamented the change in Idaho's Republican Party, saying, "We have a new right spawning in Idaho. It's getting stronger. The John Birchers are very strong, but the new right is overwhelming them." Ideally, Duffin continued, the LDS church and the state "should be separated; here they go hand in hand." And the outsiders, not just LDS and homegrown Birchers, were working to make Idaho politics ever more extreme. "The new right is beaming a lot of information heavily into Idaho," said Duffin. "I feel like I'm being overwhelmed by all this rightist propaganda, all these people backed by big bucks... They're propagandizing people through churches and other institutions. They're capitalizing on the idea of the nation as weak." Duffin, now deceased, recognized this fearmongering trend in his state over thirty years ago. The same narratives are only more potent in influencing Idaho policies today.

Bob Pedersen, founder of Rally Right, a precursor to the Idaho Freedom Foundation, ventured to Idaho in the mid-nineties because California, he said, felt like "Armageddon," the site of the final fight before the Last Judgment in the prophecy of Revelation. Too liberal, too many regulations, too much rioting in urban California, so he fled northward. Pedersen told reporter Sierra Crane-Murdoch that Idaho seemed the right place to begin again. "I believed Idaho was the new Promised Land. It was beautiful. It was a new place to start." A land for the taking, for the reshaping, for the mastering.

The history of the United States is a long narrative of similar taking, expanding, and reshaping, and the West has long been considered a last frontier: a mythic place of untrammeled, untracked lands, unoccupied, unowned lands, and unending abundance of resources. The truth was always otherwise, of course—this continent was long peopled with nations, economies, and an ongoing resistance to waves of colonialism. For folks such as Bob Pedersen—and another California refugee named Brent Regan, who arrived in Idaho five years later—the illusion of a wonderland free and available for the grabbing could be bent to their political vision. The irony is that their movement, with its religious overtones and its hyper-patriotism, is contriving a promised land not based in American democratic principles or Christian charity, but on factionalism, intimidation, and skullduggery.

Regan has lately established himself as a dominant figure, perhaps the most dominant, in Idaho's Republican Party. A tall, trim, and mustachioed man who rides a Segway and boasts a membership to Mensa, Regan came to North Idaho from California in 1999, and has since blistered the state with his confrontational politics. According to his Twitter account, Regan is a "Mad Scientist, Inventor, Chairman Kootenai County Republican Central Committee, and Chairman Idaho Freedom Foundation." Journalist Anne Helen Petersen, in 2017, wrote that "people come to him, as if before a ruler, or a king. He has the confidence of a man who's rarely challenged but always has the upper hand, when he is; he's used to others agreeing that he's the smartest person in the room." As the chair of the IFF, a group that only endorses candidates who fall completely in line with hard-right positions (pro-guns, anti-abortion, pro-medical freedom, accusations of LGBTQ folks grooming children, anti-critical race theory), and the chair of the Kootenai Republicans, Regan has considerable power in the state. He's trying to drive moderate Republicans into extinction. His minions include bigots of all stripes, from anti-Semites, to misogynists, to anti-LGBTQ, to white supremacists. Despite their prominent role in state politics, the members of this network are not devoted to democracy, nor are they above dirty tricks. They also engage with some of the most extreme figures in the country.

In 2022, Regan's Kootenai County Republican Central Committee (KCRCC) plotted to infiltrate the Kootenai Democrats, appoint their own people as precinct captains, "install an 'antisemitic troll' as party chair and channel funds raised to Republicans," according to the *Idaho Capital Sun*. The plan was discovered when another Republican, John Grimm, recorded the call during which this idea was discussed. Grimm told the *Sun*, "I know from personal observation that certain members of the KCRCC are masters of deception with an ability to twist the meaning of even their own statements." Months after this came out, David Reilly, a Regan associate whom the KCRCC bankrolls, worked to interfere with "Pizza and Patriots." This was a gathering to support so-called RINO Tom Luna, a Republican candidate for Idaho Republican Party chair. Reilly, who was involved in the Unite the Right event in Charlottesville and thinks it was a mistake to give women the right to vote, handed out bogus Tom Luna flyers at a homeless shelter in Twin Falls. The leaflets promised "Pizza for the Hungry" and gave the time, date, and address of Luna's rally. When a family from the shelter showed up at Luna's event, surprised organizers welcomed and fed them, foiling Reilly's expectation of a cruel embarrassment. Reilly was later excoriated for turning struggling families into political pawns, but Luna still lost the election to a hard-right candidate, Dorothy Moon.

Vincent James Foxx, another transplant from California with violent nationalist ties, spoke to the North Idaho Pachyderms the morning of January 6, 2023, at JB's Restaurant in Coeur d'Alene. Foxx most recently lost his bid to chair the Idaho Young Republicans. He maintains a cozy relationship with notable white supremacist and has a long history of hate speech on topics from antisemitism, to anti-LGBTQ, to anti-immigration. Though the breakfast talk focused mainly on increasing the social media presence for the Kootenai County Republican Central Committee (with some mention of election denying and Jewish elites for taking over), some months earlier Foxx had said, "This is the era of Christian nationalism. Christian nationalism is on the rise...We are the Christian Taliban and we will not stop until *The*

Handmaid's Tale is a reality, and even worse than that." It's in Idaho he sees the possibility of this materializing.

Alicia Abbott, an activist with the Idaho 97 Project—an organization whose name signifies a contrast with the militia group The Real Three Percenters Idaho—told me that Brent Regan and his associates use other dirty methods, such as doxing, to achieve their ends. We spoke on a cool morning in Sandpoint, Idaho, a place in the grasp of American Redoubt and the town where Abbott grew up. We sat outside at Evans Brothers Coffee in the Granary District, not far from the deep blue waters of Lake Pend Oreille. Wearing a dark, wide-brimmed hat that dipped over one eye, her voice hoarse, her pace quick, Abbott explained, "That man [Regan] hands out folders with people's personal information, what kind of car they drive, driver's license information, license plate information, home address, what you look like," to get his followers to harass his adversaries. Like so many others I've met who work in this field, Abbott has a wonderful sense of humor; her laughter is frequent, and her good cheer belies the serious nature of her work. She has faced threats to her life as she fights hate and misinformation in North Idaho. But she's stalwart in her cause because it's deeply important to her to protect her hometown. She joked that extremists love to characterize her as a snowflake liberal, "but no one loves guns more than me!"

Just a couple of weeks before my meeting with Abbott, thirty-one members of the militia group Patriot Front, a national white supremacist group intent on the creation of a new ethnostate, were arrested an eighth of a mile from Coeur d'Alene's Pride in the Park, a gay rights celebration. Abbott volunteered to watch over the event and create "visual barriers" and "obstacles," so that potential shooters didn't have a "direct line of sight." It's crucial, she told me, "for people like me to volunteer at events like that because I actually recognize extremists. I go into their spaces and I learn about them so I visually can recognize people who I know have said the most horrible things about gay people."

Texas-based Patriot Front had been active in the area for a while leading up to the community celebration, spreading their message and recruiting new members. Reporter Daniel Walters, writing in the *Inlander*, described their posters and stickers showing up around Spokane and Coeur d'Alene. On June 11, 2022, a U-Haul carrying members of the militia group, all in uniform—navy shirts, masks, baseball caps, and khakis, some with shin guards, shields, long poles, and at least one smoke grenade—was pulled over. Men in two other vehicles were also stopped. Investigators later issued a statement about the Patriot Front's objective, explaining they recovered plans indicating "the confrontational intentions of the group to antagonize and cause disorder." Due to an anonymous tip—someone called to report "a little army" piling into a U-Haul at a SpringHill Suites—as well as the collaborative efforts of the FBI, Coeur d'Alene Police Department, Idaho State Police, and Kootenai County Sheriff's Department, all the militia members were apprehended and charged with conspiracy to riot. All later pleaded not guilty.

Abbott marveled over the arrests because, until then, the local police had never done anything like that. The cops had been pretty chummy with militia at other local events, she said. A few of the Patriot Front members arrested that day had ties to the area, including Mishael and Josiah Buster, the two sons of Matt Buster, who leads the Real Men's Ministry at Matt Shea's church.

Patriot Front wasn't the only group headed to disrupt the Pride gathering. On her way to the event, Abbott left for Coeur d'Alene to set up at 5:30 a.m. and saw a "white Chevy truck barreling down on Highway 95" with Boundary County plates and a Nazi black-sun decal. After Richard Butler lost the Aryan Nations' compound, the Nazis scattered, though some still live in North Idaho, including

Boundary County. Anticipating trouble, she said to herself, "Well, this is going to be a day…" The Panhandle Patriots Riding Club of Bonners Ferry, whose members had been involved with Screwy Louie's imaginary sex camp and the January 6th insurrection, were planning to mess with Pride celebrants as well. They are a regional group, separate from the Patriot Front, whose members, according to Abbott, "literally just drive back and forth on the freeway all day long, weaving through traffic, doing patrols." The night before, Brent Regan had spoken to the club as they prepared for their own Pride protest—an event they called Gun d'Alene (yes, really). A Patriot member named Jeff White announced in advance, "We intend to go head-to-head with these people [Pride attendees]…Stand up, take it to the head. Go to the fight." The Panhandle Patriots Riding Club had "made it very clear that they were going to confront people at Pride in the Park," Abbott told me. It was all over social media. "Of course, that shit gets picked up by things like Libs of TikTok with its millions of followers," an account followed by the alt-right, QAnon believers, groypers (white nationalist trolls), and others who thrill in mocking people different from themselves. David Reilly, of the pizza fiasco, and Matt Shea were also planning to protest at Pride in the Park.

But after the arrest of the dozens of Patriot Front members, Pride celebrants saw no further trouble, other than a few annoyances, Abbott said. According to organizers, the event drew the biggest crowd ever in its six-year history. The Panhandle Patriots stood back, presumably spooked by the crackdown on the Patriot Front, though Reilly went ahead and led his prayer group, rosary in hand, trying to sanctify his contempt for the Coeur d'Alene's gay community. While celebrators strolled among rainbow flags, catching performances and sampling food from vendors, Pastor Shea told those tuning in to his livestream that it had been Antifa, not Patriot Front, who'd been arrested earlier that day. Though two of the men in custody had ties to his own church,

Ministries on Fire, he cast blame on a favorite scapegoat. Maybe his ministries *are* on fire, but on that day, so were his pants.

— — —

IN 2021, MICHELLE MALKIN, AN ARDENT ANTI-IMMIGRATION activist, spoke at the annual Lincoln Day Dinner sponsored by the Kootenai County Republicans, which Brent Regan chairs. She focused on the evils of critical race theory, the lies of Anthony Fauci, and threats to democracy in the unfolding of the "Great Replacement"—an imagined campaign said to be launched by elites, especially Jewish people, who want to supersede white people with non-white immigrants. Malkin, herself a first-generation Filipino American, her parents immigrants, is prominent in the extreme right-wing movement and known as a muse to one of the most influential white supremacists in the country, *America First* activist Nick Fuentes. A twenty-four-year-old Holocaust-denying, rape-promoting, agitator, Fuentes thinks that burning women alive is a good idea. He has described his single most important goal as seeking "revenge against my enemies and a total Aryan victory... I'm just like Hitler." Alongside Kanye West, he dined with Donald Trump in November 2022, to discuss Jewish people and political strategy. Malkin is known as the mother of groypers—those rancorous, young, white Christian nationalists like Fuentes. It hard to say what's creepier, that's she's considered the mommy of these misanthropes, or that she was the speaker for the Lincoln Day Dinner.

During Malkin's talk in Coeur d'Alene, she touched on homeland, warning the Kootenai Republicans to maintain their demographics (read: issuing dog whistle after dog whistle). You will safeguard this culture only through "strength in numbers," she said. "*Our* numbers. Protecting *our* neighborhoods. This slice of heaven that you have, in this beautiful county, in this beautiful town." In order to guarantee that this culture is maintained, she said, make "sure that if you do welcome newcomers, that they share your same values. Unfortunately, you can't wall off all the bad Californians"—an ironic slur, considering that Californians have been responsible for much of the enormous shift rightward in the area. She joked, "I do promise when I go back to Colorado, I'm going to talk about what a terrible experience," she had in Coeur d'Alene to keep liberals from coming and overrunning Idaho. "And then I'll secretly be meeting with a real estate agent." This brought warm laughs from an audience keen to have prominent extremists join them.

A year after Malkin doled out her advice on segregation to the receptive audience, I talked to a real estate agent who has followed the trend of newcomers moving to the Panhandle, bringing with them corrosive ideologies. He asked that I not use his name, due to the tense nature of this subject and his concern for his family, so I'll call him Broker X. Regan and the American Redoubt are not the first to try to bend Idaho to their will, but they are having more success than Bo Gritz and Richard Butler ever did. As they do their best to establish a base in the West, they are luring others to join them, making Idaho the fastest-growing state in the country. Their ideology has created a niche business—survivalist/Christian nationalist real estate—and Broker X filled me in. There are agents who will only sell properties to those who uphold far-right ideologies. Parroting a sales pitch from one such agent, he said, "Let me get you your bunker. Let me fly you over homeland." Then he added, "They do well—a ton of people are doing that." He regrets his industry's role in the trend, but he said that he actually sells to "a lot of nice people" not affiliated with Redoubt ideals. Still, according to him, eight out of ten prospective buyers hail from "Orange, Riverside, or Ventura counties—[that include] ultra-conservative communities" in California. It seems, he said, that everyone leaving Washington and California are moving "to Idaho if they're conservative and Colorado if they're liberal." The pattern is so strong as to inspire a joke among Idaho real estate sellers that Gavin Newsom and Jay Inslee, governors of the two feeder states funneling folks to North Idaho, should be named realtors of the year.

Broker X is seeing real estate and other regional businesses prosper, spurred by the influx of right-wingers. Coeur d'Alene, once considered a sawmill town with few prospects, is thriving. Problem is, the anti-tax crowd is gutting infrastructure and imperiling residents. Since the 1990s, Mark Fuhrman, the disgraced LA policeman, has led the way for California cops to retire in Idaho's panhandle. Broker X pointed out that retired law officers and firefighters tend to "vote against roads and schools," adding, "they are crippling the next generation."

These "promised" lands, these "wide-open spaces," these "blank slates" for rewriting the narratives of frustrated lives, toward which interlopers are flocking, are already occupied by families who want livable, safe, civil communities. People who yearn to pay lower taxes, or none at all, who are reluctant to contribute in any way to state and county coffers, arrive along with similar anti-government agitators and religious zealots, and the result is schools and infrastructure projects stripped of funds. The broker added that newcomers have "taken over everything from dogcatcher to library, and now run the place in the image and likeness" of a separatist state, one that's white, politically rigged, and bigoted. He is not conservative, and he supports a number of liberal causes, but he hasn't been particularly political in the past. Now things have gotten so factional, he worries about the soul of his region. As I was finishing up this book, there was a rumor circulating that Kyle Rittenhouse, the teenager who killed two people during a Black Live Matter rally, had been looking for property in North Idaho. Broker X shared, "I had one woman tell me, 'I'm a Republican. I moved here, but you are crazy. I'm outta here!' It's really too bad."

Another Coeur d'Alene Republican, Christa Hazel, is in it for the long haul, fighting Regan and his brand of politics. She beat him in 2013 when she ran against him for school board, and since then he has seen her as an adversary. She too serves on the Kootenai County Republican Central Committee, and has been trying to save North Idaho College, a community college by the lakeshore that sits in Regan's crosshairs because he thinks it's a bastion of liberalism. His cronies have taken over its board of trustees. The region just feels so different since Hazel was a kid, she told me on the phone. Regan is unapologetically building coalitions with the ugliest members of the far, far right. Together they signal to others, come forth, this is homeland. A website linked to Regan's network, Action Idaho, beckons: "Thousands are moving in, seeking freedom and fleeing state and local governments that failed them. Our cities and towns are growing fast. Our state is changing. Politics matter more than ever. Let's not forget why we're here. Let's not repeat the same mistakes." Advance. Entrench. Swarm every board, committee, and office. The New Apostolic Reform (NAR) movement and Redoubt in action.

Hazel laughed as she told me of a recent snowstorm that made many newcomers unhappy. "They don't want to pay taxes, and they don't understand how the government works," but they freak out when snowplows create snow berms in front of their homes. Solving the problem requires what are called "snow gates," but these attachments to plows are expensive and new people don't want to foot the bill, so snow stays piled in front of driveways. Also, winters can be gloomy in North Idaho, when gray skies hang for months like dark, heavy lids. Newcomers with ideas of hyper-liberty find "less D in freedom," Hazel joked, referring to the sunlight-generated vitamin so scant during northwestern winters. Having grown up in North Idaho, Hazel finds it "difficult to see what's happening in my community." The proliferation of hate comes close to home. "My daughter is gay," Hazel said, "and she's a Democrat." Community culture has changed so much from the days when the Aryan Nations was run out of town. Her father, Wayne Manis, worked for the FBI to foil members of another group, the Order, murderous white supremacists who terrorized parts of the West in the 1980s. But in the last ten years, aspects of a culture once beaten back has become mainstream.

Liberty Pastors Boot Camp, a training for fanatical ministers, was held at the usually expensive Coeur d'Alene Golf and Spa Resort in 2022; their three-day, all-inclusive stay cost a measly ninety-nine dollars per couple, thanks to a subsidy by dark money. The organizers were a group calling themselves the Black Robe Regiment (BRR)—a name based on a myth that militantly Christian leadership played a key role in the events of the American Revolution. The goal of the BRR is to prepare pastors for battles against perceived tyranny: from vaccines. to IRS threats against tax-free status of churches, to LGBTQ rights. BRR eschews sissified versions of their faith, and espouses manly cowboy Christianity, biblical literalism, and preparations for a holy war, those shared inspirations of James Wesley, Rawles, Ammon Bundy, and Matt Shea. They felt this region was suitable for their lessons and hoped to draw in locals already marinating in their ideologies. The Idaho Panhandle, eastern Washington, and western Montana have attracted a culture that follows a version of Christianity wrapped in warped patriotism and cruel intolerance. They're guided by Joshua 10:19 in their fight to hold what they perceive to be their own slice of God's promised land: "Pursue after your enemies and smite the hindmost of them; suffer them not to enter into their cities." What's been pushed to the wayside, is Matthew 22:39: "Thou shalt love thy neighbor as thyself." In North Idaho, it seems there is only a particular type of neighbor that appeals to the ultra-nationalists in their quest for a white Christian homeland. The others, Democrats, RINOs, or as Ammon Bundy calls them, the "woke mob," are the enemy. During his unsuccessful campaign for governor, Bundy ran an ad that featured hooded fiends screaming into the night—this so-called woke mob—scurrying from the then-candidate's approach. "They're still lurking in the darkness. But this battle has just begun," says Bundy who himself has only lived in Idaho for five years. Then he grabs a crispy Constitution from smoldering ashes and heads back to his truck, cowboy hat worn like the helment of a Christian Crusader.*

---

*   Just before this book went to press, Ammon Bundy, recently back from a vacation in Mexico, was on Eric Moutsos' podcast, *American Moutsos* in May 2023. The host, a former cop who quit after he refused to escort a Pride Parade in Salt Lake City in 2014, discussed Bundy's eight arrests in the last couple years and his arrest warrant for consistently being a no-show at St. Luke's court hearings. In addition to Bundy, the nonprofit health care system business is suing his gubernatorial campaign, the People's Rights Network (PRN), Diego Rodriguez as well as a couple of Rodriguez's affiliated entities. In seeking damages, the hospital's legal team has looked at campaign funds that were channeled into LLCs connected to Bundy and his associates and PRN donations. SPLC's Hatewatch recently determined that PRN received $93,000 in cryptocurrency from an anonymous donor. In the spring of 2023, to keep a sheriff from executing the warrant associated with the civil suit, Bundy People's Rights members attended cookouts on his property—a situation on Twitter known as the BBQ Standoff. Others have visited the home on and off to keep law enforcement at bay.

Bundy and Moutsos, both members of the Church of Jesus Christ of Latter-day Saints, ended their podcast parlay discussing secret codes in the Book or Mormon, which they said indicated an impending war. Bundy specifically disparaged judges, lawyers, and members of his own Church. Bundy's next trial date is July 1, 2023, and he remains out of custody.

CHAPTER 5

A SHORT HAPPY LIFE

ERIC PARKER, A MEMBER OF THE REAL THREE PERCEN-
ters Idaho whom Greg Graf is suing for attacking his family on social media, lives in Hailey, Idaho, a nearly ten-hour
drive from the Panhandle—a circuitous route, thanks to the giant road-
less area in the middle of the state named after Senator Frank Church.
Despite that distance, Parker is closely connected to the radical right
in Idaho. Known as the Bundy Ranch Sniper for his role in the 2014
standoff, he had lain in wait, flat on his belly behind a concrete barrier
with his long gun aimed at law enforcement during that tense event.
Parker, and another Idaho man, O. Scott Drexler, pled guilty to a misdemeanor in a deal that ended up with eleven felonies for his involvement in the Battle of Bunkerville dismissed. After the plea, he visited
the Idaho capitol building, and Rep. Dorothy Moon from nearby Stanley, now serving as the chair of Idaho's Republican Party, glowingly
introduced him, to the applause of state legislators. Parker hasn't physically joined those who are taking hold in North Idaho, prepping for
end-times under the thrall of nationalist homeland, at least not yet.
More about him in a bit, but for now it's enough to say that he lives in a
place where people embrace other western myths. There are plenty on
offer, and sometimes they tangle together as closely as braided latigo.

The upper Wood River Valley is a graceful little slot running south out of the Sawtooth Range that includes not only Parker's home ground, Hailey, but also the towns of Ketchum and Sun Valley. The short journey north from Hailey to Ketchum, a dozen miles, brings us to another western myth: Hemingway's. Except for the pheromones of hypermasculinity, it shares little else with American Redoubt, the Panhandle Patriots Riding Club, and that ilk. In the Hemingway saga you find oversized virility layered, not with extremism, but with big living and short declarative sentences. The Hemingway myth still enchants people who make this part of Idaho their home, though Ernest Hemingway himself seems to have gotten crushed under the weight of its impossible expectations.

Hemingway crafted some of his most beautiful work, such as *For Whom the Bell Tolls* and *A Moveable Feast*, in this little valley known for the glamorous Sun Valley Resort. People nowadays come here to carve snowy slopes, not homelands. Back when the writer tromped the foothills and fields of eastern Idaho, carrying out robust gentlemanly activity, he and his hearty pals hunted ducks, fished for salmon, slurped cocktails, and cast an aura of manly renown across these mountains. And yet this stunning place, with its sunshine, clean air, bracingly cold waters, and invigorating wilderness, evidently could not ease Hemingway's demons—including chronic injury, alcoholism, and despair. The sublime embrace of immeasurable bravado was his own myth. Papa, as he had come to be known among his intimates, committed suicide in his Ketchum home, just shy of age sixty-two, leaving those who would follow in his outdoorsy footsteps, from skiers to militia, accompanied only by his despondent ghost.

What really is Hemingway's West? Once it was just a fine place, not a myth, much as Pamplona, before *The Sun Also Rises* appeared in 1926, had been just a Basque city with a religious festival and a bull-running tradition. Before the fashionable sports set ever skated the rink at the Sun Valley Lodge, or dipped their lines into shimmering nearby trout streams, the place was much different—first it was the home to the Shoshone Paiute and the Shoshone Bannock people who for countless generations hunted buffalo and gathered camas root. Then miners came to the Wood River Valley in 1878, after the Bannock War had forced the Northern Paiute and Shoshone to surrender to the US Army. The next chapter was that of a fetid landscape of slag heaps and trash. Ketchum and Hailey started as mining towns.

In the West, remember, myths are built atop other myths, like new buildings atop the old ones. Think Athens, Petra, or Persepolis. It was gold fever that once brought outsiders to Idaho's mountains, and for most of them, striking it rich was a prospector's myth. Fourteen-carat dreams faded into the squalor of mining camps as men spent days fruitlessly picking and panning, and nights bunked up beside the sewage and the tailings that befouled thrown-up towns. Those miners and the others who catered to them—the saloon keepers, the dry goods retailers, the soiled doves, and the bankers—went about their business in scattered camps and settlements such as Hailey, Ketchum, Galena, Sawtooth, Carrietown, Gimlet, and East Fork City.

Bellevue was another, just down the valley from Hailey. *The Idaho Tri-Weekly Statesmen* wrote of Bellevue in 1880, that the town was crammed with "men from every quarter of the globe, bronzed and bearded miners, merchants, professional men, uncouth bullwhackers, profane mule skinners, quartz experts, stock sharps, gamblers and desperados," all there to "crowd the sidewalks and throng the saloons." In spite of the fact that the West is viewed as healthful, disease too has a history here, like everywhere on earth. Smallpox, carried along by the waves of whites who moved with the expanding frontier, killed enough Indigenous people to destroy entire populations. Cholera and typhoid were also common amid western mining camps. Historian Clark C. Spence sketched a portrait of Hailey and Ketchum when he wrote, "Butchers dumped offal in the nearest stream; Ketchum sawmills did likewise with their sawdust, killing fish in the process. Out-houses and livery stables were an affront to the olfactory nerves. In narrow streets, spring thaws brought to light accumulated layers of manure (five tons per horse per year)." This place, drunk with notions of strapping fitness, is draped atop stories of rubbish, miasma, and disappointment—Hemingway's West before Hemingway.

When the gold was gone and the silver market crashed in the late 1880s, agriculture, primarily sheep-grazing, became the main eco-nomic driver in the area. Then the recreational industry came on the heels of farming and ranching, and spurred a reinvention of mining towns that were never really built to outlast their booms. Throughout the decades from the 1930s to the 1970s, alpine resorts sprang up atop the vestiges of mining operations, not only in the Wood River Valley but from Aspen to Taos to Park City. Developers co-opted some of the most stunning landscapes in the West to reinvigorate collapsed econ-omies that had drained rural communities of livelihoods. Mountains became valued, not for the riches buried in foothills, but for the verti-cal feet of their slopes.

In the mid-1930s, Averell Harriman looked to renovate his com-pany, the Union Pacific Railroad. He engaged Count Felix Schaffgotsch to scout the American West and pick a place for a European-style ski village. Together the men settled on the Wood River Valley in south-central Idaho, from which Harriman's company had been haul-ing ore since 1883. In 1936, their joint venture, Sun Valley, became the first American destination ski resort, and in the years since, its broad bare mountains have attracted the rich and the famous, from Clark Gable to His Holiness, the Dalai Lama. Marilyn Monroe filmed *Bus Stop* there. Adam West, the star of television's *Batman* of the 1960s and later of soft porn, entertained visiting friends and guests with charades. Lucille Ball, Arnold Schwarzenegger, Demi Moore, Bruce Willis, Bill Gates, Justin Timberlake, and Rupert Murdoch have all basked in the sunshiny ritz of Blaine County. Yet of all the celebrities and dignitaries who have visited or lived in the place, none defines it more than writer Ernest Hemingway. He helped give Sun Valley an allure and a story, which still beckon decades after he blew his brains out.

— — —

IN NOVEMBER OF 2021, I WAS ON MY WAY TO THE COMMU-nity Library's writer-in-residence program at the Ernest and Mary Hemingway House in Ketchum to work on this book. The house had been donated to the Nature Conservancy, who then passed it on to the library in 2017. Long before moving into this house, which was built in 1953, Hemingway had been invited there by the Union Pacific to add some cachet to the new Sun Valley Lodge, and cachet he brought indeed. He and his beautiful war-correspondent mistress, Martha Gellhorn, drove to Ketchum along the same road I traveled that fall. Though eighty-two years apart, we passed by the same jumbled black lava fields and along broad stretches of irrigated ranch lands, skipping from Arco to Carey and into the town of Ketchum. But I came to a place very different from the one he and Gellhorn had first encoun-tered all those years ago. Theirs had been a rustic Ketchum at a time in history between the offal-thrown-in-the-river of the heedless mining days, and the era of multi-million dollar homes.

Hemingway did instinctively what Union Pacific had paid others to do—he marketed himself, and in doing so also marketed Sun Valley, helping turn a string of once-seedy mining towns into a coveted des-tination. Since the 1930s, the population of Blaine County has more than quintupled, and now some four hundred thousand skiers come every year to make tracks down its dreamy slopes. Ketchum and Hai-ley are full of hotels, Vrbos, condos, mansions, second mansions, third mansions, fourth mansions, cabins, and cottages to house people from all over the world. There are also more modest dwellings, abodes of the working class, and even professional class, who can't afford the ridiculous prices to buy or rent. Although we think of fancy resorts as places for the monied, they are places for people who work extremely hard, sometimes in multiple jobs, to accommodate the whims of the rich and famous. We'll get to this in a few chapters, but the outward image of a resort is a dark fairytale itself.

I was just beginning research for this book as I drove to the Hemingway residence. Rolling down the highway, I filled my driving time listening to an audiobook, *Plague of Corruption* by the anti-vaxxer and *Plandemic* star Judy Mikovits. It was newly released and already widely discredited. Mikovits had been a topic at home while my husband worked on a COVID book that was intended, in part, to address misunderstandings about the virus of the sort she so lavishly spread. I knew her deceits would figure into my own first two chapters, as the inspiration behind Debra Weber's network of conspiritualists, so I had cued up her book. Imagine my surprise to find—sheer coincidence—that the woman reading the audiobook was none other than Mariel Hemingway, Ernest Hemingway's granddaughter.

Later I came to find out that the younger Hemingway and her partner, former Hollywood stuntman Bobby Williams, are devotees of "natural health." According to the *YouTube* channel for a show called *The Doctors*, in which they both appeared, the couple swears that "air, sun, water, earth, nutrition, exercise, and rest are the seven doctors of nature," noting they are "available to everyone 24/7 and are free." These Ketchum residents, Mariel Hemingway and Bobby Williams, are not themselves doctors. But their prescription of natural elements to induce potency echoes the ideas that the West conjures among many—a geography both nurturing and rehabilitating. The prospect of air, sun, and exercise as palliatives against disease made Hemingway's West a sanctuary during pandemic.

The year before my residency, around the time Americans were just realizing the scope of the pandemic, tourists poured into many western hamlets for holidays, weddings, and outdoor recreation. Some brought skis. Some brought skates. And some brought sickness. In early 2020 it was vacationers, a few months later it was COVID refugees, who carried the SARS-CoV-2 virus as they arrived from elsewhere and put pressure on resort communities and their small western health clinics, exposing residents to the new infection. The people affected by this route of transmission included financially comfortable retirees, young recreationists operating ski lifts, and local families, many of them Latino, working and raising children in pricey communities. Many ultra-rich lingered in their Ketchum second-home residences during COVID, rather than return after vacations to their primary addresses. After the first wave, even as community leaders watched in horror while their medical facilities and personnel were overwhelmed, outsiders continued to come, seeking safe haven but making locals feel less safe.

Across the West, resort towns such as Aspen, Colorado; Jackson, Wyoming; and Park City, Utah, were hit hard by the pandemic. Crested Butte, Colorado, actually directed "visitors, tourists and part-residents to leave," even those who owned property in the valley, to the consternation of many Texans. By April 2020, Blaine County, Idaho, had over four hundred COVID cases. Ketchum had been busy with events in the months preceding the sharp increase in cases, with thousands of people enjoying restaurants, shops, and hotel amenities, breathing in and breathing out, as humans do, while the virus floated through the air from one person to another. Michael Ames of the *New Yorker* wrote of an early interaction in February 2020 between a tourist and a group of locals. As these friends settled themselves inside the Roundhouse Express gondola for a day of skiing, just as the door was about to shut, a stranger jumped in. A few minutes into the ride, he answered a call on his cell phone. The friends heard him tell the person on the other end of the line to "shut everything down. Send everybody home. We're closing down shop." There had been someone in his office with COVID, a scary notion at the beginning of pandemic. After the man hung up the phone, the whole group talked together in the enclosed car, carried two thousand vertical feet up the ski mountain, breathing in and breathing out. The virus had gripped this ski community.

In the first weeks of the pandemic, some very uncomfortable finger-pointing occurred over who was to blame for disease ravaging the county. The *Idaho Mountain Express*, for which Ames himself had once been a writer, linked the outbreak to a gathering of the National Brotherhood of Skiers, an association of African American winter athletes. Their annual winter conclave, known as the Black Summit and starting on February 29, 2020, brought some 3,500 Black skiers and snowboarders to town. A hundred of their members, as well as many locals who attended the summit's events, fell ill during the week. But the paper's speculation was tenuous and wildly unfair—Sun Valley, Ketchum, and Hailey were bustling with tourists, such as the phoning man on the gondola. Local residents were also traveling out from the community, domestically and abroad, and returning, possibly with their own contagions. Blaine's high infection rate was one of the reasons that Idaho's governor Brad Little, like some other governors across the country, issued a stay-at-home order. In Idaho's case, that was a twenty-one-day shutdown that began on March 25, 2020.

Though Little's order provoked Ammon Bundy and his supporters into acts of revolt, it reassured others, such as retired Ketchum doctor Scott McClelland, who started a webpage on Facebook with daily updates, which I followed for more than a year. McClelland told me, by phone, that he had worked seven to eight hours a day reading the literature on SARS-CoV-2. Even Eric Parker, the local militia member down the road in Hailey, voiced concern in one of his more rational moments (though he later changed his tune). Parker told the *Idaho Mountain Express*, "If you watch Fox News, this thing [COVID] doesn't exist. If you watch MSNBC, we're all going to die and it's the orange man's fault. There's a third group out there: people who just want to make sure their community is safe." The beginning of the pandemic was terrifying for the residents of Blaine County, who were inundated with those seeking sport, then refuge, and with them bringing disease.

The arrival of COVID wasn't the first time the Rocky Mountains have been regarded as a healthy getaway, beckoning to those escaping disease. People have long come to the region for fresh air, exhilarating activity, hot springs, and even radon therapy, earning the West its reputation, real or imagined, as a restorative place. Mountain air, big skies, and rigorous pastimes, from ranching to hiking, keep bodies and minds in tip-top shape—or so goes the belief. People escaping the high rates of COVID in urban areas sought out Montana, Idaho, Utah, Wyoming, Arizona, and Colorado, trying to flee both sickness and imposed restrictions. Some communities tried to stave off the onslaught. New Mexico, for a time, strictly forbade tourists and returning residents who had traveled out of the state from leaving homes, hotels, or Vrbos for two weeks upon entering or reentering. Still, in 2020, the Navajo Nation had a higher per-capita infection rate than New York or New Jersey. This, of course, was due to many factors besides people bringing in the virus—notably including widespread economic and healthcare inequity on reservations, the reverberation of Teddy Roosevelt's brutality and contempt validated as the "winning of the West."

This wasn't the first time, as I've said, that people looked to the West as a sort of rustic sanatorium and a refuge from infection. In the late nineteenth and early twentieth centuries, thousands of people suffering respiratory ailments were drawn west, including my great-grandfather William Meyers, who brought the family to Alamogordo, New

Mexico. While he recovered from a far less contagious airborne disease, tuberculosis, my grandmother was born. Also known then as consumption, TB was a killer in that era before antibiotics—but not such a transmissible killer as COVID-19. A tubercular patient spreads their germs after coughing for hours, whereas a person infected by COVID can be asymptomatic and yet pass along an infection in short order. Most famously, Doc Holliday, that emblem of the Wild West, traded a dentistry practice for cards and gun-slinging when he came west to ease his own consumption. By 1900, twenty thousand people annually were seeking help for their TB-riddled lungs, creating a western industry—tuberculosis tourism. According to a statement from the Colorado Springs Chamber of Commerce in 1915, "The climate of Colorado contains more of the essential elements which effectively promote health than that of any other country. These requisites are found in the chemical composition of the atmosphere; in the dry, pure, clean, soft, yet stimulating breezes which quicken circulation and multiply the corpuscles of the blood; in the tonic effect and exhilarating influence of the ozone; in the flood of its life-giving germ-destroying sunshine." More than a hundred years later, the same sentiments can be heard in Mariel Hemingway's prescription for good health: earth's elements, rest, and relaxation. Add the lax protocols in many western states, and you get COVID tourism.

There are many reasons why the West has been seen as a panacea. One of Hemingway's inspirations, Teddy Roosevelt, in addition to participating in and perpetuating the brutal myth of conquest, also remorselessly saw the West as a place to build a man's character. In his 1885 book, *Hunting Trips of a Ranchman: Sketches of Sport on the Northern Cattle Plains*, he writes, "The charm of ranch life comes in its freedom and the vigorous open-air existence it forces a man to lead." Not only a vital place, this West, but a virile one; a romanticized place of remedial freedom. Historian Jared Farmer explores the idea of western wellbeing in his book *On Zion's Mount*, an account of Latter-day Saints settling Ute lands. He writes of Eugene Roberts, an athletics coach at Brigham Young University, who took the notion of "muscular Christianity," a connection between exertion and morality, and started the tradition of climbing Mount Timpanogos, in the Wasatch Range near Provo, in 1912. As Farmer points out, the strenuous hike was as much an act of devotion as it was athleticism. The West helps build sturdy constitutions while testing one's strength and confirming one's manhood in a place of robust freedom. In part it was this notion of a salutary West that swamped places during the pandemic. Mountain bikers to Moab. Skiers to Crested Butte. Anglers to Bozeman. The rich to wilderness retreats.

— — —

DURING MY MANY VISITS TO THE WOOD RIVER VALLEY OVER the last few years, I've thought a great deal about Hemingway and his mixed legacy as writer, egotist, bully, and generous friend. In Sun Valley he palled around with Gary Cooper, possibly the most iconic movie cowboy ever. From *The Virginian* to *How the West Was Won*, the handsome six-foot-three Montanan embodied the masculine hero that Americans might picture when they imagine this place. The two men hunted together in Idaho, their wives were on friendly terms, and Cooper starred in two movies based on Hemingway's books. It's fitting that they were friends, though they differed on politics. Cooper was a conservative Republican and Hemingway a liberal. Hemingway saw Cooper as a specimen of an ideal man and even modeled Robert Jordan, the hero of *For Whom the Bell Tolls*, on the actor. But his admiration for this kind of manhood, shaped in western culture, the kind to which he so aspired, came at a great cost to him and others as it became harder to maintain with age. Both Cooper and Hemingway suffered under the weight of such expectations and went through professional rough patches, leading to speculation that they were both washed up by their fifties. Then, at nearly the same time, they both saw soaring success, with *The Old Man and the Sea* and *High Noon*—stories of aging men facing challenges with different degrees of success. Hemingway and Cooper were both dead ten years later, dying within seven weeks of one another, each barely into his sixth decade.

I'm reminded of something my grandfather, Bo, used to say. A picture of him, my mom's dad, taken when he was working at a cattle ranch in New Mexico, sits in a frame on a bookshelf in our dining room. This is not the great-grandfather who recovered from TB—these men come from different branches of the family tree. In his picture, Bo stands in chaps and a cowboy hat, holding the halter of a horse, looking handsome, young, and healthy. His thin legs look longer than those of his mount. After the ranch, he went to serve in the navy aboard the *US Devilfish*, the only American submarine to survive a kamikaze attack. Long after the picture was taken, Bo repeatedly told me, "Old age is a tragedy." This was when he had reached his fifties and seen his own huge strong body grow slow, thick, and cumbersome. Like it had with Hemingway, there came an inevitable time when the extreme masculinity that defined Bo's own young life, in both the West and in war overseas, was no longer physically possible. To live a life made mythic by American culture, first as a cowboy and then as a war hero, became for Bo an impossible expectation that followed him like a melancholy shadow.

According to Paul Hendrickson, author of *Hemingway's Boat*, "three weeks short of his sixty-second birthday, Papa was prematurely old, multidiseased, mentally bewildered, delusional, slurred of speech…" He had come to live in Ketchum by force of circumstance—in Cuba, his primary site of residence in the 1940s and 1950s, Castro had confiscated his home and all of his belongings. Forced to decide between Castro's draconian Cuba and the United States during the beginning of the Cold War, Hemingway opted for the latter—he bought the Ketchum home in 1959—but it broke his heart to leave the place that had inspired one of his most famous books and launched his beloved adventures at sea. Though to many, Hemingway's West is one of full-bodied exertion and healthy fresh air, to him it was exile. On the morning of July 2, 1961, he awoke, "slipped a red silk dressing robe over blue pajamas, put on slippers, moved past the master bedroom where his wife was sleeping, padded down the red-carpeted stairs," writes Hendrickson. In his basement he grabbed some shells and a double-barreled twelve-gauge shotgun, set it on the floor, bent over, placed the muzzle to his head, and ended his myth.

— — —

NOT ALL STORIES TOLD ABOUT THE WEST ARE MYTHIC. AND not all who live here have tragic or radicalized lives. Some move west to retire, enjoy life, appreciate this corner of America that Hemingway loved, and live in companionable peace. At the invitation of Clare Swanger to speak to her book club, I drove to the Wood River Valley in late spring of 2021 to stay with my old friend Ann Down, an octogenarian philanthropist with a keenness for Pilates, yoga, and mountain climbs. The next day, I was greeted by our host, meeting Peggy Grove, with her bright eyes and dazzling smile, in the front garden of her home, with beds full of peonies just a day or two past their glory.

The group calls itself More Than Just a Book Book Club, reflecting their breadth of interests and heartfelt connectedness. They were gathering for the first time since the beginning of COVID and were thrilled to be together again. We bundled up against the chill, sat in the milky sun, and discussed militia maneuvering, Idaho politics, national polarization, and ranching. I shared in their reunion and in their relief at receiving vaccines.

I spent a good deal of time with this group of friends and later heard from a couple members that the pandemic had almost put an end to their decade-long tradition. Many were in their seventies and eighties, and they had tried to meet using Zoom, pandemic's tedious mechanism, to discuss their monthly readings, but a few of the members just couldn't make the technology work. Though the technophobes got coached by others, confusion led to an exasperation that nearly finished their shared connection. But the members stuck it out, in spite of Zoom and everything, and are now fully back to their routine of discussing books.

Grove, who spent years researching ancient communications on rock walls in Australia's Arnhem Land, started the club in 2009, when she and her husband moved to Idaho. Posting signs urging readers to join her to mull over books on science, history, culture, and current events, she cast a net that landed a vibrant and accomplished group—a collection of learned, adventurous, mostly retired folks from varied professional backgrounds and wide-ranging experiences, with a shared inquisitiveness. They hail from all corners of the United States and travel together, dine together, some go to church together. They hold differing income status and political views, but they don't let that interfere with their friendships. Most have come to the West as adults, though a few grew up nearby. Brent Robinson's family settled in Brigham Young's Deseret, the geographical label for another western myth, Mormon empire. His grandfather even spent a bit of time in jail in Boise for polygamy. Elaine Phillips remembers lively dances with the Latter-day Saints while she was growing up in Jerome, Idaho, on a dairy farm, though some of her earliest memories from childhood are of visiting Minidoka, the Japanese internment camp, to drop off sandwiches for families being held there.

Bob Probasco, a retired professor from the University of Idaho, taught music and computer science, and loves to run rivers, especially the Middle Fork of the Salmon. At seventy-nine, Jorjan Sarich, whose father grew up ranching in Fairfield, a town about an hour from Ketchum, is pursuing a PhD in comparative religion focusing on Zoroastrianism. Clare Swanger spent years working on land conservation in Taos, New Mexico, and now trains dogs. Julie Driver is an artist. Patti Lindberg is a retired nurse.

This book club is also invested in community projects in ways that others are not or cannot be. Most members live here year-round, unlike seasonal residents, and most have time and resources to give nonprofit groups, unlike those working multiple jobs. Jeannie Cassell helped found a crisis center for domestic violence after being told, "It's a beautiful resort area, you don't need a women's shelter!" She also attends St. Thomas Episcopal Church, where her congregation helps provide affordable housing for families and works to engage the Latino/Hispanic population more fully into the community. On January 6, 2022, exactly one year after the insurrection in the US Capitol, the church celebrated the traditional Latino holiday called Three Kings Day, or the Feast of the Epiphany, embracing South American workers and their families, the lifeblood of the resort. That's a far cry from what's happening in Brent Regan's corner of Idaho, where people fear immigrants and resent their presence in America. While people with dreams of homeland drift into this part of Idaho, members of this book club look for ways to contribute, not to revamp, radicalize, and rule.

The lives of these people are rich and their stories joyful. After my first occasion with the group, I visited some members several more times over dinner, on walks, and at their annual Christmas party, when they ponder the book selection for the following year. On one late afternoon, with sun shafts piercing Peggy Grove's living room, a few of us gathered together as Dick Springs told the story of meeting his wife, Melinda. He was ranching in Oregon and a friend set him up with a woman lawyer from back East. The two shared a whirlwind romance and he proposed to her. But not long afterward it became clear that this Chicago lawyer was not going to be happy on a ranch in rural Oregon. After a few icy interactions during trips with her family, Dick called the relationship off, telling the woman to keep the ring. He was sorry it didn't work out, he said. This didn't sit well. She turned around and sued him for hundreds of thousands of dollars for breach of contract. By the way, this woman is not Melinda.

The story became a national news item in 1992, when the ex-fiancée won a court judgement, but not the full sum of money. Journalist Jane Pauley covered the ruling and the story on the CBS *Morning Show*, where Melinda first glimpsed Dick. In spite of the strange circumstances and the sensationalism, she decided to write this man a letter, and tucked in a picture of her horse. He had received other correspondences, he said, and wrote back to everyone, but with Melinda, and her horse, he picked up the phone and called her office. Four times. She told her assistant that she was tied up each time he rang, but finally relented. She laughed, recounting, "Well, I was the one who started it!" They ended up grabbing coffee, finding that the relationship clicked, and getting married.

They now live in Bellevue, near Silver Creek, a stream famous for being a favorite hunting spot of Hemingway's. They have a ranch they share with Norwegian Fjord horses, some chickens, a cat, six dogs, and a flock of rescued emus, courtesy of a neighbor's failed emu oil business. During the first years of the pandemic, with the help of Grove and another club member, Mardi Shepard, Dick and Melinda Spring raised potatoes, raspberries, cauliflower, eggplant, winter and summer squash, green beans, spinach, Russian kale, cucumbers, green cabbage, rutabagas, leeks, and broccoli to give to the senior center. Growing food gave them purpose and focus, and together they made it through the pandemic, while living in a county which at one point had the highest per-capita COVID rates in the country.

Other book club members weren't as lucky. Lynn Bockemohle was the first person to pass away from COVID-19 in Blaine County, in March of 2020. He was followed by Bill Cassell a year later. This was a disease unkind to people of a certain age, vulnerable even in the supposedly salubrious West.

— — —

HEMINGWAY KNEW PANDEMIC. HE LIVED THROUGH THE horrific influenza of 1918-1919. In Italy, as an ambulance driver for the Red Cross during the First World War, he was wounded himself at not yet twenty years old, and watched the brutal death of a young man who succumbed to the flu in a hospital in Milan. It haunted him. War was a catastrophe that felled mostly the young, as he knew well by then—but here was something else, an invisible microbial killer that could also take down a lad in the first flush of manhood. So, Hemingway took note and opted to live big and fast in the years that he had. The writer acted as though neither illness, nor crashes in small airplanes on the African savanna, nor the horns of dangerous bulls in Spain, nor the even more relentless diminutions of old age, could ever take him down. That was enticing but impossible. In other words, a myth to embrace.

Just over a century later, in 2020, the natural-health and anti-vaxxer crowd—encouraged by Hemingway's own granddaughter—had begun filling the airwaves, school boards, and town halls across Idaho and the rest of America. It was now the era of instant expertise, of Googling "researchers" who mistake themselves for virologists, of internet misinformation and cheap "wisdom" available with the ease of a click. Ernest Hemingway, a tragic soul but a great writer, belonged to a different world: one of books. And there in his town remained a group of sane, steady elders—Peggy Grove and her friends, the More Than Just a Book Book Club.

They have lost two members to COVID, but to them, old age is not a tragedy, not by a long shot. In a place so associated with Hemingway's virility and stamina, a myth that outlived him, they live lives that make this community better. The writer's broad, handsome face covers the wall of Ketchum's Starbucks; his stone memorial lies off Trail Creek Road; his Swiss chalet, solid and square, sits perched above the Wood River; his specter lingers everywhere. Blaine County has suffered some darkening, thanks to COVID. The disease arrived, taking up where smallpox, TB, and the great influenza left off. Extremism also has a foothold in the community. Though he lost his bid for the state senate in the 2022 primary (and lost in the general election two years earlier to Democrat Michelle Stennett), Three Percenter of Idaho Eric Parker continues to try and seize political power, like Brent Regan has in Kootenai County. But there's good news: At least in this valley of central Idaho, some people have built deep relationships in spite of political differences. They are invested in their community. A shared respect connects this dear group of friends who engage in civil discourse, help the marginalized, treasure friendships based on goodwill not ideology, grow peonies, rescue emus, and read books. They vote. These are all signs of community health. And the most severe syndromes of political polarization, vituperative rhetoric, a contempt for otherness, and the fevered adherence to toxic of western myths, have met, in a small way, a bulwark in this little book club.

CHAPTER 6

THE BIG BAD WOLF

←—— — — — — ——→

O KAY, I'VE BEEN TELLING YOU ABOUT PANDEMIC, rebellion, politics, western history, rural pressures, cultural expressions, machismo, and strange takes on science. But, wait…if you think this book is bulging with a vast variety of subjects, you ain't seen nothing yet. Try watching Steven Seagal's movie *The Patriot*. Filmed in the 1990s at his ranch in Madison Valley, Montana, as well as in the nearby towns of Ennis and Virginia City, the story goes something like this: The leader of a group of gun-toting insurrectionists, Floyd Chisholm, played by Gailard Sartain (a good-ole-boy character actor and former regular on the television show *Hee Haw*), is holed up with a bunch of guys in camo. He's in the middle of a prolonged standoff with the Feds and decides to inject himself with a lab-created virus, turning his own body into a biological weapon. Then he surrenders to federal agents, thereby starting the murderous spread of pandemic.

Seagal plays a friendly, well-loved, anti-vaxxer doctor, Wesley McClaren. Doling out various holistic treatments, he cares for ailing townsfolk, who are played by actors with bewildering accents. I mean seriously weird. McClaren is a former government immunologist who may have inadvertently developed this virus for US biowarfare, and he's also a cowboy rancher who wears vaguely karate-esque outfits and beats up bad guys with his sick martial arts moves. His father-in-law, a Native man, drinks mysterious herbal teas made from local wildflowers and encourages friends and family members to do the same. The flower-tea drinkers seem to be immune to the new virus, while amoral government officials arrive in biohazard suits to quarantine splotchy, sweaty people who are dropping dead because of Chisholm, the Trojan horse. Chisholm's militia members have gotten themselves injected with a federally recommended vaccine as a precaution for this attack, but it doesn't work because the virus has mutated!

The movie has all things western. Panoramas showing cloud shadows move across the foothills of mountain ranges. People on horses riding to places. Poor folks paying bills with chickens. Trucks.

It all comes to an exciting conclusion when our cowboy/doctor/ martial arts hero kills some bad guys, and then shares the secret of his father-in-law's curative tea. In the final scene, wildflower petals are dropped from helicopters because vaccines are silly. The End.

Although our last couple of years have not starred Steven Seagal, we too have been living in a place populated by militia, vaccine skepticism, an untrustworthy government, rumors of a manufactured virus, and misplaced patriotism. This mix of ideas has clearly been around for a while, as evidenced by *The Patriot*, a movie shot twenty-five years ago. It's a film that remade a wide range of myths about the West—simple western folks, wide open spaces, natural health, nationalist homelands—but it omitted a big one: the myth of the big bad wolf. We're only halfway along on this tour I promised you, through the museum of western myths, and it's time to inspect the wolf exhibit. That's where Roger Lang comes in.

Seagal sold his Sun Ranch to Lang in 1998, not long after *The Patriot* went straight to video. It's a gorgeous place in Madison County, Montana, comprising thirty thousand acres of deeded land and public lands grazing leases, that stretches across one of the most important wildlife habitats in the Yellowstone ecosystem. With a history of practical agriculture, and then of hobby ranching, the Sun has fattened not just cows but also pronghorn, deer, and elk. It offers an uneasy corridor for predators along the crest of the Madison Range—critters who don't obey "No Trespassing" signs or understand private property. They move with the seasons in search of food, across lands that they don't care who owns. Grizzlies, wolves, and cows all share, sometimes uncomfortably, this corner of the West. It is a wonder that such a mix of wild and cultivated can coexist, and the mixing isn't easy.

I've known Roger Lang since he moved to Montana in the late 1990s. Endlessly conversant on any number of subjects, he was one of the last people I shared a restaurant meal (sushi) with before COVID brought the world to a standstill. Then, during the first year of the pandemic, Roger and his partner, Lisa Lenard, hunkered in the Madison Valley to maintain social distance from the crowds mobbing Bozeman. I went to visit them in 2021 on one of my first jaunts away from home. During my stay, we were memorably mobbed in a pasture by incredibly friendly horses looking for treats, which they got.

Months later, he and I were meeting in my living room with my three large dogs and Lang's ancient Yorkshire terrier, Jupiter, whose tiny tongue drooped from a mouth long absent of teeth. The two of us talked about his new business endeavor—an Icelandic gin distillery, one of his many irons in the fire. We also spoke of the increasing flotilla of anglers on the Madison River that runs past his property, and the hatches of insects that make trout reckless, fishermen happy, and property owners exasperated. We covered the upheavals of American politics, his quirky and conspicuous persona in rural Montana, and his time on the Sun Ranch.

When Lang moved with his then-wife Cindy, he told me, unlike cutthroat trout in the Madison, he was a bit of a fish out of water. "It's like, okay, I am who I am. I wore Hawaiian flower shirts and drove an Audi convertible down to Sun Ranch and everybody is like, 'That's that crazy Californian.' And I didn't care." But it's not the shirts for which he's now known in the Madison Valley—it's his work on collaborating to keep down noxious weeds and his wolf-friendly ranching practices. Lang grew up visiting the Madison Valley as a kid and it's dear to his heart. "We'd visit every summer like clockwork," he said. "To Yellowstone country and fly-fish. Catch and release." His family ranged from Wyoming to Montana. They always stayed with the same family in Pinedale, the Olsens, and fish the Green, then they'd head over to Ennis and try their luck on the Madison. One of Lang's favorite memories is stuffing bills into a little slot at a fishing access called Three Dollar Bridge, a revered fishing spot for generations of anglers. So finally, when Lang was able, he returned to the waters of his childhood. The Sun went on the market, and he bought it. He'd come into a considerable sum of money through the sale of stock in his company, Infinity Financial Technology, and he wanted to try his hand at being a cowboy. "I love the ranching community and the nature," he said, adding, "without consuming it." By which he meant that he didn't want to exploit the land, but rather wanted to take care of it.

Lang proceeded to operate the Sun as a working ranch. He leased some of his grazing rights to a local man, who ran cows on the property, and he supported other ranchers in combatting invasive plants, left in abundance by Seagal's neglect. Tall buttercup, spotted knapweed, hoary alyssum, hound's tongue, leafy spurge, Canada thistle, and yellow toadflax were all scourges, and Lang's focus on battling them endeared him to the people of the Madison Valley. He decided to try his hand at community organizing and in 1999 held a party for his neighbors to raise money towards weed eradication. This led to the creation of a local weed committee as well as the annual Noxious Weed Fundraiser or "Weed Party," the most popular social event in the area. When I attended the affair held in 2021 at a riding arena, a woman behind me, dressed to the nines, told her friend that she looks forward to the Weed Party all year. But Lang also remained committed to coexistence with the abundant wildlife of nearby Yellowstone National Park, just a mountain ridge away. Like his Hawaiian prints and his Audi, his predator-friendly practices set him apart.

In addition to hosting cows, Lang hosted humans, offering elk hunters guided trips, and built a high-end ecotourism lodge. He worked to "cut deals" with nearby luxury developments such as the Yellowstone Club, an elite compound of zillionaires just eastward over the crest of the Madison Range. He stood ready to "helicopter wealthy people into Sun Ranch for a real ranch experience, or hunting, fishing, glamping, whatever you wanted." Lang explained, "Sun Ranch was a real cattle ranch. We had anywhere from 2,200 to 3,000 cows, depending on the year, in terms of anticipated dryness or wetness, and grass bank. We did a whole bunch of things from carbon sequestration to native, threatened trout restoration." Lang started a hatchery for westslope cutthroat, a species displaced or hybridized by non-native rainbows and browns in the Madison River among other waterways. As he told me of his work on the Sun, we sat beneath two-story walls of books, him on the couch, me in my red leather chair, as the four dogs occasionally demanded our attention. "We wanted a ranch with wolves. It was very avant-garde." It was more than avant-garde. Not only was it novel, it was difficult. Many factors made running a cattle ranch hard, but Lang wasn't susceptible to one of the most fervid of western myths about that: the myth of the wicked wolf.

Wolves, extirpated from this region in the early twentieth century, were reintroduced to Yellowstone National Park in 1995 and have since fanned out through the ecosystem, dispersing beyond park boundaries. The species has been incredibly successful in its return, but packs need lots of territory and lots of food. When Lang owned the Sun, the Wedge pack moved into the eastern flanks of the Madisons and lived with the cattle for years before they began to kill them. Throughout the Northern Rockies, wolves prey on elk in good times and rabbits and rodents in meager times. A wolf pack can take out a moose or a bison but it's hard work and costs lots of calories. It's also perilous for pack members. What isn't as hazardous to a wolf's welfare is preying on cattle. At least until the rancher seeks retribution.

In the Madison Valley, one can look across the landscape and see rangelands, or one can see wilderness. Lang sees both. That is why he loves the place so deeply. Raising cows in the presence of wolves and grizzlies takes patience, grit, commitment, and the ability to recover from financial loss and a broken heart. Though there are nonprofit organizations and government programs ready to reimburse owners for wolf and grizzly kills of livestock, most ranchers don't want to deal with predators killing their animals, nor with the hassle of filing for reimbursement. Lang accomplished something remarkable, but not without a toll on cows, wolves, and his ranch hands.

Bryce Andrews worked for Lang in 2006. In a memoir published in 2014, *Badluck Way*, Andrews recalls his year on the Sun, managing both cattle and wolves. The book captures the pain of embracing two seemingly contradictory mindsets: a genuine appreciation for wolves and the understanding that this apex predator is deadly to a domestic animal in one's care. You can love the wild, Andrews tells us, while feeling anguish at its ferocity.

Andrews worked hard, moving cattle, tending fence, all the while watching the Wedge wolf pack run like phantoms through the draws and sinuous edges of Lang's place. There had been a series of cattle predations, and Andrews's direct boss, not Lang, pressed him—would he shoot a wolf if he saw one? The Montana Department of Fish, Wildlife and Parks issued a permit, giving the ranch permission to kill pack members. It was a very troubling request, killing a wolf, and Andrews himself wondered if he would be capable of it. When he later saw the individual male thought to be responsible for the predations, Andrews shot him twice, killing him. That night, he went back out to find the wolf's body. Sitting in the beams of his truck's headlights, he touched the carcass, finding the hole in the wolf's side where a bullet had ripped its way through silvery fur. The next day, he drove to Jackson, Wyoming, for a two-day bender.

Another incident took place some months later, when Andrews found two heifers attacked by wolves, one mortally wounded, her backside in shreds. The ranch had been asked to keep the cows alive until officials could examine them, so Andrews watched the heifer struggle to get back to a barn as blood dripped from her torn hindquarters. Her staggering gait and her evident terror nearly made him vomit, so horrible was it to witness. This was an animal under his care and seeing her in such misery wrecked him. Due to the attacks, more wolves were killed.

A year later, after Andrews had left, the ranch was cited for a violation of Montana law when Justin Dixon, another hand, driving a four-wheeler, chased the pack's alpha female suspected of attacking livestock. Lang told me that Dixon had shot the wolf a couple of weeks before the incident without telling him, injuring the female and making it more difficult to hunt. When Dixon caught up to the female, he ran her over with his all-terrain vehicle, crushing her body under its wheels as she yowled in pain. When Lang got the call about her capture, he also heard ranch dogs snarling and snapping as she lay pinned. Wedged, still alive, between the dirt and 700 pounds of metal, the wolf struggled while someone went to find a rifle to finish her. It was crushing to Lang, who couldn't sleep well for three months. A blow to his ranching ideals and a stab in his heart. He later issued a statement saying, "I am very sorry that this event happened on any ranch let alone our own. We condemn all inhumane treatment of animals."

Lang later told me that, at the time, the population of wolves on his ranch had totaled fifteen and that "anything north of ten created problems." As in problems when predators tangle with livestock and myths of agrarian cultivation are confronted with the hungry wild.

There is a history of disregard for wolves in the American West. As land was settled in the 1800s, white newcomers wiped out elk and deer populations through overhunting, forcing wolves and other predators to livestock as a source of food. European agriculturalists brought their culture to America, so the lobo was reviled on American soil as immigrants streamed West. These beliefs are still firmly held. Lang's ranch hand, Justin Dixon, hails from a small Mormon town in northern Utah and grew up in a culture with deeply ingrained biblical notions about nature that Christians carried with them from the old country.

John D. Lee, an early western settler and an infamous figure in Utah Territory, also shared this culture and set of beliefs. He wrote in 1848 about the critters slavering over livestock and wild animals, noting in his journal, "Among the Many, the wasters and destroyers was taken into consideration, to wit, the wolves, wildcats, catamounts, Pole cats, minks, Bear, Panthers, Eagles, Hawks, owls, crows or Ravens & Magpies, which are verry numerous & not only troublesome but destructive." To rid themselves of these "wasters and destroyers," Lee and others organized a hunt, beginning on Christmas Day in 1848, to wipe out predators. The campaign was recorded in Latter-day Saint records as "Articles of Agreement for Extermination of Birds and Beasts." When tallied in March 1849, the total number of animals exterminated was 2057, including 331 wolves and 216 foxes.

Yes, wolves can threaten domesticated animals, but their vilification far exceeds their offenses. In European fairy tales, wolves eat grandmothers and menace little girls, while in the Bible, the wolf threatens shepherds and their flocks, serving also as a metaphor for a false prophet. In other words, in Judeo-Christian myth, wolves are dangerous and mendacious. Considering the disregard that Dixon showed towards the female wolf on Lang's spread, it's impossible to ignore another biblical myth, dominion, an idea also mentioned by the Bundy family to substantiate their range war. At a rally in 2018, Ammon Bundy, who is LDS, told an audience, "I first need you to know that I'm a Christian." He then invoked Genesis, while claiming his own dominion in subduing the earth. Earlier that year, his brother Ryan Bundy, dressed in a tight leather vest, spoke to a group in Paradise, Montana, telling the crowd (which included me) that Genesis gave "man" full sovereignty over the land and authority over every "creeping thing that creepeth upon the earth." Man (his word) was given the freedom, Ryan continued, to do whatever he pleased with the animals, plants, landscapes, all placed here for his use, his pleasure, and his disregard.

After one of my several meetings with Roger Lang, I was reminded of Jaren Watson, another member of the Church of Jesus Christ of Latter-day Saints, who grew up in southeastern Idaho, not far from Dixon's origin. In an essay published in *Origami Journal*, Watson wrote of his own experience in encountering a fox, another one of those wasters and destroyers, when he was a kid. Like Dixon, Watson pursued the animal on a machine, a snowmobilie in his case, with his brother. The boys chased it to the point of exhaustion, then ran the poor creature over. "It merely ran," Watson wrote. "It ran through belly deep snow with heroic effort. It ran and ran and kept going, churning the snow under foot. Eventually, it tired." The animal finally became resigned and just stood in the snow, head bent. The boys gunned the engine. "It wasn't much, running over that small fox. The sensation was like swallowing some too large thing, a momentary catch, a pressing against the soft flesh of the throat…We had broken its bones. Its slender front legs zigzagged at severe angles. Some of its insides were outside. We had smudged it."

Writing as a grown man, Watson conveys both experience and regret for his needless callousness. He had come to understand the loss of this animal, a small predator making its living in the wild, and his youthful role in its brutal and heartless end. "Of what consequence, this mere fox? Passing over this bit of fur, this bit of bone. Noticed by no one, perhaps, save only him, who notices the fall of every sparrow. Good God in heaven, who among us had not where to lay his head, forgive me. I was a boy then. I was only a boy, and I took unto myself a lump I couldn't swallow. I cannot swallow still." Watson asked God to forgive him for the senseless killing—one accomplished because as a human, he had the tools, and God-given dominion, to take its life.

That humans kill things wantonly embodies the myth of a God-given dominion over all. It's an idea that humans are somehow superior because humans are created in the image of God, while wild nature, wild animals, are inferior, just as a cultivated garden is "superior" to a native grassland or forest. This myth makes it easy to kill wild things and to hate undomesticated animals. Without reflection like Watson's, a harmless fox, let alone a fierce wolf, remains for many people something to distain, to torture, and to kill.

Actions like running over a wolf or a fox are certainly not confined to southeastern Idaho or the Sun Ranch. Though wolves are well loved by tourists who see nobility in their pack loyalties, family bonds, and social interactions, they are hated by many westerners. Though predation by wolves has a small impact on livestock overall, ranchers who do experience livestock loss have a unique and personal exposure to wolves' prowess at killing. That said, there is a big difference between an animal trying to take down its dinner, even if that meal is a cow, and a human trying to take down a perceived enemy, driving it to exhaustion and death. Judging from how the wolf gets treated by predator eradication programs, and how those programs are legislated by politicians, it's clear that science isn't driving wolf management.

When Lang owned the ranch, he and his team tried to find a balance. They lost only one percent of the stock, though at cost of other losses. Hands lost sleep, cows failed to gain their expected weight, and wolves were shot. Livestock, workers, and the wolf pack itself were traumatized, each in its own ways. When the rancher who leased the Sun from Lang weighed his cattle at the end of the summer, the herd was thousands of pounds light due to the stress of living in wolf country. The man was livid. No matter how careful ranching operations are, wolves can kill livestock. That's why so many ranchers detest them. Packs hunt in ways that can be difficult to witness, attacking from behind and occasionally leaving mortally wounded members of the herd disemboweled and suffering. As beautiful and charismatic as wolves are, they are considered menaces by those who work livestock. Wolves are killers. But they are not evil—no more, anyway, than a human is evil for raising cattle to kill and eat. But humans, in rearing those animals, have an obligation to act respectfully towards wildlife. Acts of malice towards critters who are just trying to stay alive are gratuitous and mean.

In his memoir, Andrews wrote, "I was tempted to construe ranching as nothing more than a protracted act of violence…Cattle got eaten. Wolves met bloody ends. Ranch hands arrived, sweated, and tried to stand against the wilderness long enough to make a living. Owners came and went, leaving their legacy in the form of strange structures and a mixed bag of place names. There was an element of tragedy in it, of course, but the main thing was the land kept on." After reading this stunning memoir, I contacted Andrews. He's still writing and running cows. Now in Montana's Mission Mountains, big wolf and grizzly country, Andrews continues to live with this difficult paradox.

And the land does keep on. Despite his mixed results with the Wedge pack, Lang's time on the Sun left an enduring legacy through his commitment to contiguous habitat and protection from development. Before Seagal bought the ranch, it was owned by two San Diego land developers, explained Lang, who "subdivided the shit out of Sun Ranch, then never developed it." When the housing market went south in 2008, Lang was hit hard. If he had gone through with the developers' plans, he might still own part of the ranch, but he had put it in conservation easement instead, legally protecting the land from future development forever. Then, under pressure of circumstances, he sold the Sun in 2010 for just under $30 million to a mining executive named Richard Adkerson and a couple of partners. I asked Lang if the ranch was now using his management recommendations. "Well, we set it up for them, so they didn't really have a choice. I mean, we replaced eighty miles of barbed fence with high-tensile wire that was wildlife friendly so that they could run through and not get tripped up. That's all still in place." So is the work of the weed committee and the impact of the conservation easements some of Lang's neighbors put in place, protecting lands in perpetuity.

Lang's wildlife ethics aren't shared by the most recent wealthy out-of-state owners. In 2019, a ranch hand on the Sun was fined for lacing the body of a cow with strychnine, an act that killed a wolf and a dog. According to Steve Primm, a wildlife biologist who was on the Sun the day that Bryce Andrews shot the male wolf, the new owners don't have the same commitment to coexistence. Primm, a patient and professional scientist whom I've known since the 1990s, when we both worked on grizzly bear protection, is with the Northern Rockies Conservation Cooperative and has a long history in the Madison Valley. He tried to establish a relationship with the new owners of the Sun Ranch when they bought the place, but they showed little interest.

"The wolves are still denning up there," Primm told me, "so there are some wolves on the property." But notwithstanding Lang's efforts, he added, the Wedge pack was gone. "Wolves are smart. They're huge, but they literally disappear into the sagebrush, and they still kill livestock in spite of predator-friendly efforts. I think it was a shock to Roger that he couldn't manage them." The losses were real; the predators remained predaceous. The myth abides, and the complexities receive little attention. Wolves barely kill any cows compared to other lethal threats livestock face, but wolves remain the boogeyman. The US Department of Agriculture recorded that, of the 6,000,000 cows that died in Wyoming, Montana, and Idaho, wolves killed 136. These states also contained 820,000 sheep. Wolves killed only 144. Respiratory and digestive disease, complications during calving, poisonous plants, and weather accounted for many more dead cattle. In a 2017 report, the US Department of Agriculture found that 98 percent of all deaths in adult cattle and almost 89 percent of all deaths in calves were non–predator related in 2015. The hype over wolves is wildly disproportionate to the damage they do, but they are still hated by many ranchers surviving on the slimmest of bottom lines.

Though Lang has since sold the ranch, both Steve Primm and Linda Owens, the program director of the Madison Valley Ranchlands Group, think he made a lasting contribution to ranching culture in the valley. Owens grew up near Ennis, "but I'm only third generation," she told me self-consciously, referring to the measuring stick of credibility in multigenerational white ranching families. The more generations, the more standing. I met her in Ennis, in the old building that once served as headquarters of Moonlight Basin, a ski resort and housing development later acquired by Boyne Resorts and CrossHarbor Capital Partners LLC, and now based over the mountain in Big Sky. We chatted in a partially finished basement office, a sharp contrast to the elegantly appointed upstairs, but given Owen's demeanor, the bare-bones décor seemed to suit her just fine. She's direct, with pretty blue eyes and a keenness that makes it clear that this woman sees through any sort of pretense. I really like her. She works alongside the valley's old boys' club, a mixture of local ranchers, who make a hard living, and hobby ranchers, who fly into town and don't need the income. "Roger [Lang] brought his integrity with him. I trust him implicitly. He was a first-generation rancher who wasn't trying to honor misguided ideas." Owens has seen Lang have a good effect on the valley—people are more open to conservation easements, those binding agreements that protect lands in perpetuity. Lang also convinced some ranchers to replace barbed wire, which can be fatal to animals that get entangled, with wildlife-friendly fencing. But none were willing to follow Lang's lead regarding wolves in the Madison Valley.

Despite the fact that wolves occasionally kill cows, the ranching community has not been the central force behind the recent loosening of wolf protections in states like Idaho and Montana, according to Primm and Owens. It's a political issue. The ever-broadening rift between Democrats and Republicans has taken a retaliatory turn. The erosion of wolf protections and the increase of licenses, said Primm, is "really about owning the libs—hurting people you don't like by killing things they care about." This was the point Paige Williams made in her April 2022 piece in the *New Yorker*, appropriately titled "Killing Wolves to Own the Libs?" She covered the wolf issue in Idaho, but her points ring just as true in Montana. As politics in these neighboring states have become more and more polarized, officials take to the most extreme positions, including in wildlife management. Politicians have constituents who like to kill things, but these constituents are not necessarily from the ranching community.

Still, there are certainly agriculturists who live to kill critters. "Some ranch families' younger members," Owens told me, will kill anything moving other than livestock—rabbits, skunks, coyotes, wolves. But there is a reason for this inclination that sits atop a culture where the idea of dominion sits deeply seeded. Young ranchers are sometimes left in an "awkward" position, either "perceived or real," she explained, and there's "peer and family pressure to ride hard, be aggressive and push determinedly to prove their worth and mettle to become the next generation to steward the family farm or ranch." When the younger generations look to less aggressive means of working and tolerating/accepting wildlife on and near the land they are responsible for, they risk losing respect from a generation that did not often deal with large carnivore conflicts during the decades between wolf eradication and before reintroduction. Young ranchers are left to act with neither guidance nor inclination to deal humanely with predators from an older generation, and they carry the burden of proving ability to both livelihood and culture. One way to do this is killing what are considered "varmints," because varmints can kill cows.

Ranching is hard in the West. Always is, always has been. Last time we spoke, Linda, herself, had just lost two calves, not to wolves, but to a late spring storm.

In looking at the current situation, Roger Lang is philosophical about what he accomplished. "I haven't totally given up...I'm going to still do philanthropy in my valley, Madison Valley, but basically, I came to the following conclusion: I've protected thirty thousand acres, I've given tens of millions of dollars away to conservation, and do I say that to brag? No, I say it actually because it hurts. Because guess what? We need twenty *million* acres saved in the Greater Yellowstone, *not* thirty thousand."

Lang still owns a long stretch of Madison River streambank with no structures at all. "There's probably 120, 140 acres, maybe three miles of the Madison. I'll put like 98 percent into conservation easement, so it can never be subdivided. It's the kind of place that somebody would want to put an eighteen-hole golf course. And I'm not going to, you know, do that, of course. I'm going to protect it all. Because I've seen wolves take down elk there...I've had encounters with grizzlies there. I've seen wolverines there." And most importantly, it's across the highway from his beloved Sun Ranch. A place that he misses in his bones. "I still dream of it," he told me.

— — —

IN 1886, "A WOLF-LIKE CREATURE" SKULKED ACROSS THE Hutchins homestead, which later became part of the Sun Ranch. It was a large critter, black, and tapering from high shoulders to low hips like a hyena. According to Israel Amon Hutchins, the patriarch of a Mormon family settled along the banks of the Madison River, this animal lurked around his spread, screaming into the night. Hutchins finally shot and killed it, then gave the carcass to his pal Joseph Sherwood to taxidermize. The mount sat for years on a shelf in Sherwood's general store, on the nearby Henry's Fork of the Snake River, then folks lost track of it. If it was a wolf, its disappearance in mounted form only presaged the disappearance of the species from these parts altogether.

By the 1940s, wolves around Yellowstone had all but disappeared due to endless campaigns of extirpation, scrubbing the land of the predator for the sake of ranching and farming operations, in yet another version of winning the West. One or two solitary animals would occasionally make their way down from Canada, but breeding pairs were killed by ranchers and, at that time, also by Yellowstone park rangers, because the park itself had a misguided anti-predator policy. The gray wolf was listed as an endangered species in 1974; in 1982, the act was amended to include a special category, designated "experimental, nonessential population," for controversial endangered species that were reintroduced to an area, but not with full endangered-species protection. This made way for wolf reintroduction in Yellowstone National Park, under that clinical-sounding "experimental, nonessential" status for individuals whose loss would not impact the survivability of its species. It was a compromise arrangement, which allowed ranchers to shoot wolves that left the park and messed with cows, but mollified opposition to wolf-reintroduction enough to make it possible. Fourteen Canadian wolves were loosed in the park in 1995, and a year later, seventeen more were set free. In 2008, wolves were considered to have a robust population in the region and were removed entirely from the endangered species list. This meant that, when individuals loped beyond the park's boundaries, whether they stalked livestock or not, they could be killed on sight. For years since, states and the federal government have fought conservation groups over the protection status of wolves, while many of these animals were shot and trapped across Wyoming, Idaho, Montana, eastern Washington, eastern Oregon, and northern Utah. As of 2022, the US Fish and Wildlife Service was considering a petition to relist the Northern Rockies populations, following a new lawsuit by environmental groups. In Colorado, voters passed legislation to reintroduce wolves there.

The West is no monolith. As Colorado made plans to accommodate the wolf, Montana adopted measures in 2021 that allow hunters to kill wolves in unlimited numbers, including by baiting to shoot, and by neck-snare traps. Montana's Department of Fish, Wildlife and Parks also reinstated some for bounties on wolves, and permitted hunting them at night. During the 2021-2022 wolf-hunting season, twenty wolves that left Yellowstone National Park boundaries were shot by hunters, the most wolves killed in a year since they were reintroduced to Yellowstone. Montana's Republican governor, Greg Gianforte, killed a radio-collared Yellowstone wolf, an animal that park biologists had been monitoring, after it strayed out of the park.

Conservation groups are hard at work to stop the ongoing slaughter. A temporary restraining order to cease wolf hunting was issued in November of 2022, but overturned a week later, allowing the "2022-2023 hunting and trapping season to move forward unabated," according to a press release from the litigant, WildEarth Guardians. This gave the green light to "Montana's efforts to kill 456 wolves—nearly 40 percent of the state's entire wolf population, based on potentially unsound modeling."

—   —   —

THE MYSTERIOUS ANIMAL KILLED ON THE HUTCHINS RANCH back in 1886, mounted as a curiosity and then lost for decades, made its own return not long after the wolf returned to Yellowstone. My husband, David, who once lived in Ennis, remembers hearing about the Hutchins *beast* from a fellow who had lived in the Madison Valley all his life, his pal Ralph Paugh. This old rancher—whom David loved well, even serving as a pallbearer at his funeral—told David about the wolf-like thing that was said to scream in the night, and showed him an old snapshot of the mount. Paugh knew it, from old Ennis lore, by the name *guyasticutus*. Others have referred to the beast as *ringdocus* or *shunka warak'in*. The mount disappeared for 121 years until some-one found it in a museum in Pocatello, Idaho. In 2007, *guyasticutus* returned to Montana, where its first stop—a courtesy, by those who brought it—was to Israel A. Hutchins's grave, to let the old rancher's bones know *that the creature was back*. It now resides in the Madison Valley History Museum.

In its glass case, this animal looks like it was a wolf with genetic abnormalities or subjected to funky taxidermy nearly 140 years ago. Or maybe, as some suggest, it might have been a wolf that suffered dis-figurement by falling into a Yellowstone thermal feature. Its identity is in the eye of the beholder. To Israel A. Hutchins, it was a monster that menaced the Madison Valley. To others, it is a stuffed wolf, long ago shot by a rancher. His family demurred when the museum suggested genetic testing because they like the idea of everyone having their own notion of the thing. In some ways that reflects the ambivalent reputa-tion of the wolf as a species—everyone has their own version of it.

Over the centuries, museum collections have become places to visit empirical realities. Cabinets of curiosities gave way to scientific displays. For example, after Charles Darwin presented his theory of evolution, the American Museum of Natural History (AMNH) in New York City, as well as the Smithsonian Institution in Washington, DC, focused on explaining aspects of his work and findings. This emphasis lasted until evolution seemed to take root in mainstream America. According to Stephen T. Asma's *Stuffed Animals and Pickled Heads*, the public's increasing embrace of evolution posed to curators a dilemma. What was newer and weirder than evolution? What could draw more visitors? American natural history museums cast around for a next attraction. "After evolutionary theory crossed from novelty to established fact, natural history museums, with the fight already won, seemed confused about their future function," Asma wrote. What they did was turn to "exotica merchants" with strange stuffed taxidermy, and later, as paleontology digs yielded prodigious fossils, a focus on dinosaurs. "Instead of taking up the increasing challenge of educating the public about the need for environmental concern—about delicate ecological relationships—the museums tried to distract and entertain patrons with the exotic lions of faraway Africa or some other novelty." This trend held until William Hornaday, a zoologist and taxidermist who became the first director of the New York Zoological Society, offered a new raison d'être for the AMNH and the Smithsonian—conservation of American wildlife. Hornaday himself had taxidermized some of the last bison in the West for an 1887 exhibit and he hoped museums might take a role in saving them from extinction. Museums worked to galvanize a movement that combined patriotism with preservation—America's great fauna such as bison, its citizens could gloat, trumped the less robust and impressive wildlife of Europe. And unlike the passenger pigeon, bison still existed as a (barely) viable population in the wild. Although Hornaday's bison were dead, killed and stuffed for the purpose of being displayed, they gave museum-go-ers a glimpse of the American West and the charismatic beasts that helped mythologize this region. With the momentum that Hornaday and others generated, monied and powerful folk took measures to bring the buffalo back from the edge of extinction.

But not all American fauna were thus treasured. Hornaday himself wrote, "Of all the wild creatures of North America, none are more despicable than wolves."

Although *guyasticutus* now stands stuffed in a museum, mute and solitary amid other displays, the Greater Yellowstone ecosystem, of which the Madison Range is a part, is a living and interactive system, functional, dynamic, populated with a vast diversity of wildlife. These are not museum specimens that sit quietly in the corner of an institution, but wildlife that cross a giant landscape when they get hungry. They share that landscape with people—including folks such as Roger Lang, who embraced both wild and cultural values, and Linda Owens and Steve Primm, who implement conservation measures in the Madison Valley. Such people are essential players in places where land status varies between public and private. Living wolves present ranchers with headaches, but they belong here. Lang might have lost ownership of his ranch, but through his conservation easement, protecting the Sun Ranch in perpetuity from development, he kept it from being subdivided. With that agreement, he ensured a future owner of the Sun could live like Lang did, with the wolves.

While wildlife practices rooted in ideas of dominion have endangered or even eradicated animals, dominion also includes elements of stewardship—as in the responsibility to shepherd God's creations. According to the Church of Jesus Christ of Latter-day Saints Environmental Stewardship and Conservation statement, "This beautiful earth and all things on it are the creations of God. As beneficiaries of this divine creation, we should care for the earth, be wise stewards over it, and preserve it for future generations."

The Madison Valley, which carries with it a long history of LDS ranching families, is not a museum of lifeless specimens that stare at visitors with glass eyes. It's a place chock-full of wildlife—life, to stress the obvious, that is *wild*. Wild means not subject to imposed rules. Wild means unpredictable. Wild means taking food where it can be found, not waiting for it to be given. Wild means inconvenient and unbridled and crafty and magnificent. Wild means, sometimes, dangerous. Yes, there are cows, but also elk by the thousands, browsing grassy hillsides. Trout rise from watery depths to grab at flies, both real and tied. Sandhill cranes, looking ancient and elegant, walk on long thin legs across stubble fields, joined by mates with whom they remain paired for life. Wolves den, produce litters, and the pups get hungry. Each of these critters lives a hard-won existence while giving the impression of glorious jubilance, not frozen in place, but soaring, singing, foraging, rutting, roaming, battling, leaping, racing, dancing, snoozing, grooming, howling, loping, and pairing.

Amid all of them lives another species, *Homo sapiens*, also crafty and dangerous, also accustomed to taking what it wants. Unlike the others, this creature possesses the formidable capacity to reconfigure perceived reality as abstraction, distort the abstraction into an ideal, then try to impose that ideal back on reality. In other words, to make myths.

CHAPTER 7

DONKEYS TO JACKASSES

SAW HIM, MORE THAN ONCE, WALKING DOWN BOZE-
man's Main Street in front of the expensive boutiques. He wore a
dark cadet cap, a light red down jacket, and held a cardboard sign.
It read, "Please sell me a home."

I later learned that his name was Sean Hawksford, he was twen-
ty-seven years old, and he had lived in Bozeman since college. He now
wanted to raise his son, due soon, in the town where his wife, Jessica,
grew up. Jessica's parents run a local Christian camp, and they have
also been struggling to find an affordable house, after living on the
camp's church-owned property since 1995. Sean and Jessica had been
approved for a $500,000 bank loan and were actively making offers
on homes. But by the time he walked down Main Street, sign strapped
to chest, the couple had been outbid for homes eighteen times. Sean
worked—he'd been a rafting guide and the owner of a construction
company, and is currently working to become a financial advisor at
Edward Jones—but as people with more wealth from large, faraway
cities poured into the West during the pandemic, newcomers beat out
locals with cash offers. In 2022, the median home in Bozeman was
almost $900,000. Still, Sean's sandwich board worked. A local man
whose son had passed away in an accident a few months prior was
moved by the young couple's plight and sold them his son's house for

a price they could afford. The Hawksfords got lucky in a place where many have not. Housing costs in appealing western towns like Bozeman are through the roof.

Kathleen McLaughlin is a journalist based in Butte, a bighearted working-class town ninety miles west of Bozeman. In a 2021 piece in the *Guardian*, she wrote about Hawksford's plight, also noting that "in the last couple of years, Montana has become a destination among both the traveling and remote-work class—and my home is changing as fast as in any previous western land rush." Outsiders with deep pockets are making things very hard for local residents trying to build lives. Housing prices over the 2020-2021 period jumped 57 percent in Montana, 46 percent in Idaho, and 37 percent in Utah and Nevada. Over the last couple of years, people who can work remotely have resettled in large numbers in western communities. Others have bought properties as investments—then leased them out at exorbitant rates, or made them into Vrbo rentals that leave communities bereft of real resident housing. Bozeman itself offers too many examples of what happens to a town when land speculators move in, inflating the real estate market and making it harder for people who work here, who attend school here, or who have even grown up here and hope to stay. Visitors bring money into mountain towns, yes, but a proliferation of Vrbos can turn a neighborhood into a social desert. So can second homes that sit empty for much of the year. Additionally, rents have gone sky high, yielding gentrified zones where neither working-class people nor even professionals can afford housing. Like the old gold rushes, this land rush has brought barons to the West, widening disparity between the haves and have nots.

As McLaughlin notes, as Bozeman's fancy new developments pop up atop former agricultural lands, tucked away in quiet streets, service workers are living in their trucks or trailers, sometimes even pitching tents in the grass. "They're the picture of displacement out west, the collateral victims of an affordability crisis created by Montana's booming popularity as a place for people with money." In the winter of 2023, I saw dozens of these RVs and cars lined up behind a new gas station and casino, plywood covering the windows to keep the subzero temperatures and icy winds from creeping inside. I'd seen people living out of trailers in Bozeman here and there in the past, but never so many, closely parked, in various states of disrepair, down multiple streets.

COVID-19 was an accelerant in this new western land rush. COVID refugees, escaping both the disease and the strict protocols imposed in some places against it, have stampeded into western towns, many working remotely, or not needing to work at all, as even richer people bought giant ranches and estates within compact communities in the foothills. The rush has been painful in many ways, as rents increased and housing prices soared. Montana has the fastest growth of income inequality, according to a recent report based on US Census Bureau data. Of course, land rushes are nothing novel. Métis poet and writer Chris La Tray, a member of the Little Shell Tribe of Chippewa Indians, tweeted a comment in response to the phenomenon in 2022: "You know, this sucks, people being forced away from where they've gotten cozy. But welcome to the last five hundred years, Mo-foes." Still this current rush, hurting so many western communities, doesn't ease the pain that came from the dispossession of Native lands—pain that has ongoing repercussions. And in ways, it makes it worse.

The 1800s saw white settlers pushing ever westward. Fur traders, prospectors, cowpokes, land speculators, robber barons, railroad workers, loggers, uranium miners, roughnecks, and merchants poured out along and across the ever-expanding frontier. Later, when some Americans had enough money in their pockets and the free time that comes from prosperity, tourists arrived by rail, roaming the Rocky Mountains to visit the lands taken from Native people. Thanks to

Ralph Waldo Emerson, Henry David Thoreau, Walt Whitman, and others whose writings inspired the preservationist movement, land came to be best appreciated when empty of people and void of utility other than leisure. Within the mad rush to settle the West, lands too difficult to access for extraction had other forms of appeal. Some possessed great beauty and others held opportunities for high adventure. These remote and rugged destinations came to be valued in a new way, that of parks and wilderness. Wealthy people eyed lands not just for resource exploitation, but as private hideaways with stunning scenery, fresh air, and opportunities for sport. Hunting along foothills, fishing in glittering rivers, and riding horses through grasslands drew the well-heeled to the Rocky Mountains. The Harrimans, the Guggenheims, the Rockefellers, and other titans began acquiring their own homes on the range, following in the footsteps of Teddy Roosevelt. And during COVID rose still another form of appeal: remote properties as sanatoria. That wasn't new either, but it hadn't had such force since the nineteenth century and its "Come West and Be Cured" vogue of easterners in flight from their consumption. Get away for your health and safety.

The West still beckons. In tourism campaigns—Jeep commercials, movies, novels, and other forms of cultural influence—the myth of the boundless and empty West calls to people. Most recently, *Yellowstone*, the television series starring Kevin Costner as the patriarch of a ranching family, has become the dreamscape, as evidenced in the endless references to it I've heard from people who do not live here. Most people I've talked to who do live here are not fans. The West gets romanticized ad nauseam, but it's still woefully misunderstood by other Americans. This isn't surprising. As in *Yellowstone*—the show, not the park—it's a place portrayed in silly, skewed, and grievous ways.

Before Kevin Costner, there was Lorne Greene of *Bonanza*, and before him there was Hopalong Cassidy and John Ford and Zane Grey.

But the most impactful and woeful portrayal of this place was courtesy of historian Frederick Jackson Turner, in his 1893 essay, "The Significance of the Frontier in American History." Turner's work enthroned some of the most dangerous of western myths as well as some of the most stubborn. Real Americans, Turner contended, were ever expanding their horizons and wants; were shrugging off their urban, or European, pretensions; and were chasing new opportunity in the forever-opening frontier. They sought the "simplicity of primitive society," and the "hither edge of free land," forging in the process of their efforts what he understood as the authentic "American character." Turner contended that the "true point of view in the history of this nation is not the Atlantic coast, it is the Great West."

Turner's assertions reduced an understanding of the West to a matter of white settlement, resource extraction, and infinite abundance. Although his view is no longer the prevailing narrative in the field of western history—he himself conceded that there was no more "frontier" after 1890—his 130-year framework certainly influenced the way the West has been perceived, commodified, and consumed. According to Turner, to be a westerner is to have "dominant individualism," a "buoyancy and exuberance which comes with freedom," and an interest in "incessant expansion." He construed an entire geographic region as empty land in which to plant stakes signifying ownership, an unmarked canvas on which to paint success and claim dominion. That's why people see the West as a place in which to build homelands, escape disease, and buy trophy ranches, without acknowledging the stories and lives of those people already here. Turner saw the West as an empty page, but it's actually a palimpsest.

Turner's notion has a corny and distressing abstractness, as it lingers in the minds of people who have little understanding of landscape. The West is a real place, but it's also a tall tale. Although Turner touted a region where settlers can find "free land," there is no such thing and there never was. Land was pilfered from Native peoples and sold cheap, effectively given away, to settlers by the government under the Homestead Act. Turner's idea of free land has its echoes in the current western land rush, as acreage is grabbed up by those who come with more money than those who are struggling to make their livings here. Instead of rushing westward in a wagon train to lay claim to a desirable 160-acre patch, they make calls to agents or shop online, sometimes buying sight-unseen. The land is still free, not as in gratis, but in its availability to those who can afford it. This time people are moving to the West, or visiting second homes, not to tame the wild in pursuit of pasture and farmland, but to consume it as aesthetes, connoisseurs, and recreationists. This has increasingly made western communities unaffordable to many locals, gentrified rural towns, increased pressure on limited resources, and created shifts affecting everything from politics to economics to cultural perceptions. Old, familiar drugstores disappear from Main Street seemingly overnight, replaced by real estate offices and art galleries selling expensive western kitsch. There's a notion in certain monied circles in America that the West is theirs for the taking. Because, sadly, it is.

Turner once wrote that the West has been a "miner's frontier," a "farmer's frontier," a "rancher's frontier," and a "trader's frontier." The latest iteration of Turner's thesis might be the frontier of exclusivity. About fifty miles up the road from Bozeman, Montana, sits the Yellowstone Club, a 13,600-acre resort, offering golf and "private powder"—that is, rarefied and untracked snow on its ski slopes. This place exemplifies the multiple issues that come with tailoring the West to the expectations of the highly wealthy. It's a gated community, safeguarded by former Secret Service agents, founded in 1997 by one Tim Blixseth, a developer, songwriter, and onetime Oregon timber baron who left behind bankruptcies there to try new tricks in Montana. Blixseth had the instincts and the ethics of a western Trump. He had money and land from sales to, and swaps with, the US Forest Service. He also had chutzpah. He sought high-profile investors, like former bicycle racer Greg LeMond, three-time winner of the Tour de France. At the YC nowadays, you might bump into Justin Timberlake or Bill Gates or Jennifer Lopez.

The man behind this vision of a luxury wilderness retreat, Blixseth, lorded over the place in the early stages of its existence. In the passing years, he dressed variously—in smart suits, modish black turtlenecks, and sporty ski getups that finally gave way to orange prison coveralls. This one-time billionaire, who made headlines with his opulence and his hardball methods, went from being one of the most influential entrepreneurs in the country to being an inmate at the Cascade Regional Detention Center.

Blixseth, himself a westerner, grew up dirt poor as an only child in what he describes as a religious cult. His dad was the preacher for a group called Jesus Name of Oneness, an Oregon Pentecostal sect of around seventy people who spoke in tongues, engaged in full submersion baptism, and performed ongoing acts of repentance. Determined from an early age to escape poverty, he schemed to get rich and pursued that goal by whatever means necessary, including shady maneuvering. His first racket, at age thirteen, involved three donkeys that he bought for $25 each. A few days after his purchase, he saw an advertisement: Pack mules wanted, $75 a pop. Hmm, he thought, who's to say my donkeys aren't pack mules? In a 2008 interview with *Forbes*, he told a reporter that he decided to place his own announcement in the paper, advertising his new acquisitions as mules. "The phone rang off the wall." When he sold his three donkeys to some chump for $225, "a light bulb went on and I went, 'Huh, okay.' All we did is rebrand the donkeys into pack mules," and the wheeling and dealing went on from there.

Graduating from asses to timber, timber to real estate, Blixseth came to Montana in 1992 to buy land from the big logging company Plum Creek, thinking he would focus on timber harvest and property sales. He ended up trading 164,000 acres in the Gallatin Range, an exquisite stretch of mountains running along Yellowstone National Park, for 100,000 acres in the Spanish Peaks, closer to Big Sky Resort. Journalists Todd Wilkinson and Scott McMillon have both written about this agonizing deal between Blixseth and the Forest Service—a checkerboard land swap that, on the bright side, protected contiguous habitat for many species in an area called Porcupine Creek. Blixseth couldn't have cared less about the area's high value as habitat for grizzlies, elk, moose, and bighorn sheep, famously declaring that he was "tired of people saying clear-cutting is a bad word." He considered this corner of southwestern Montana a "tree farm." In 1997, he renamed the tree farm the Yellowstone Club, a la donkeys to mules, and turned around to sell the hell out of it.

At this 15,000-acre sanctuary for the rich, members buy homes or building sites along the flanks of the Spanish Peaks. Just beyond their front yard is Yellowstone National Park, and in the backyard is Big Sky Resort. In 2020, $18 million would get you a six-bedroom house, with 12,500 feet of room to store your skis. According to *Celebrity Net Worth*, which touts itself as "the website future billionaires read every day" (this I seriously doubt), the Yellowstone Club offers "serious skiing, a Wild West Montanan vibe, and someplace members can relax and not worry about being watched, followed, or hounded. For the rich and famous, that is worth the price of admission." The website shows video clips of fly-fishing, skiing, horseback riding, and golf. It beckons, "Your Mountain Sanctuary Awaits."

But here's the rub. This playground for the affluent, so exclusive and expensive, has a lousy track record as a neighbor in many ways. In 2004, the Yellowstone Club was fined $1.8 million for sixty violations of the Clean Water Act, after wetlands were damaged during the building of the golf course. YC was ordered to "restore five acres of damaged wetlands and reconstruct 1.5 acres of new wetland habitat." When billionaires want wilderness, they want it gilded. Amenities get gouged onto fragile places ill-suited for luxury development. Sixty violations of the Clean Water Act didn't stop the transgressions. There would be more offenses washing downstream.

In 2005, Blixseth and his wife, Edra, took out a $375 million loan from the bank Credit Suisse. This was, in part, to finance Yellowstone Club World, an expansion of the original concept in the form of a string of high-end destination properties, nine in all, scattered around the world. The *New York Times* described it as "an opulent time-share program for the richest of the world's rich." Courts have since ruled that $286 million of the loan was used personally by the couple. In 2008, during the global financial crisis, enormous upheaval almost pulled the legs out from under this club for millionaires and billionaires. The Blixseths' acrimonious divorce further whittled down the couple's net worth, even as the mortgage market went bust and the consequent collapse of real estate values across America sent their investments underwater. They filed for Chapter 11 bankruptcy protection and later CrossHarbor Capital Partners acquired this Montana property. Blixseth continued to evade creditors but spent almost fifteen months in jail for civil contempt of court in 2016. After years of legal battles, in 2022 he filed a lawsuit against the Montana Department of Revenue for hundreds of millions of dollars in damages and legal fees. The old mule trader is still bucking, though he has nothing to do with the Yellowstone Club any longer.

After emerging from bankruptcy in 2009, the Yellowstone Club and Big Sky Resort bought Moonlight Basin, another ski area and development that had been slammed by the 2008 recession. Over the years, more and more people moved to this constellation of developments, increasing pressure on the waters of Gallatin Canyon, in which it lies, and the Yellowstone ecosystem generally, of which the Gallatin Canyon is part. Again in 2017, the club was fined hundreds of thousands of dollars after thirty million gallons from a wastewater storage pond spilled into a tributary of the Gallatin River, a gorgeous and vulnerable ribbon of water draining north through the narrow canyon. This constituted two legal offenses, "discharging sewage, industrial wastes or other wastes into state water without a permit; and contamination of state waters, stemming from exceedances of established water quality standards." With all the growth around Big Sky, three tributaries of the Gallatin have been deemed "impaired" due to "excessive nutrients" (read, sewage). The result is an ongoing profusion of algal blooms in the Gallatin and its tributaries. Notwithstanding those explosions of green gunk in the Gallatin, the encroachment into wildlife habitat, and the ever-growing economic inequity, high-end developments keep sprouting, like toadstools.

Cultural sociologist Justin Farrell, in his 2020 book *Billionaire Wilderness*, discusses the pressures the uber-rich put on places— the cost to community culture, the carbon footprint of private jets, and the economic hardships imposed on the working class, many of whom are from Central and South America and struggle to find places to live. Additionally, enclaves such as the Yellowstone Club, carved out of wild landscapes such as the Gallatin Range, result not just in loss of habitat and decrease in population numbers of wildlife, but also in habitat fragmentation, further detrimental to biological diversity. A grizzly bear can't travel to its reliable, crucial October food source if it finds a swath of luxury homes and ski villas blocking the way. As more and more people are lured to the Yellowstone Club, Big Sky, and the ever-growing slate of new luxury resorts in the region, nature is diminished in richness, fractured into pieces, and degraded in other ways. In a 2022 piece in *Mountain Journal*, Todd Wilkinson detailed all of the crushing ecological issues that go with rampant subdivision. When developments are pushed into wild places, "there is no going back." Elk migration is thwarted and herds abandon their efforts to reach seasonal habitat; females have fewer calves; animals are hit and killed by people residing in these developments, commuting to work, or coming to recreate. The Yellowstone ecosystem, a mix of both public and private lands, is home to sixty species of mammals and three hundred bird species have been spotted in the area. Sixteen fish species, six reptile species, and four amphibian species make this place their home. Rich people share the space with a lot of biodiversity. Dave Hallac, Yellowstone Park's one-time chief scientist, saw the multiple factors affecting this ecosystem as "death by a thousand scratches." Wilkinson wrote: "The science is clear: what happens on six million acres of private land in Greater Yellowstone can devastate or impair the ecological function of eight million acres of public land adjacent to it; understanding this, in fact, is the modern cornerstone of true ecosystem thinking, of which the greater Yellowstone is held up as paragon." But, like housing inequality, ecosystem health is not a priority among many people flocking to the frontiers of exclusivity.

There are three new and jaw-droppingly expensive projects in the area, including the Montage, where rooms start at $1,745 a night. In early 2022, Lori Rippstein, director of sales and marketing for this high-end resort, told the *Billings Gazette*, "We're a combination of leisure and group guests, mostly corporate right now. We are hopeful we will attract Montana residents to come and do a staycation." The average household income in Montana is less than $57,000 a year, and although the resort boasts adding five hundred new jobs to the Big Sky area, it's hard to imagine that those jobs will afford workers a staycation at their place of employment. Another nearby property, the Saudi-financed One&Only in Moonlight Basin, lists residences beginning at $8.45 million—as a woozy tagline entices buyers to "surrender to nature." But it's nature, and many locals, being forced to surrender to the whims of the wealthy.

The mountain sanctuaries, hotels, employee housing, and new businesses, plus a new school and tourist amenities, are severe challenges to Big Sky's water and sewage system. Several measures are in process to address sewage coming from all the older and newer development in the area; for instance, a new sewage treatment plant will produce cleaner effluent that will be used to make artificial snow (which has a large carbon footprint) on the local ski slopes. There is continuous monitoring of effluents, thanks to the Gallatin River Task Force and the Montana Department of Environmental Quality. Further, a campaign is underway to replace old septic systems that leak directly into the Gallatin River. Currently, Upper Missouri Waterkeeper, whose mission is to employ "strong science, community action, and legal expertise to defend the Upper Missouri River, its tributaries, and communities against threats to clean water and healthy rivers" (this includes the Gallatin River), is pushing to designate the Gallatin River as "impaired," which would require a state-mandated cleanup plan. A statement from that conservation organization said, "Prolonged and widespread algal blooms have the potential to cause serious harm to the physical, chemical, and biological integrity of the Gallatin River, the consequences of which could impact Gallatin County's outdoor economy, drinking water supplies, ranching and agriculture, and wildlife and trophy fish." The summer of 2022 marked the fifth year in a row that a form of bright green algae proliferated in tributaries to the Gallatin and in the river itself, an iconic waterway featured in the movie *A River Runs Through It.*

— — —

THE STORY OF BIG SKY, THE RESORT THAT ANCHORS THE YELLOW-stone Club, Moonlight Basin, and all of the condos, houses, and hotels surrounding it, is one that the writer Ray Ring called a "test site for the idea that government and anything public should be shrunk down to libertarian size, allowing money, private property and market forces to dominate." The town is unincorporated and decisions are made by the Gallatin County and Madison County commissioners, as well as several boards, from the sewage board to the resort tax board. Developers and realtors hold enormous power in a place without a central government.

In a noisy Bozeman café, I sat down with Scott Bosse, whose boyish looks belie a long experience protecting regional waters. As the Northern Rockies director of American Rivers, Bosse is well qualified to offer an overview of ongoing work in the region and the pressures that the Gallatin watershed has faced and is currently facing. "I've been involved in Big Sky water quality and wastewater issues for about twenty years. Before I worked for American Rivers, I worked for GYC"—that's the Greater Yellowstone Coalition, still another conservation organization—"and I was engaged in that process," Bosse explained. "Big Sky Water and Sewer District at one time had a discharge permit and they wanted to discharge all their treated wastewater directly into the Gallatin River," he said. "It was really controversial." During the legal proceedings, officials of the district agreed not to dump wastewater directly into the Gallatin. "And since that time the goal of a lot of influential community members in Big Sky has been to make Big Sky a zero-discharge community." Continuing this would help curtail further algae blooms that affect trout and the aquatic insects they eat. Fishing tourism generates $350 million every year in Montana—in addition to feeding trout, this river feeds families.

To uphold its agreement, Bosse explained, the district recycled and reused water for various things, such as landscaping, golf course irrigation, and snowmaking "because if you can do that, then you can close the loop on water use." Wastewater needs to be held to a very high standard in its treatment, or nutrients will remain, making it unusable for such purposes. "And then the only alternative really is to discharge into the Gallatin River, which, like, 99.9 percent of communities in America do. They discharge treated wastewater into rivers. In Jackson, Wyoming..." He paused before continuing. Jackson, another getaway for the rich, Bosee explained, has been discharging treated wastewater into the Snake River for decades.

Even so, Big Sky has a nutrient problem, due to leaky septic systems, climate change, overwatering of golf courses with wastewater, and voracious development. The wealthy want their fancified nature, and the resort and real estate developers want their money. As an activist, Bosse does not take funding from this sector nor anyone else he feels would expect him to turn a blind eye to environmental problems. Though some conservation organizations in the area do accept funding from such sources, Bosse believes that it undermines their effectiveness. Over his twenty years in Gallatin County, he has seen many people—people he was certain would work forever to protect the values that drew them to the area—sell off their integrity, as Tim Blixseth once sold off his donkeys. Bosse, whom I've also known for a long while (we attended the same graduate program, but during different years), confided that these people know that they are selling out, but they do it anyway. "I've talked to people that are really high up in the development community, including at the Yellowstone Club," he told me. "I've talked to them over campfires after several drinks and heard them say things about...regretting what they let happen to Big Sky. I totally heard it." But, he pointed out, people start making money and their values get chucked.

Asked why people are buckling in a place that so desperately needs protection, Bosse offered: "It's kind of like Patty Hearst. You fall in love with your captors." Especially if those captors are making you cash. "And I think the people that moved to Big Sky twenty, thirty years ago had good intentions back then." It wasn't just real estate salespeople and developers who have abandoned their principles, he said, but also hydrologists, surveyors, consultants, even environmentalists. But, he added, there were decent folks still fighting for this precious corner of the Greater Yellowstone ecosystem, "people with truly good hearts that want to do things differently, that recognize that we still have some of the things here that have been lost everywhere else in the Lower 48."

He's right. I've talked with water conservationists and residents of Big Sky who are concerned about their community and avidly working to safeguard it. They love this place. Another friend of mine, for instance, is an enormously philanthropic man who owns a lot but no dwelling, at the Yellowstone Club. He's a modest and soft-spoken midwesterner who serves as a great champion of healthy rivers the world round. Yet there are many people profiting richly from swelling the affluent population of Big Sky. So the expansion continues, and so do the detrimental impacts to communities, and watersheds, and ecosystems.

If the Big Sky area, and Bozeman for that matter, continue to push ill-considered development into one of the most important biological systems in the world without regard for the impacts, then the very things that make the place precious—such as clean waters with abundant fish, migrating elk, and livable communities—will disappear. Wildlife can't relocate. They can't go to second homes. Neither can many of the people who live and work here who can't even afford a home at all. Wilderness retreats are presently being built on lands, high and steep, dramatic and severe, that weren't settled earlier because they were too hard to access. Now these lands are being commodified based on their very remoteness. Some illegal environmental actions draw fines, but those are small prices to pay—small, anyway, for high rollers who feel entitled to their hunk of nature. As developers and real estate interests turn parts of this ecosystem into playgrounds for the rich, the economic disparities and the environmental degradation undermine the very myths they are selling. These lands are anything but free, and eventually the "wilderness" roundabout is just an illusion painted on fancy walls.

Nowhere is this better exemplified than at the Yellowstone Club. I remember, one day, walking out of a discussion on the wastewater situation with a YC employee. It was in the early 2000s and I was working for the conservation group American Wildlands. The meeting itself had been unmemorable, but I recall coming out of a Quonset hut into a white rip of sunshine that sparkled the snow. This is where it all happens, I thought. This broad bowl within the glorious Spanish Peaks, a magnificent locale to which some of the richest people in the world flock. Here they build enormous homes, retreat to luxuriate amid these ever-shrinking wildlands, distance themselves from the hoi polloi, congratulate themselves on their exclusivity, and poop in a river.

CHAPTER 8

THE COWBOY

←——— – – – – ———→

MOST WESTERN TOWNS AREN'T RESORTS AND most westerners aren't billionaires. It was only certain corners of Colorado, Wyoming, Montana, Idaho, New Mexico, Arizona, Utah, and Nevada that saw an influx of people during the pandemic. In many rural communities, life seemed to change little—no mask-wearing, no telecommuting, no private jets. People lived day-to-day, as they always had. Still, a deep seismic movement was afoot. In a period of quarantine, the rural West became more culturally and politically isolated, largely due to the discord being sown via social media and news networks. As with the rest of the country, people grew ever angrier as political aisles widened and lies fueled mistrust. As people severed relationships, either intentionally or inadvertently, with those who saw things differently, the result was a divergent sense of reality. I saw this in Idaho, where polarization created splinters in the community. Parts of Montana show signs of following suit.

This brings me to a story about a cowboy—the real McCoy, not a cartoon version portrayed by John Wayne or Kevin Costner. On the day I met him, it was hard to tell if Lance Kalfell was completely enraged, or just on a roll. He seemed spitting mad, telling me how he hated Biden and the Democrats. This was a man who had lost faith in any federal policy intended to address issues affecting him and his community. Kalfell was raised in the town of Terry, Montana, the seat of Prairie County, a little place built amid the breaks and sage, and folded between the Powder and Yellowstone Rivers. The Old Milwaukee train depot in the middle of town once served passengers coming west, but now Burlington Northern Santa Fe trains sail through without stopping. There are a great many stories inscribed on the lands around Terry, from the conflict between Sitting Bull and his Lakota people with the US Army to the state's deadliest train wreck. Although the population is small, just 549 people, Terry boasts two museums. That's a whole lot of museums per capita, a curious point to which we'll return.

When Kalfell and I met, Joe Biden had recently canceled the Keystone XL pipeline project, an enterprise commissioned by a Canadian oil company that would have delivered eight hundred thousand barrels of crude oil per day from where they were extracted from Alberta's tar sands, across Montana and South Dakota to Nebraska. Though many Indigenous leaders, farmers, and ranchers were against the project, Kalfell had been counting on taxes that, he said, were attached to the pipeline's revenue and which he was certain could benefit Terry's schools.

This wasn't his only bone to pick; lots of things were troubling him. "I've become radicalized," he told me. He had joined the NRA and bought some guns. Kalfell is a man about five feet and ten inches tall who wears rectangular glasses with tinted lenses that adjust to the light. He speaks with a gravelly, fast-paced authority. I confess his word "radicalized" gave me pause. He listed the issues that pushed him toward his so-called radicalism—hypocritical Democrats, wildly off-base media, environmentalist "carpetbaggers," and public land managers, specifically those from the Bureau of Land Management (BLM). Although I've interviewed many people with similar opinions, I've never heard someone be so forthcoming about them and I wanted to understand his frustration. For the last several years, I have worried that people in rural communities are feeling so disenfranchised that they would embrace the ways of the Bundy family and other anti-government agitators. I feel it's important to hear them out because so much of the country has stopped listening. With Kalfell, although it seemed especially worthwhile it was also a bit stressful; his candor unsettled me.

I had been introduced to him by Mike Bugenstein, who wrote a book about Kalfell's family, *Since the Days of the Buffalo: A History of Eastern Montana and the Kalfell Ranch*. It includes the story of Gottlieb Kalfell, Lance's great-grandfather, who settled in eastern Montana on lands once roamed by buffalo before starvation campaigns and the hide trade nearly wiped them out. Gottlieb acquired a scrip, a form of credit used to buy land in the federal public domain, in 1882, and with it, he launched a legacy that Lance Kalfell now shares. For nearly one hundred years, his parents, grandparents, and great-grandparents raised cattle and sheep on this parcel of sage-and-grass range, a hard place to make a living as a rancher. For instance, the winter of 1886, shortly after Gottlieb arrived, was a bad one. The ferocity of the storms that winter buried lands and downed animals. Blizzards scattered and killed thousands of cows and sheep across the state of Montana, leaving ranchers helpless as their animals froze in drifts. The tribes suffered even more, as corrupt government agents left them to starve, forcing people to eat the horses found dead in the snow. Nelson Story, the man who inspired the novel *Lonesome Dove*, lost thousands of heads of livestock that winter and decided to quit the cattle business altogether. Several people across Montana's eastern plains—mostly Native people—froze to death.

Over the years, the Kalfells raised livestock, fought brutal snows, endured crippling droughts, and engaged in quarrels between the generations who worked the land. The family almost lost their place during the 1980s, due to debts and reduced income from failed crops, and plummeting prices for livestock. But they persevered, experimenting with various livestock management styles, implementing no-till farming practices, and digging extensive trenching that provided water to dry corners of the property. Unlike the hobbyists of the Madison Valley, most ranchers in eastern Montana live at the mercy of commodity market prices, weather, and their relationships with banks. Ranching is a hard livelihood, especially in a land so unforgiving.

— — —

AS WE TALKED OVER COFFEE, KALFELL TOLD A STORY ABOUT the time in the 1990s when he became a member of the Foreign Agricultural Service, an arm of the US Department of Agriculture. As part of a multi-day training program in Bozeman, he'd been instructed on the service's sexual harassment policy, a requisite for his membership. At the time, this exercise bothered him, though he has since come to find it funny. "I've always respected women," he told me. "They wanted me to go through sexual harassment training?" he asked rhetorically. "This was during the Clinton administration!" The training mandate convinced him, Kalfell said, that Bill Clinton himself was deflecting his own lasciviousness onto others. He felt resentful and mistreated. The whole thing persuaded him that liberals were downright dishonorable—another reason why he can't stand Democrats.

The restaurant where we met that first morning in June 2021 was very noisy, making the exchange difficult to record on my phone. I took notes instead, sitting at a long wooden table next to the busy kitchen. Bugenstein, Kalfell's biographer and a progressive from Ohio who had moved to Montana decades ago, joined us. During the hour or so we were together, Bugenstein pushed back on Kalfell's political perspectives in ways both cajoling and quarrelsome. I'm prone to woolgathering when others argue, even when among friends. I was only half-listening to their conversation, but it grew louder as Bugenstein talked more and more vociferously over Kalfell.

"Are you going to take it down?" Kalfell asked.

"Sorry?" I replied.

"I've asked you three times," he said. "Are you going to take down my information?" He wanted to know if I would be interested in visiting his ranch, the Kalfell spread between Miles City and Glendive. He also asked if he could read my book, *American Zion*.

"You'll hate it," I told him. I had given Bugenstein a copy the day before, in reciprocation for his gift of the Kalfell family book, and he had suggested that I give one to Kalfell as well. *American Zion* is a history of Mormonism and public lands battles in the West, including Cliven Bundy's fight with the BLM and federal law enforcement over public lands ranching. I wasn't sure that I wanted this man, who had told me he was radicalized and buying guns, to read what I'd written about certain ranchers. The Bundy family, even though they are hardly typical, had gained sympathy among those tired of government oversight. Nonetheless, I walked out into the hot mid-morning to grab Kalfell a copy from my car. We then exchanged contact information, and I honestly didn't know if I'd see him again. I thought he might rescind my invitation to his ranch after he read my book. But when I arrived home a few days later, I emailed him and asked when I might come and visit. This was his response:

Betsy,

We must be on each other's mind!

I was about to send off an email. I couldn't decide if I wanted to finish the book first. I am a little over half done. (which surprises me)

Your book is very engaging. (like being in a battle for survival!)

Not an expert, but your writing is charming, witty and filled with sarcasm.

Reminds [me] of a ranch woman, on which I am an expert! (this statement is a compliment to you)

My ranch wife says that the apartment is open, so I look forward to seeing you on the 26th.

I will chill some red wine and see if I can find some tofu.

Don't forget your white board, I am a slow learner.

I will lock up my guns, if you promise not to shoot me in the back.

I will brush up on my pocketbook "Rules for Radicals".

I might even call Saul.

Feel free to contact me at any time.

Your friend, Lance

It's hard to explain how much this note moved me. It showed me that this was a curious man, capable of irony and good humor, who was also familiar with Saul Alinsky, the pioneering community organizer who wrote *Rules for Radicals*, a book I've never read. A few weeks later, I found myself touring land that has been in the Kalfell family for five generations. When I arrived, Kalfell told me that I should have talked to him before writing about ranching and chastised me for being way too easy on the government. His admonishment was breezy, but his consternation was not. I met his wife, Lisa, a funny, vivacious retired nurse and the very woman who had helped her husband earn his expertise on ranch wives. She had moved with her family from California in the 1970s and attended high school in Terry, where she met Lance. The couple put me up in the place where his parents, Bruce and Merry, had lived until Bruce went to a nursing home in Miles City. Bruce died in 2020, and Merry followed less than a year later.

During my visit, we spent a day seeing the best of Terry, a town named after General Alfred Howe Terry, a full-bearded man with a prominent forehead and the wild eyes of Edgar Allan Poe. He served with the Union Army during and after the Civil War, and later as military commander of the Dakota Territory. General Terry's troops were the first to come across the bodies of Custer and his men following the Battle of the Little Bighorn in 1876.

Our first stop was the Kempton Hotel, established in 1902 making it one of Montana's oldest continuously operating inns. Russ Schwartz, who owns the hotel, collects western art and maintains a private library filled with books on the West that he ships to other collectors throughout the world. In addition to accommodating lodgers, over the years the Kempton has served other functions too—as an infirmary near the end of the First World War, for example—and is said to be haunted by nurses who died tending victims of the Spanish flu. Schwartz tells of guests hearing the disembodied sounds of spurs dragging heavily along the second floor—presumably worn by the phantom of some long-dead cowpoke who showed little regard for woodwork. We took a quick turn around the narrow, spook-filled halls, glancing into small tidy rooms, before settling together in the lobby. As guests wandered in and out, asking questions of Schwartz, we began a wide-ranging dialogue on current headlines.

Schwartz, like Kalfell, grew up in Terry. A libertarian who left Montana to embark on a career in engineering, he came back with his wife, Linda, to run the Kempton (named for a local family to which Schwartz is not related). Sitting around a table, we discussed the issues of 2020 and 2021—political conflicts, protests, and climate. As we moved to the subject of the pandemic, both men expressed disdain for Anthony Fauci. "He's a clown," said Schwartz. "I liked him until I found out that he was a big liar. Politics should not be in medicine, or we aren't going to get anything done." Yes, politics should not have gotten into medicine. On this, we agreed. On Fauci, we didn't. It was politics that divided our country into vaccine skeptics and those who felt confident in Fauci's expertise and leadership. The politicization of COVID has been a tragedy, but while Russ Schwartz and others might blame Fauci, I blame Fox News, Judy Mikovits, Del Bigtree, and Donald Trump.

We're all ensnared in confirmation bias. People trust political affiliations more than expertise, and even doctors are villainized, and diseases politicized. Round and round it goes...but there are always surprises. When I asked these two men "the V question," they told me that, yes, they had reluctantly been vaccinated, though Kalfell later confided that he wished he hadn't. Schwartz only got jabbed so he could travel to see family.

The talk turned to the Bundys, a hot topic out west. Schwartz and Kalfell are both familiar with the family's takeover of the Malheur National Wildlife Refuge and the death of LaVoy Finicum, who was shot and killed during the Oregon occupation. A group of Oregon state police had recently stayed at the Kempton during a hunting trip in the area, and they told Schwartz that Finicum, though he'd courted a violent confrontation with law enforcement, did not need to be killed. After hearing from the officers, Schwartz felt that Finicum's death could have been avoided.

"What about George Floyd?" I asked. Before Derek Chauvin knelt on his neck for over nine minutes, he'd been resisting arrest, Kalfell said, though witness testimony differed. "LaVoy was resisting," I pointed out. I wouldn't wish death on anyone, but I reminded them that Finicum didn't comply with officers during his arrest and had reached into the pocket holding his gun.

It was different, they said; Derek Chauvin didn't wake up wanting Floyd dead, Schwartz contended, implying that Finicum's death may have been premeditated on the part of the government. I told them about Finicum's apocalyptic novel, in which the hero goes out in a blaze of glory, exalting in violence as well as martyrdom. It may have been the way Finicum envisioned his own end.

"Death by suicide?" Schwartz offered.

"Maybe," I said. "I don't really know."

Both men also expressed doubt that climate change was behind the West's soaring temperatures and parched lands. Kalfell later sent me home with several *Wall Street Journal* articles by climate skeptics. "I think it's a natural phenomenon," he told me. Schwartz brought up the Dust Bowl of the 1930s and remarked that weather statistics only go back one hundred years. Still, we agreed that it was a rough time, and that prolonged drought was particularly problematic for agricultural communities.

It felt good to be talking face-to-face, rather than sitting at home and stewing over social media hot takes on political differences. Though Schwartz, Kalfell, and I we were coming at these divisive issues from different angles, we were able to discuss them without anger. Sitting at a table in an old hotel in very rural Montana, we talked about police violence, race, and climate while listening to one another. Though perhaps no minds were changed, this discourse felt like headway in a country paralyzed by fury.

Schwartz suggested I read *The Worst Hard Time* by Timothy Egan, a book on the Dust Bowl and the prolonged drought that defined the High Plains during the 1930s. I picked it up after our visit and read of the record-breaking heat and drought, when waves of dirt rose from homesteads on lands ill-advisedly sod-busted. Dust choked the roads and buried whole communities, from the Texas Panhandle to eastern Montana. It was clear why Schwartz had suggested it—the Dust Bowl stands as a shocking story on the ferocity of Mother Nature. Though I know he mentioned the book to show that we have seen extreme weather patterns in the past, what struck me was that the dusters of the 1930s, like our recent emissions-driven climate change, were a phenomenon brought on by human actions—in the older case, breaking up the plains and planting crops in place of wild grasses. Now we know better, and do better, in our agricultural practices, though we have a way to go—we still spew too much methane, carbon dioxide, pesticide, and herbicide.

We also spew too much bile. Real dialogue is different. And as we experience more extreme weather, no matter what people think is the cause, it's going to be essential for us to be talking to each other about it. Ongoing drought, floods, and fire are affecting food production, damaging property, and killing people and animals, both wild and domestic. We are going to need to plan together, take care of, and rely on one another as we consider our future. Tim Egan's book, in addition to being a great read, emphasized the story of communities and neighbors who supported one another through hard times. We need to be ready to do the same.

—   —   —

TERRY HAS MANY OUTSTANDING FEATURES FOR SUCH A TINY town, and Kalfell has a hand in much of the good stuff. He's involved in Terry High School, where he coached football and wrestling. (Go, Terriers!) He and his family have hosted numerous AmeriCorps VISTA volunteers over the years, one of whom married his son. He has collaborated with Wild Montana, formerly the Montana Wilderness Alliance, and together they created trail maps outlining paths through the broken, otherworldly country near his ranch along the Powder River. Kalfell has also played key roles in Terry's museums.

The Prairie Museum is a collection of tightly packed objects from Terry's bygone eras. Hodgepodge cabinets are arranged in the former State Bank building, a high-ceilinged, sturdy structure that, according to the website, had the "only steam-heated outhouse this side of the

Mississippi." Farm implements necessary to the business of home-steads sit alongside archaic typewriters, animal horns, an old stove, desks, inkpots, pens, and manikins dressed in garb over a hundred years old.

The Evelyn Cameron Gallery is part of this museum, but it's in another building and has an entirely different feel. It's open and bright, with walls of black-and-white prints from the gallery's namesake. Kalfell and a jovial man named Rich Miller showed me her work of which the town is so proud.

Cameron was a woman who first visited eastern Montana as a well-heeled tourist on a hunting trip. She returned four years later to become an irrepressible homesteader in a fickle landscape. Photographer and frontierswoman, Cameron had a remarkable eye and a clear sense of humor, both on full display in her work showing moments of hard-won survival on the Montana prairie.

In 1889, with her new Scottish husband, Ewan, an amateur naturalist, Cameron traveled from Britain to hunt game along the Yellowstone River. By that time, the country was empty of the millions of bison that had roamed here. She was the daughter of a wealthy merchant who raised his many children in rarefied English circles south of London. Her half-brother, Cyril Flower, married Constance Rothschild of the famed Rothschild banking family—the same often scapegoated by anti-Semitic conspiracy theorists. Cameron had an inheritance from her father, but she and Ewan, a spoiled and disobliging partner, struggled financially. This put her through ups and downs, swinging from merry to "blue." According to her journals, she took pleasure in raising a garden of potatoes and corn and delighted in entertaining guests, but she and Ewan continually struggled to pay their bills. There was never enough money, despite Evelyn's small inheritance. An initial plan to raise and sell polo ponies went bust, so the couple resorted to providing for lodgers in their small cabin. It was in the quest for some extra income that she bought her first camera; one of her boarders taught her the basics of photography.

Her pictures had nearly been lost, forgotten for decades while moldering in the basement of her best bosom friend, Janet "Jeannie" Williams. The trove was rescued in the 1970s by Donna Lucey, an editor and writer for *Life* magazine, when Williams invited Lucey to Terry. Lucey arrived by bus, and Williams, then in her nineties, finally shared her precious collection, something she had been loath to do with others. Lucey later published much of this work in a book, *Photographing Montana, 1894-1928: The Life and Work of Evelyn Cameron*.

A year after my introduction to Cameron's work in Terry, I went to examine her letters and journals in Helena, Montana, sorting through boxes in the Montana Historical Society archives. Behind me stood a taxidermized buffalo named Big Medicine, a sacred member of the Salish Kootenai herd that had been honored for his white fur and blue eyes. A few months after I sat with him, it gave me great joy to read that he was leaving Helena to be returned to the lands of the Salish, Kootenai, and Pend d'Oreille people, where he had been born. Under the gaze of Big Medicine, I read Cameron's journals, and also correspondence between her and Williams, who inherited Cameron's photographic work and other property after her death in 1928. Cameron bequeathed 1,800 glass plates, 2,500 prints, and bundles of letters and diaries to Williams, all of which she held closely private for over fifty years. Lucey, after her fateful bus trip, convinced Williams to hand over Cameron's possessions and then helped secure a permanent place for those precious items.

The photographer spent years lugging around her large Tourist Graflex and glass plates to take family portraits, shots of immigrant railroad workers, images of laughing women, and pictures of wolves, horses, dogs, and raptors. She captured scenes that seemed incongruent with the severe landscape. Her shots were intimate, funny, and quirky. A child riding a pig. A smartly dressed accordionist perched in the thick crux of a tree. A self-portrait of Cameron smiling, standing on the back of a white horse, wearing a crisp cotton shirt, a fine leather belt with a tooled buckle, and a little bow tie. There are pictures of cowgirls, picnic parties, cattle drives, and sheep wagons, all taken by this woman who was to the English manor born but embraced life in eastern Montana. Cameron captured moments that most male photographers of her time did not. As Kalfell pointed out to me, many of Cameron's portraits carried her own long shadow across the frame—a no-no for many photographers, but for her, a signature wink. He also showed me a portrait of his own great-grandmother and her sisters among those in the gallery.

Riding through the eroded country along the Powder and Yellowstone Rivers, Cameron had accompanied her naturalist husband as he studied various western bird species. There are pictures of goshawks, eagles, and herons in her oeuvre, providing images for journals to accompany his writings. She sometimes spent hours inching ever closer to nests and perches, moving slowly to assure the birds, and their chicks, that she was no threat.

Cameron noted changes to her corner of Montana in her diary, as waves of newly arrived folk sought opportunities there. Her wild places gave way to agriculture, and as she explained to one reporter in 1906, "The great hunting days are over in Custer County and the ranchman and granger will see to it that they never return. About all that is left to the sportswoman today is to hunt with a camera." Later, in a 1910 letter to her sister, Hilda, she wrote, "Of course, the country has settled up very rapidly and deprived us of range, but on the other hand, some of the settlers are very nice." The ebbs and flows of land rushes have been happening for some time.

In 1907 Cameron met the woman to whom she would bequeath

her ranch and photographs, Janet Williams, a young newcomer who had just moved to Terry from Minnesota. Williams enchanted both Camerons, and the couple delighted in her piano performances, including compositions by Cameron's mother. When Ewan died in 1915, the two women grew ever closer. Together, they witnessed the horrors of the First World War and the Spanish flu; influenza, but not from Spain. Williams, who worked for the Red Cross in 1918, asked Cameron to join her in Europe. Cameron demurred. In a letter to Williams, she explained that "it is futile to think of going to Europe, sweet child, while the war lasts unless the individual is a professional expert in the occupation useful to the allies...Better for you to do less for your country's welfare and for me to grow food for returning heroes." The flu, raging in Europe, was by then also gripping eastern Montana, including Terry and the nearby town of Fallon. News of neighbors dying rattled these communities. For a while, Terry's churches, schoolhouses, and saloons closed their doors (sound familiar?), while the Kempton Hotel served as a hospital, as I've mentioned, and the ghosts of flu victims still walk its halls. Williams, on her return to Montana, even brought Cameron a gauze mask to wear.

Williams, who never married, was evidently cherished by Cameron. In her diary, she noted how she grew "fonder of her every day, as if that were possible." The two "confided in one another" and sometimes stayed up "chatting in bed," according to notes and journal entries that the photographer left behind. Cameron took numerous pictures of her apple-cheeked friend—sitting on her horse, Zip; holding a coyote pup in a crate; posing prettily with her sister, Mabel. There are also portraits of the two women together. One, in particular, captures the comfort they took in each other's company. Posed side by side in this self-portrait, sitting snugly in a doorframe, Cameron and Williams, dressed in blouses and long skirts, press their heads together at the temples. The photographer smiles at the camera while Williams gazes dreamily into the vastness of the Montana prairie.

There are many references in Cameron's journals to Williams, wistful scribblings even from the time before Ewan died. On January 10, 1913, she "sat in the gloaming and thought of Janet." Other entries indicate that she had stayed up late reading Williams' letters, spending hours crafting responses and recording the lengths of time she took writing them in her journal. There were endless references to her feelings for Williams tucked among her meticulous observations in the last diary—accounts, crops and yields, meals prepared, errands crossed from lists, and Janet, Janet, Janet...

I found, tucked in boxes of Cameron's possessions, two cards. One read, "Love's message: Somebody Loves You deep and true. If I weren't so bashful I'd tell you." The other side of this card is inscribed, "My love I'm sending you this date. Will see you soon and demonstrate." The word *demonstrate* is underlined. Though not signed, the handwriting looks like the same lovely cursive as Cameron's diaries—her *y* is very distinctive. There is another card I found that read: "Unspoken thoughts are sweetest, unwritten songs are best, and love that lies the deepest is often unexpressed." This love letter was signed, "Janet."

The Prairie Museum's Evelyn Cameron Gallery is filled with portraits of people who admired and trusted a photographer. During her life in eastern Montana, she had captured friends and neighbors— those coming West trying to make living in a land of fierce weather, drought, and locust plagues. Kalfell introduced me to the rail workers, farmers, and ranchers that hang in frames next to his own ancestors. Among Cameron's body of work are the Kalfell women; unsmiling, raw-boned mothers and the blurred faces of children; hoodoos and natural bridges; roughhewn shacks on forlorn homesteads; and a pronghorn dangling from a tree branch just before its gutting. I was lucky to see these photographs and later to read intimate letters with clues to the life beyond the photographer's camera. It seems Evelyn Cameron fell for this corner of the West, and also for a woman named Janet Wil-

liams. That's among the many facets of a person this community celebrates. It was also a dent in yet another myth: small-town intolerance.

—   —   —

WE VISITED TERRY'S OTHER MUSEUM, EVELYN CAMERON HER-
itage, Inc., an elegantly renovated building displaying Cameron's
photographs in much smaller prints than the first gallery. This place
apparently exists because the Prairie Museum board had little interest
in working with a group that received an economic development grant
from the state of Montana to promote Cameron's work. A committee,
including Lance Kalfell, created the second museum. Upon entering
the large room of highly polished wood, I tucked a twenty-dollar bill
in the donation box and walked the hall, again admiring this woman's
lovely work. Then we headed to the next stop on the Terry tour, the
Prairie Unique.

This old-fashioned curio emporium is the best kind of shop.
Crowded with Montana products, its shelves stand laden with salves
such as goat's milk lotion and Terry's Own Wool Wax Cream; polished agates from Kalfell's ranch; antler art; and books such as *Fla-
vors Under the Big Sky*, *Montana Trivia*, and *Make Mine a Ditch*,
about bars in Montana, of which there are many. Overhead, large and
multicolored model planes hang from the ceiling, above walls stacked
with model radio-controlled monster trucks and drag racing cars. Dale
Galland, who owns the store with his wife, talked with me about the
varied inventory. We realized we have a friend in common—also a fine
photographer—Lynn Donaldson. "We love Lynn," he said. "I do, too,"
I said. I had just come from a joint memorial service for her parents, in
Denton, Montana, a town even smaller than Terry, with a population of
296. They'd died within three months of each other. Galland expressed
his condolences and his hope to see Donaldson again soon. "I'll let her

know," I said, and left with a pile of books, some huckleberry taffy, and a couple of bags of Montana Farver Farms Lentil Crunchers.

Just outside town, the landscape gives way to broken country—the buttes, hoodoos, natural bridges, and spires that define the Terry Badlands. Kalfell loves this place, though he's not crazy about it being a Wilderness Study Area. That's a restrictive designation prohibiting projects like road building, but cattle grazing is still permitted. Kalfell gives out maps to these trails, serving as an active booster for hiking in the washes and draws. It's a great spot if the day is not too hot, or if rain hasn't turned the dirt roads into truck-eating gumbo—something that happens when water turns bentonite clay into sticky, impassable mud. We talked together in the cab of his pickup and together gazed on forty-four thousand acres of sage- and juniper-flecked tabletop mountains and scoria escarpments. By then Kalfell and I had fallen into an easy repartee, both of us comfortable with each other's considerations, even when we did not agree. During the day (and on subsequent phone calls), we've discussed the North American Free Trade Agreement (Kalfell does not support it); Standing Rock (Kalfell thinks paid agitators from Seattle came to protest); methane emissions escaping from landfills vs. methane from the burps and flatulence of cattle in feedlots (Kalfell doesn't think cows should shoulder all the blame); drought in the West (Kalfell contends this is consistent with historically extreme climate fluctuations rather than climate change); women's right to choose (Kalfell is for it, though he has concerns about abortion after three months); and the federal government (Kalfell is not a fan).

On and off during the day, he ribbed me. "You think I'm a white supremacist and a racist," he said, repeating what Republican politicians and pundits like Tucker Carlson often tell their audiences. Well, I responded, I think Trump is. I pressed a bit and asked him if he thought there were barriers in the United States that made it historically more difficult for Black people to succeed. Like the process of buying property, I suggested. Kalfell went into some detail about the GI Bill and how it was highly unfair to Black vets, who couldn't buy property they had been promised for serving overseas. He knew a lot about this issue—owning property is a big deal to Kalfell—and he understood the history of injustice in real estate.

He also mentioned his best friend growing up—a migrant who had crossed the border to come with his family to Montana and pick sugar beets. You know, he later told me, in rural communities we see the hardships that itinerate farm workers face more than those living in larger towns. "I saw their poverty," he said. When Kalfell encountered his friend a few years later in Billings, the boy had changed. "He was quiet. Life had been hard."

As we stood by the side of his truck, looking at the raw break country, he said, "You know, there is something we could all agree on. The Amazon." This was about the Brazilian rainforest being slashed and burned to make way for raising cattle and creating steep competition for Montana ranchers as well as destroying an essential ecosystem. Ninety percent of cleared rainforest has been turned to pasture in Brazil. In 2018, the US banned the import of Brazilian beef, but this decision was overturned in 2020. If Biden can stop the Keystone XL pipeline, Kalfell mused cynically on a recent telephone call, then why can't he reimpose the ban on rainforest beef?

I later mentioned my conversation with Kalfell to Wyatt Nelson, president of Wild West Local Foods, which sources regionally raised meat. Is rainforest beef a big problem for western producers? "First of all, Brazilian beef is on the market here," he said, as is "beef from all over the world. It's cheaper, and what do Americans want? Cheap food." Montana ranchers have trouble competing with countries that can raise animals inexpensively, even though the meat is transported thousands of miles to wind up in the US market. Farmers and ranchers are paid far less in Brazil than they are in the US, making their products more competitive. In Europe, according to Nelson, consumers are "educated on the farming and ranching practices, and they understand that it costs a lot of money." In other words, shoppers expect higher meat prices, just as they do higher gas prices. In the US, most people are reluctant to spend money on a product if they can find something that's cheaper, even if it means that one of the most important carbon sinks in the world is being cannibalized while Montana ranchers are being squeezed. Those who have wanted to consume only local beef have trouble. A short-lived program known as COOL (Country Of Origin Label), which called for packaging to indicate the origin of meat, was repealed by Congress in 2016 after trade disputes. So what can we do? I asked Nelson. He laughed a little, realizing he was undercutting his own business. "Buy directly from the ranchers. Get a group together and buy a side of beef." Foreign, cheaply raised, environmentally destructive beef hurts western ranchers and global ecosystems. Certainly, we could begin discussions with western agricultural communities around this topic.

Without slogans and stereotyped assumptions, Kalfell and I covered polarizing issues and found common ground. If he had really been drifting towards extremism, as he asserted during our first meeting, I saw little evidence of it when we spent time together. I know he has grievances, but he's smart and fair-minded in ways that many of the fanatical folks I've met are not. Still, there is undeniable anger in our country. Politicians and social media platforms are benefitting from that anger, winning votes and clicks by shilling resentments and blame. Perhaps this sounds too obvious and incremental, but I think it must be up to us—as friends, neighbors, and members of communities—to push back and fight damaging falsehoods, not one another. One key to staving off polarization might simply be healthy relationships. Given the huge problems we currently face, we must be able to talk to one another, no matter on which side of the aisle we stand.

I was reminded of an exchange I had when I first started researching this book. I was talking to a liberal acquaintance about the themes
that I meant to cover, from COVID to polarization to my interest in
engaging rural communities. Of the latter topic, he had asked: Why
bother? implying an insurmountable ignorance among such folks.
Again, the myth of small-town minds. As much as liberals like to think
they are open-minded and magnanimous, among some of them there
lingers a disdain for rural people. There are certainly folks in the rural
West who are equally scornful of liberals from larger communities like
my own. But either way, this contempt is toxic to our culture, communities, states, and the fabric of our nation.

After a full day of wide-ranging conversation, Kalfell and I had
dinner at the Roy Rogers Grill, a lively restaurant across the street
from the Kempton Hotel. To wash down his burger, Kalfell ordered a
Mango Cart wheat ale, which seemed a bit tropical for a tiny town in
drought-stricken rural Montana, but he just kept surprising me. I like
fruity beer, he later explained.

He then surprised me again. In 2020, the Republican-controlled
Montana legislature voted to allow open and concealed carry of firearms on college campuses. Seeing folks with a sidearm didn't sit well
with Kalfell. It made him uncomfortable. On this, we agreed. This
man, who told me that he was buying guns when we first met, now
declared he didn't like seeing them on the hips of others. Seeing folks
with guns in public is unsettling, especially in a college environment,
he said. After the legislature's action, the board of regents sued, and
the plan was overturned as unconstitutional. On Montana campuses,
the state constitution grants the board of regents, not the state legislature, "full power, responsibility, and authority to supervise, coordi-
nate, manage and control the Montana university system." So no guns
on Montana's quads.

A couple of weeks after my visit, I sent Kalfell an article from the

New York Times (not his favorite paper), describing political parties becoming ever more oppositional—something that's really hurting Americans. He emailed me back:

> *So much truth. But yet, we as a people, see the evils differently. (Like Nancy Pelosi ripping up government property, State of the Union address)*
>
> *We can't decide who started this "war" or will end it. For sure, we are all mad (because we are very afraid, of the unknown). I believe we have hope. People like you and I, have to keep hope alive. I hope this is just a dust-up, and we can see the error of our ways.*
>
> *I genuinely, very much like you. And have enjoyed our conversations. Too bad they don't put us in charge!*
>
> *Please keep me in your heart, you will always be in mine.*
>
> *Looking forward to hearing from you again.*
>
> *Your friend, Lance*

I do keep Lance in my heart and have continued a friendship with him, which I treasure. I appreciate his devotion to his small town, his integrity, and his complete sincerity. There's a current notion out there that we can't get along with others beyond our own political ideologies. It isn't true. We've fallen prey to misperceptions about one another. In that criticism, I include myself. Our ignorance has trapped us in eddies of pique and inertia and made us incurious and unwilling to engage. This is a cultivated divide, thanks to various bad players and insidious social media. It stifles the joys of connection and halts steps toward healing a gaping wound. Amputation is not the answer and recovery is possible. Though the process may be slow, it's necessary as we face toxic politics and ever more severe pressures on quality of life, community health, and resources. I recommend one way to start: with a talk over coffee at the Kempton Hotel. Take a spin through the Prairie Unique. Drink a mango beer with a local at Roy Rogers. And tour the museums of Terry, including the portraiture of Evelyn Cameron, with your favorite interlocutor.

CHAPTER 9

MATTERS

←—— – – – – – ——→

C RAIG HEACOCK IS TALL AND LANKY, WITH BLOND hair dusting to gray. His field is psychiatry, and his particular focus is ketamine therapy, a psychedelic treatment that he has seen work miracles for patients with deep wounds and traumas. Heacock's office sits in a nondescript, squat building in Fort Collins, Colorado, at a cross street along a wide boulevard of stately old homes. It's somehow soothing in its prosaicness. I've known this man, with his clarion and contagious laugh, since we met during my freshman year at Colorado College. We were sweethearts for two and a half years and have kept in touch on and off over the decades. I came to Fort Collins to interview him for this book, and we spent the first few minutes catching up on news of mutual friends, his three kids, a recent backpacking trip, and his work bringing people "back from the abyss," a phrase that also serves as the name for his podcast. Heacock has never been busier. With a deep compassion for humans, especially those with severe traumas, and a fascination with the power of psychedelics, his job couldn't suit him better. The pandemic was difficult, as some of his clients regressed into old patterns and substance abuse. For several of those people, Heacock was the only lifeline in their involuntary isolation. He witnessed older folks who lived by themselves wrapped in utter loneliness. At times, he felt their enforced seclusion was more debilitating than coming down with COVID. Addictive behaviors, divorces, heightened fury, paranoia, and deep fear were all among the behaviors he observed increasing during this time.

"So, here's a good example," he said. "I see a guy who's the manager of a gun store." When the pandemic hit, he told Heacock that work had become too stressful. Assuming the voice of his patient, Heacock said, "'I hate it…every bozo in the world is coming to buy a gun!'" Heacock's patient had loved his job before COVID, telling him that he had mainly sold guns to collectors, "like fine wine or something." But the experience changed during COVID and the Black Lives Matter protests of 2020. His patient saw a different clientele altogether, and he told Heacock, "We are just inundated with people who have never owned a gun, and they're coming in like, 'Hey, give me one of those AR-15s.'" The man had pleaded with his new customers to chill out and at least seek training, telling them to practice shooting and go to a gun range. But that wasn't what they wanted to hear. "And they're like, 'No, no, I need this for protection. And I need the most powerful gun you got.'" The circumstances of 2020 made people jump at shadows, so afraid were they, and so uncertain of the times.

The man has come to dread his own business. "I mean," Heacock added incredulously, "this is someone who loves guns!" But now, out of ammo and firearm inventory, his patient worried he had sold "guns to people with no business having guns because they're just a bunch of idiots! And they have no plan for how they're going to safely store or practice using their guns," Heacock continued. "It's weird to think he's having an all-time sales record and he's like, 'I hate my job now.' Because we are just selling mountains of guns to people who have no business having them."

Since 2020, Americans have been further rocked by a pandemic, mass protests, polarization, and misinformation. Some hoarded toilet paper; others, assault rifles. According to a study published by the *Annals of Internal Medicine*, "An estimated 2.9% of US adults (7.5 million) became new gun owners from 1 January 2019 to 26 April 2021. Most (5.4 million) had lived in homes without guns, collectively exposing, in addition to themselves, over 11 million persons to household firearms, including more than 5 million children." Also alarming is that half of all suicides in the country are committed with firearms, with Wyoming (first), Montana (third), New Mexico (fourth), Idaho (fifth), Colorado (seventh), and Utah (ninth) seeing some of the highest rates in the country according to Statista's 2020 rankings. So much for the myth of the salubrious West. People here kill themselves at alarming and heartbreaking rates and have a lot of guns, especially in Wyoming, the state with the highest suicide rate per capita in the US

The last several years have made people anxious and outraged, and they are now literally up in arms. Many took things further, joining militias of varied forms, deputizing themselves as community protectors, and even, in extreme cases such as that of armed teenager Kyle Rittenhouse, killing people in the streets of a Black Lives Matter rally. Stewart Rhodes and the Oath Keepers hauled nearly $40,000 worth of weapons to the US Capitol on January 6, 2021. Ammon Bundy— who has been involved in two armed conflicts with the federal government—formed an organization called the People's Rights Network just before the pandemic hit, and promptly amassed fifty thousand members. Together, these groups harassed officials, doctors, and politicians, all trying to do their jobs. "Let's face it, our governmental systems of defense are deteriorating quickly!" exclaimed Bundy's website. "Government officials, more and more, are becoming the type of people we must defend ourselves from. As people in government deteriorate our traditional defense systems, you and your family become less and less secure from all types of criminals. Government criminals and street criminals. We must not be left defenseless!" And so, gun stores were mobbed, and Craig Heacock's gun-shop-owner patient fell into despair.

I asked Heacock what he thinks this frightened and terrifying sociopolitical environment is doing to us. He remarked that there are two paths folks take when experiencing trauma: fear and fury. COVID has been traumatizing for so many. The seclusion, the confusion, the emotional and economic insecurity, the distrust of science, and the overwhelming nature of a deadly pandemic have caused collective emotional damage. This combined with the way some media outlets portrayed the protests after the death of George Floyd—many saw endlessly looping footage of riots. Fear and sadness, Heacock explained "can feel so helpless and vulnerable and despairing and disempowering and impotent. Anger can feel so good. I mean, anger is about adrenaline." Some felt a need to build an arsenal for self-defense. Some imagined themselves genuine vigilantes amid social unrest. And some, enflamed with anger and adrenaline, just felt a need to shoot people.

— — —

THERE WERE 647 MASS SHOOTINGS IN 2022, DOWN FROM the record set the previous year of 693. Right-wing rhetoric continues to center ideas of exceptionalism and unimpeded freedom as excuses for unending bloodshed. Collateral damage in the form of murdered schoolchildren, grocery shoppers, and partygoers is the price for the right to bear arms without sensible guardrails. This notion is modern, not historical. The exaltation of the Second Amendment as a bulwark for democracy is a new idea manufactured by those profiting from the arms industry. Sensible gun laws once existed, even in the Wild West. The shootouts and standoffs of movies were uncommon and unpopular in the real West during the period on which western myth-making is largely based, roughly 1860 to 1890. Specific steps were taken to avoid orgies of violence inside white settlements during those years, notwithstanding the imaginings of Sergio Leone. Of course, campaigns of genocide by settlers and the United States Cavalry against Indigenous peoples were carried out by men with guns, and this violence leaves a crushing ache that still runs deep in the West. But within the limits of frontier towns it was mandated that visitors check firearms at inns or with law enforcement. In addition to bans within city limits, guns were specifically prohibited at polling places. Montana Territory's first act of legislation was banning "the carrying of concealed deadly weapons." Western papers such as the *Black Hills Daily Times* touted protective measures in the 1880s. "Perforated by his Own Pistol" read one headline, and a Helena paper called a man with a gun "more dangerous than a rattlesnake." Back in the Wild West, some gun restrictions were seen as common sense. Today, we see long guns at peaceful protests, rifles at Arizona polling stations, and assault weapons in schools, nightclubs, and sometimes produce sections at the supermarket. The idea of guns as an emblem of freedom is both confounding and lethal. Wyatt Earp, Tombstone's marshal, famous for his role in a shootout precipitated by a breach, in part, of his town's gun law, must be rolling in his grave.

— — —

LIKE SO MANY OTHER AMERICANS, GEORGE FLOYD'S MURder spurred westerners to swell the streets, from Heacock's hometown of Grand Junction, Colorado, to Cedar City, Utah, and from Idaho Falls, Idaho, to Gillette, Wyoming. In Bozeman, Judith Heilman, a formidable and brilliant Black former police sergeant, helped organize a peaceful protest with her organization, the Montana Racial Equity Project. Partnering with Bozeman United for Racial Justice, the event drew an estimated five thousand people or more—approximately ten percent of the town's entire population. My family and I marched among the protesters and encountered the counterdemonstrators who carried their shotguns and long rifles on Main Street. Across the West, most of these rallies were largely calm, with a few exceptions. In Salt Lake City, protesters turned over a police car and lit it on fire. In Denver, police fired pepper balls and lead-filled bags at demonstrators, who later sued and were awarded $14 million in damages. In Coeur d'Alene, armed counter-protesters showed up to defend a WinCo grocery store from rumored Black Lives Matter-supporting Antifa protesters from Seattle and Portland—only to encounter a single local man carrying a crowbar, according to journalist Daniel Walters. But that was enough to reinforce the anger, fear, and assault rifles of the men lured there by internet hearsay of Antifa crazies.

Spokane saw disruption on the evening of May 31, 2020, after a day of Black Lives Matter protesters marching through town. As the majority of demonstrators chanted, "We want peace!" a rogue group broke away from the gathering and began to loot a Nike outlet. Skirmishes and confrontations with police erupted. An artist named Nicholas Sironka attended the protest, though he didn't witness any violence. A member of the pastoral Maasai Tribe of Kenya, Sironka became a naturalized US citizen in 2018 and now lives in Spokane, working as a drug and alcohol counselor. At six feet and five inches tall, he's hard to miss—I met him in a parking lot by the mural he helped paint in celebration of Black Lives Matter. Warm and perspicacious, Sironka moved to the United States as a Fulbright Scholar in Residence, teaching batik and Maasai culture at Spokane's Whitworth College during 2000-2001. He was one of several artists who added a panel to the mural—he contributed an image of an African warrior joyfully drumming. He explained to one reporter, "This is the heartbeat of every person of African heritage." He told me his image was later singled out and splattered with white paint by two female anti-BLM protesters who haven't yet been identified.

We walked together to find coffee at a busy Starbucks in downtown Spokane, not far from the mural. While he's happy to be in this country, he said, he has become discouraged over many things, including the fighting between Republicans and Democrats, growing nationalism, police violence, and the breakdown of civil discourse. "There's a lot of people looking for justification for their animosities," he told me. "I am from a country where we had a dictatorship regime for twenty-four years. We looked up to America as a yardstick for civility, for rightful thinking and human rights." When Sironka arrived in Spokane, he told me, he thought, "We are going to make it!" The heady feeling of chasing the American Dream. "Then you come here and these men are choking people." He reflected on the response to George Floyd's murder. "I painted that mural, how wonderful!" he had mused to himself, and at the time he was pleased to be part of the citywide effort to address social injustice. But the pushback bothered him. He explained, "You're painting a mural that says, 'Black Lives Matter.' Somebody says, 'Everybody matters.' Of course, everybody matters," he explained with exasperation. "But if you have children in the house and only one child doesn't always have a jacket," or is constantly being slapped, he went on, or does not get to ride in the car but is forced to travel by foot—then "you have to say, '*This child matters.*'" Black Lives Matter is a movement seeking justice for a population that needs protection. According to a 2020 study from the Harvard T. H. Chan School of Public Health, Black people are 3.23 times more likely than white Americans to be killed by police. And that matters.

The protests that drew armed counterdemonstrators really bothered Sironka, as has the increasing frequency of people walking around with firearms. "I was in Coeur d'Alene yesterday, and I see this guy walking on the street with a gun." He told me what went through his head. "You're not hunting deer, and anyway, who goes hunting for antelope or deer with a machine gun…What are you going to do with a shredded deer?" There has been a growing phenomenon of intimidation in western towns, and he wonders what these tactics accomplish. "If you come up with a machine gun and give me a machine gun, what happens? We just shoot each other. Does that solve the problem?" he asks. "We have a saying in my culture. 'No two people can speak at the same time.' When two people speak at the same time, you cannot understand…one has to be quiet and listen," he explained. This is the first step toward understanding where another person is coming from, defusing anger, and listening. Guns don't do that.

— — —

A BISTABLE IMAGE IS ONE IN WHICH THE OBSERVER CAN view, alternately, two very different things. Danish philosopher Edgar Rubin produced one such image in 1915 called Rubin's vase. It's an intentionally ambiguous picture that the eye, and therefore the brain, can see in two very different ways. Glance at it and you see either a vase or the faces of two men. Both images are clear, but when you focus on the two black profiles, you lose sight of the vase, and when you focus on the white vase, you no longer see the faces of the two men.

Over the last few years, there have been campaigns to call attention to disconcerting realities, such as threats to reproductive rights, cases of police violence in the arrests of Black people, climate emergencies, and the dangers of SARS-CoV-2. Along with these, campaigns have been launched to support certain lies and illusions, such as massive election rigging and the scope of mayhem at social justice protests. People construe matters differently depending on their politics; we tend to reaffirm our own assumptions in what's called confirmation bias. This inclines us to believe only things that we already consider to be true, leaving information that contradicts our assumptions to be disregarded or scorned. This happened with Black Lives Matter—some folks refused to look at the issue in a way that challenged their standing views.

Harvard researchers in 2020 reported that, despite misleading media coverage, "The Black Lives Matter uprisings were remarkably nonviolent. When there was violence, very often police or counter-protesters were reportedly directing it at the protesters...Only 3.7 percent of the protests involved property damage or vandalism." All the same, Black Lives Matter has become Rubin's vase to people who are overlooking the shapes of their own assumptions, and it has therefore become terribly misunderstood.

— — —

AFTER DEREK CHAUVIN MURDERED GEORGE FLOYD, MIL-lions of Americans were anguished. Protests were widespread, well-attended, and broadly supported, until a combination of factors blemished the campaign, creating another Rubin's vase reaction. A mix of rage, adrenaline, guns, vigilantism, misinformation, and unrest led to dangerous situations. The idea that looting was ubiquitous at the protests, thanks to ongoing news coverage of isolated incidents in Minneapolis, Seattle, and Portland, scared people in the suburbs. Then reports of certain financial improprieties within the Black Lives Matter Global Network Foundation alienated others who, pained over the death of George Floyd, had initially embraced the movement.

It's important to know that Black Lives Matter is not a monolith—all sorts of people joined the demonstrations out of genuine anguish and a drive to support the Black community. Although financial improprieties became a focal point of the movement for some,

Sean K. Campbell, who broke the story of corruption at the foundation in *New York Magazine*, reported that the movement's moneymaking arm and the social justice movement were "two branches of activism." He continued, "There are on-the-ground, grassroots organizers...who work locally, passionately, with little money, often risking their lives and livelihood through their protests. And then there are the larger, more professionalized national groups with corporate donations and fundraising power, whose high-profile leaders can garner lucrative speaking gigs and book deals." Leaders within the Black Lives Matter Global Network Foundation engaged in sketchy misappropriations, such as the purchase of a multimillion-dollar mansion. They also, it was reported, bankrolled family members. Their actions, along with various incidents of destruction during the protests, damaged the cause—a heartbreaking turn when so many Americans felt so passionately aligned. According to the Pew Research Center, 76 percent of Americans supported Black Lives Matter in 2020. The violence connected to the protests—in many cases carried out by police and counter-protesters—was manipulated to create confirmation bias and fear.

There are reasons Black Lives Matter was roundly vilified. Some politicians benefitted by scaring voters to win elections. Other politicians had an interest in disparaging a movement that broadly united white people and people of color. And other politicians didn't want the public to know it was their own bases causing problems at Black Lives Matter rallies.

—   —   —

SCULPTURE IS SCATTERED THROUGHOUT THE GROUNDS OF the Albuquerque Museum, though one installation became a focal point during the summer of 2020: *La Jornada* (The Journey). Installed in 2004 to commemorate the arrival of the Spanish in the sixteenth century, the display once featured settlers, their families, carts, wagons, horses, cattle, sheep, oxen, and donkeys, all following their leader, the conquistador Juan de Oñate (1550-1626). Soldiers with Spanish flags, a Native guide, and a priest rounded out the full exhibit—a tribute to those who made their way up from Mexico to colonize the land. All figures remain at the museum today, frozen in their journey, except for Oñate, whose statue was removed after a confrontation at a George Floyd rally.

I spoke with Cathy Bailey, an Albuquerque teacher, in another garden, while her dogs romped happily around us. We talked about Oñate, his legacy, and stories of her Chicano family. She spoke of the difficult time during COVID, trying to take care of her students amid America's ongoing reckoning with injustice. She and I had met while serving on the board of a conservation group, WildEarth Guardians, and had gotten to know each other over Zoom during the last year and a half. It was lovely to be face-to-face now in the New Mexico sunshine, even if the conversation circled difficult recollections. Bailey is droll, solicitous, and extremely passionate about her students' welfare, especially given what they experienced during the pandemic.

In New Mexico, during the protests over George Floyd, she explained, activists focused on grievances related to colonial violence in the Southwest. The figure of Oñate has long been a bone of contention. When Black Lives Matter protests swept the country, one Oñate statue was removed from the Oñate Monument Center in Alcade, New Mexico. He had stood caped and helmeted, with metal feet shod in impressive spurs along the flanks of a muscular horse. Now only a bare cement block remains where his likeness once rose up. Over the years, people targeted this sculpture, even sawing off its right foot to call attention to Oñate's long-ago order to amputate the feet, or perhaps the toes (accounts differ), of twenty-four Acoma people. This was carried out after Oñate had already murdered eight hundred and enslaved many others over a period of twenty years. The amputations followed a failed Spanish raid on the Acoma Pueblo during which twelve or thirteen Spaniards were killed while Native people defended their homes and stocks of food. After Oñate retaliated against the locals, he was tried and convicted of several charges, including the use of excessive force, which resulted in his banishment from the Americas. He died in Spain, leaving a legacy commemorated by controversial statues. There are legitimate reasons why people resent his commemoration. These came to a boiling point after the death of George Floyd.

Following the removal of the statue in Alcade, activists focused on Albuquerque's sculpture garden and the bronze likeness of Oñate there. Demonstrators and armed counter-protesters came together at a rally at the Albuquerque Museum on June 15, 2020. The rally organizer, a Chicano Native American rights activist named Moises Gonzales, knew there was going to be trouble when members of a militia group, the New Mexico Civil Guard, arrived with weapons. It was supposed to be a peaceful gathering and prayer ceremony, but a clash of ideologies resulted in a shooting. Social justice protesters approached the Oñate statue with a chain and a pickaxe, as counter-demonstrator Steven Baca, witnesses said, forcefully shoved three women to the ground. When Black Lives Matter protestor Scott Williams swung a skateboard at him, Baca shot Williams several times. Members of the New Mexico Civil Guard, in their military and tactical gear, then surrounded Baca and the sculpture, though they later claimed Baca wasn't a member of their group. A witness who was expected to testify in the case was visited and threatened by one Daniel Carr, a member of the Three Percenters militia, one of the groups that came to the aid of the Bundys during their standoff against the government in Bunkerville, Nevada. Carr, who later pled guilty to intimidating the witness, showed up at his apartment with a gun on his hip and told the witness and his girlfriend that he knew where they lived.

Albuquerque police chief Mike Geier said of the protests, "We have done everything possible to keep them peaceful and protect the protesters, but the continued involvement of agitators, whether it's a single individual or a group of vigilantes, is resulting in this violence… We also discourage the presence of armed citizens at protests, which has the potential to escalate violence not prevent it." Law enforcement confiscated over twenty guns as well as other weapons at the event. Since the shooting, Albuquerque has banned firearms and other deadly weapons in public parks. In 2022, Bernalillo County district judge Elaine P. Lujan ordered that the New Mexico Civil Guard refrain from acting "as part of a military unit" or "assuming law-enforcement functions" at public events or protests.

Many of Bailey's students participated in the Oñate protest after being inspired by the national racial justice movement. "All this stuff happened, the horrible stuff happened, with George Floyd's death… We had a student who was part of the Medical Corps at the demonstration, who was standing by at that event and rendered aid to the person who was shot," she told me. "He was yelled and screamed at by police officers and it was just horrible." The student, she said, had received some medical training as a way to give back to the community, working with EMTs so "they can serve as medical support at different events around the city, or even across the state." The victim's own father is an EMT and was also on the scene. Given the danger and the chaos, it's understandable that the police reacted to Bailey's student administering aid, though it must have been traumatic for the young volunteer who, after he saw a man get shot, was shouted down for trying to save him.

Bailey explained why Oñate was so controversial during the Black Lives Matter protests. "There were Indigenous, Hispanic, and white people who were protesting against police brutality within the state of New Mexico, and our students were part of that demonstration," she said. "We had students coming back onto campus who had been through this horrible and traumatic event"—the shooting, from which Williams subsequently recovered—"so we knew that we were going to have to address significant issues around Indigenous and Hispanic culture, along with how white culture overlays that." New Mexico, Bailey told me, is inhabited by people who view history differently from one another, and gauge Oñate and the conquistadors according to the experiences of their ancestors. Some have far more direct causes for grievance and outrage than others. As a teacher at the Bosque School, she works with a student population reflecting the diversity of the state of New Mexico. Depending on their heritage, the students have distinctive ways of navigating a burdened legacy, from colonialism to Native sovereignty.

She explained that New Mexico is a mix of Latinos (peoples born in or descended from ancestry in Latin America); Hispanics (peoples born in, or descended from ancestry in Spain); Chicanos (peoples born in, or descended from ancestry in Mexico); Mestizo (mixed race); the Native community from various nearby pueblos (there are nineteen distinct pueblos, or sovereign nations, in the state); and people with other European, non-Spanish heritages. Black and Asian people live in the state as well. Hispanic people in New Mexico, she said, want to emphasize their whiteness or European roots. Their families were discriminated against when their territory became a part of the United States, after the Treaty of Guadalupe-Hidalgo in 1848. Over the decades, Hispanics have been harassed for being Mexicans, and have tried to distinguish themselves as Spanish descendants. "We have kids like that at our school, who have deep roots in the Hispanic culture and colonialism," Bailey said, "whose families are, have always been, part of the sort of upper Hispanic level. Then we have kiddos who are Mestizo, who came up with the Spaniards, who were not necessarily part of the upper classes, but were part of the working, farming, agricultural…And then we have Indigenous folks who have married into Hispanic families…and then we have those who are just completely living in Indigenous cultural places." A lingering anger over Oñate is shared by many Native people, due to the violence of his actions as well as an ongoing and debilitating racial injustice. During COVID, Bailey had one Native student with no running water or access to the internet; her parents drove her to Walmart from their pueblo every weekend so that she could get Wi-Fi to do homework.

Attitudes over Juan de Oñate reflect the deep cultural divides in New Mexico. Some Hispanics, like Steven Baca, are more likely to admire this sixteenth-century Spanish leader who expanded his king's interests and colonized the territory. Indigenous communities are inclined to see him as a murderer, oppressor, and proselytizer. The entangled history of land grabs and Catholicism is a brutal one among Indigenous peoples, and riddled with examples of rape and sexual abuse, separation of children from families, forced assimilation programs, and campaigns for Indigenous erasure.

Bailey lamented the aftermath of the protests and the impact on her community when the Trump administration sent in the National Guard. "I mean, he didn't just send them to Portland and Seattle. He sent them here. The protests had been peaceful, for the most part, until this one guy, who thought he was the militia, felt called out to protect the country by Trump and decided to shoot somebody." In a book titled *Frankly, We Did Win This Election*, author Michael C. Bender, senior White House reporter for the *Wall Street Journal*, recounts that Trump wanted to invoke the Insurrection Act during the George Floyd protests and goaded General Mark Milley to employ a military campaign to overpower protesters. After being asked to undertake heavy-handed measures, Milley responded, "Goddamnit! There's a room full of lawyers here. Will someone inform him of my legal responsibilities?" According to Bender, Trump repeatedly pushed violence toward protesters, not counter-demonstrators. He wanted to "crack their skulls," "beat the fuck out of them," and "just shoot" Black Lives Matter supporters, which is what people like Steven Baca and Kyle Rittenhouse took it upon themselves to do. The Black Lives Matter protests did have edges, but many counter-protesters were involved in the chaotic moments. Trump didn't want those he deemed on his side to take any responsibility, so he found a perfect scapegoat. While the militia and militia wannabes carried out his wishes, Trump made the case that the country needed a strongman to implement order against civil unrest, which he decided to blame on Antifa.

— — —

THERE'S A REASON WHY THE TRUMP ADMINISTRATION AND RIGHT-wing media tried to manipulate opinions on the movement and use Antifa as a smokescreen to obscure other issues. By blaming a small group of anarchists involved in vandalism in cities like Minneapolis, Seattle, and Portland, according to *Politico*, operatives fueled dread "by trying to redefine the Black Lives Matter movement as a radical leftist mob looking to sabotage the white, suburban lifestyle." Many compared the civil rights movement, a chapter of important upheaval now largely revered in American history, to the Black Lives Matter movement, claiming the former was a much more effective and peaceful way to go about making change. This is unfair and inaccurate. Using two sets of data, Crowd Counting Consortium and the Dynamics of Collective Action, PhD candidate, Kerby Goff, and Professor Emeritus of Sociology, John D. McCarthy, determined that "during these eight years of civil rights protests, 11 percent of the 2,681 events contained property damage. By contrast, during the 12,839 racial justice protests in 2020, only 4 percent included property damage." The Black Lives Matter movement had been inaccurately portrayed to play on white fears.

This brings us to our ugliest myth—white supremacy. This one has roots in Europe, where Western civilization was valued above all else. That value came to America with Columbus and the waves of invasion, conquest, colonialism, and slavery that followed him. In the making of America, Black people were exploited and dehumanized as property. Historians have shown how they were disregarded despite their prominent role in building this nation. Over the years, American students, including Black students, have been taught to "admire the Hebrew, the Greek, the Latin, and the Teuton and to despise the African," wrote Black historian Carter G. Woodson in 1933. Although there has been progress since then in acknowledging Black history, Florida's banning AP African American Studies and the reflexive (and misunderstood) outcry over critical race theory show an ongoing aversion to Black culture.

We see this myth of supremacy play out in many other ways as well. Black Lives Matter protests were villainized while the January 6th insurrectionists, who were mostly white, were labeled by the right-wing press as innocent protesters. We see it in the desire for some Hispanics to distinguish themselves as European to avoid racial discrimination; in ongoing police bias, leading to racial profiling, and sometimes murder; in the GI bill that didn't effectively offer opportunities for Black vets to buy homes; in the idea of Manifest Destiny claiming white people justly deserve Native land; in the redlining of neighborhoods; in Black incarceration rates *at nearly five times the rate of whites*; in non-white neighborhoods that become "sacrifice zones" for industrial pollution. And on, and on, and on. It's no wonder people continue to take to the streets.

For those with specific agendas, Antifa was a perfect group on which to pin all the disruption and looting adjacent to Black Lives Matter protests. They are easily made into fall guys because there is no central figure to speak for them. Antifa, short for "anti-fascist," is a loose network of primarily young activists who are neither organized nor have a chain of command. The oldest of the groups known by that name, Rose City Antifa, was founded in 2007 in Portland, Oregon, and focused on fighting racism and Nazism while championing feminism and LGBTQ rights. The origins of Antifa are traceable to Italy in the 1920s, when anti-fascist troops fought Mussolini's Blackshirts (*Camicia Nera*), his personal goon squad. In the United States, Antifa came to the Pacific Northwest by way of a Minneapolis group, Anti-Racist Action. The movement sprang from a punk culture that was inhabited by anti-fascists fighting with neo-Nazis. In 1991, Anti-Racist Action helped put on a conference in Portland, a liberal city in a state burdened with a dark legacy. Oregon has a history of racism that goes back to the Peter Burnett Lash Law, an 1844 statute stating that Black people had to leave the Oregon Territory or be whipped. Additionally, over the decades, the Pacific Northwest, from eastern Oregon and Washington across the Idaho Panhandle and into western Montana, has harbored members of the Order, Aryan Nations, Militia of Montana, and other racist cells and followers. Eventually, these groups, and others like them, attracted their opposite, in the form of a much smaller and far less organized aggregation of activists known collectively as Antifa.

Craig Heacock's patient, the gun dealer who sorrowed over stampedes of gun-ignorant people coming to buy his firearms, witnessed firsthand what happens with false equivalencies—Antifa was a bit player in the protests, but many, in their fear, were arming up against them. Those forces arrayed on the right—the Oath Keepers, the Three Percenters, the Proud Boys, Patriot Prayer, the Constitutional Sheriffs and Peace Officers, the Boogaloo Bois, and the Patriot Front—far outnumber the loose-knit group of any violence-inclined left-wing agitators, but the presence of the latter was usefully exaggerated by right-wingers in fear-mongering. Still, Antifa-affiliated Michael Reinoehl shot and killed Patriot Prayer militia member Aaron Danielson in Portland on August 29, 2020. Though they may be insubstantial in number, some of those violent lefties were on the front lines.

I went to Portland for a conference in 2021 and came face-to-face with Antifa myself. I had mostly discounted them, but when I took a walk during a break between panels, I saw a group of young, mostly white people dressed in black, marching through downtown. At least one had a rifle. I'd had some warning of these complexities. Months earlier, I met a man in Polebridge, Montana—a man who calls himself Thermos, having cast off his given name—who gave me some insight into Antifa. He introduced himself while I was having dinner at the Northern Lights, a bar and restaurant in a remote hamlet up near the northwest corner of Glacier National Park. An engaging, bearded, well-tattooed fellow, Thermos was born in Butte, Montana, then later his family moved to Fargo, North Dakota, from where, as a teenager, he ran away and hopped a train. This led to years of riding the rails, moving in and out of Portland, hanging out with anarchists, and getting beaten up on more than one occasion when cops found him in railroad yards. Thermos shared the boxcars and the encampments with Antifa members, hung out with them in bars, and got to know them and their perspectives. Over beers, Thermos told me about his Antifa friends, mostly kids from the suburbs around Portland. He gave me his number after our chat and we kept in touch as he moved to a job for a lodge in Hot Springs, Montana, then to a saloon in Stanley, Idaho. I called him after seeing the Antifa march in Portland and told him the story. He wasn't surprised. "Ever since the militia started showing up," he said, "Antifa has accelerated." And by accelerated he meant that some have taken up arms.

Journalist Luke Mogelson spent a month in Portland observing the clashes among police, militia, and Antifa, as recounted in his October 2020 piece in *The New Yorker*. The conflict that played out couldn't be reduced to white hats versus black hats, that old western semiotic cliché, but rather was a melee between problematic players, the writer observed. Armed militia stood opposed to Antifa, but both remained certain that they were on the right side of the ideological divide. The militia sought to protect property and Antifa sought to protect marchers and bring down fascists. They engaged in street fights overseen by law enforcement sympathetic toward militias, as earnest protesters wound up in the crosshairs.

Mogelson reported he saw no vandalism, but that newly deputized "federal marshals arrived with a large contingent of state troopers in riot gear," who fell on protesters, pushing, shoving, and wrenching the limbs of the innocent—using tactics that Trump promoted. "The show of force felt more intense than anything I'd seen in the past month. On this hundred-and-twenty-first day, it could have been a form of desperation—or of vengeance." These were brawls between people with different beliefs. Black Lives Matter, for all the genuine anguish and hope that was carried into marches, was co-opted by those with divergent agendas and vendettas.

The Department of Homeland Security issued a report that called the rallies stages for hardliners. "Anti-government and/or anti-authority violent extremists are likely to be emboldened by a perceived success exploiting otherwise peaceful protest movements and concealing violent tactics. These violent extremists are increasingly taking advantage of large protest crowds to conduct violence against government officials, facilities, and counter-protestors." As leftist radicals fought militias, right-wing extremists used the specter of Antifa to justify violence and recruit more members to the cause. Portland and Seattle became battlegrounds for these two groups. Ironically, the extremists on both sides are mostly white, detracting from the real issue at stake, Black lives.

While cynical players—from Trump and various media to militants, overbearing cops, and various agents of chaos—used this initial outpouring of solidarity as a platform for their own aims, many of the protesters were simply marching for justice. These were vigils, occasions for people to come together in support and heartbreak. They mourned with those also in pain and marched calling for reform.

A few months after the protests, on one of my many trips to Glendive, Montana, I visited a tall and amiable man named Jim Hicks. He grew up there, playing football for the Red Devils, then marrying his high school sweetheart, Becky. Together, they raised their children in a home on a shady street overlooking the Yellowstone River, where we sat one day drinking iced tea. He told me a story he had heard from one of his daughters, Teresa, now living in Bozeman in the same neighborhood where Matt Kelley was harassed by Ammon Bundy's vigilantes. Teresa had attended the Black Lives Matter rally with her son, Hicks's grandson, Henry, then just eleven years old. The boy had likely seen the men with long guns on Bozeman's Main Street during the march. Those ugly protesters in his own neighborhood, ranting about COVID restrictions recommended by Matt Kelley and parading their leashed turkey, had also been part of Henry's 2020 experience. Such jarring impressions would be just as concerning to a granddad back in Glendive as they were to a kid in Bozeman. But Henry seems to have coped.

One day Henry came home from school, Hicks told me, and announced that he was off to play with a new friend. Who? asked Teresa, wanting to know a little more about his new pal. Kids can be coy and laconic, so Henry paused a beat. He answered hoping both to reassure his mother as well as express his own steadfastness. "Don't worry, Mom. He thinks that Black lives matter."

CHAPTER 10

ACKNOWLEDGMENT

T HE NOTION OF INHERENT FREEDOM LOOMS LARGE over the American West: its vast lands, its unbroken vistas, its distant horizons, its big skies. In all its wide openness, one can feel deeply unencumbered and completely unfenced-in. This expansiveness comes with myriad opportunities—walking across deserts, riding over plains, cruising down blue highways. Town to town, trail to trail, it's not just about the destination; it's about the unfolding miles as one moves through across that vastness, inviting an expanded perception not just of space but also of time. Speeding past island ranges of looming mountains, eroded bluffs, alfalfa fields, and rivers swollen with spring runoff delivers a sense of abandon, of timelessness—and of pleasure. There is so much to take in.

One of the great joys of doing this book has been my trips crisscrossing the West. Across the plains of Wyoming and past Thunder Basin National Grassland, where many years ago I researched my master's thesis on the impacts of public land grazing. Along the Colorado River's Sangre de Cristo Mountains that frame the San Luis Valley, where I spent a month studying environmental ethics and the history of Spanish land grants. Hugging the mounded stone of Utah's Grand Staircase-Escalante National Monument, where I backpacked years before it received its controversial monument status. In Idaho's

Palouse, I once schlepped to rugby games with an old boyfriend. I spent many Christmases at the Santa Fe home of one of my best friends, an adobe full of small dogs, raucous laughter, and the smell of piñon pine. Researching *True West* has taken me back through my own history here. Colorado, Montana, Utah, Wyoming, Idaho, Nevada, Washington, Oregon, and New Mexico contain the sites of many of my own epiphanies and near-misses. Racing down western highways, watching grass bow to wind and raptors drift above fields, has been a sort of reunion for me.

But despite the joys of moving across spaces, I have often considered the costs. We're facing the impacts of climate change and its associated droughts, fires, storms, floods, and scorching heat waves. Driving a gas-powered vehicle (a hybrid, or even an electric one) cross-country contributes to our mounting environmental calamities. The more people get in their cars, vans, commercial planes, or private jets, and scoot off to destinations like Sun Valley or Big Sky, the more fossil fuel is combusted, sending carbon dioxide into the air, adding to the witches' brew of greenhouse gases and trapping heat in the atmosphere. Lithium and cobalt mining, necessary for electric car batteries, also comes with environmental costs. The allure of moving across the vast spaces of the West, of visiting its gems and playing amid its nature, is a guilty pleasure, and the guilt lies in making the planet sicker.

In her book *On Freedom: Four Songs of Care and Constraint*, the poet and critic Maggie Nelson writes about her son's adoration of trains. There is ambivalence, she notes, to the merit of railroading. The invention of the steam engine began the accelerating rate of climate change in the age we now call the Anthropocene. Still, despite the history of the Industrial Revolution and its consequences, Nelson expresses her joy at watching her son marvel over locomotives at Travel Town, a museum that, according to its website, "preserves and celebrates the rich railroad heritage of Los Angeles." Of trains, she writes that "when they get going, they impart a feel of freedom—of speed, transformation, leave-taking, escape, anonymity, rush—whether you're riding or watching them speed by." The trains of Travel Town put her in mind of "adolescent freedom...synonymous with driving my 1976 VW bug on the open road...I have since returned to the gospel of solitary driving (or so I had before the pandemic—now my car collects dust in the driveway, which turns out to be its own form of freedom—the freedom of not having to go anywhere, which vibrates uncomfortably beside the feeling of there being nowhere to go)." But with the advent of COVID vaccines in 2021, Nelson and the rest of us suddenly, once again, had places to go. I dusted off my own car and started work on this book.

I couldn't wait to hit the road and talk with people. I left in a rush. Some of this had to do with the fact I had work to do, and some of it was simply itchy feet. In the same rush that yielded a sense of freedom, though, I felt a rush of responsibility. I considered my own impacts. I may have had my professional mission, but I was still a tourist, burning gas and adding to the crowds of people pressuring western communities. I was also contributing to strains on public lands and adding my carbon footprint to the collective one, the giant stomp of humanity, squashing the rest of nature flat.

According to a 2018 study by Professor Manfred Lenzen of the University of Sydney and his colleagues, "Between 2009 and 2013, tourism's global carbon footprint has increased from 3.9 to 4.5 $GtCO_2e$." That's 4.5 billion metric tons, or almost five billion US tons, of CO_2 equivalent—"four times more than previously estimated, accounting for about 8% of global greenhouse gas emissions." In 2020 and 2021, unable or unwilling to fly overseas, many Americans loaded up their vehicles and hit the road, heading toward western national parks, mountain hamlets, and rivers. Zion National Park and the Grand

Canyon broke records. Glacier National Park went from 1,700,000 visitors in 2020, when the eastern side of the park was closed on account of COVID, to 3,000,000 in 2021. That same year, Yellowstone welcomed 3.8 million visitors.

The impact on national parks varies from place to place. Fires, erosion, wildlife-human conflict, traffic snarls, jammed parking lots, crime, search-and-rescue expenses, accidental deaths, and frustrated locals are some of the biggest headaches. Of course, there is an upside—park revenues and employment opportunities—but most of the service jobs in national parks are low-paying and seasonal. In many western communities, tourist dollars poured in while those who catered to visitors struggled to find affordable housing.

I know a woman who worked the first year of the pandemic in one of the most inundated destinations, Glacier National Park. Flannery Freund, cherubic and ruddy-cheeked in her forties, grew up in Weiser, Idaho, nestled in the foothills of the Snake River on the Idaho-Oregon border. She described her hometown of five thousand people as being "a third Mexican and a third Mormon." Enjoying a rare moment of quiet during a frantic tourist season, we chatted on the porch of her new restaurant in Polebridge, watching dust devils flit across an empty dirt parking lot—a lull in an otherwise busy season. Freund moved here in 2009 with a man she was dating and worked for a while at the Polebridge Mercantile, a popular bakery four miles down the road. The Merc, as locals call it, is usually packed with tourists looking for the pastries for which it's famous. She bought the place with her now ex-boyfriend and co-owned it from 2009 to 2014. After she sold it, Freund worked as a baker and later served three years as a ranger in Glacier National Park. She now owns a five-acre compound called Home Ranch Bottoms, with a campground and a restaurant, with her husband, Dan, a musician who has lived in this corner of Montana for two decades.

It's a remote place, but the BBC has been here. In a piece they produced, Polebridge is described as a place of "raw beauty and the boundless freedom of the vast, wild landscape." The current owner of the Mercantile is quoted describing Polebridge as "on the edge of civilization, which is when you feel most alive." Visitors come to that vivifying edge by driving down a long gravel road, along the western boundary of Glacier National Park and the North Fork of the Flathead River, which eventually takes one to the Canadian border. Now, as the COVID shutdown has given way to a sense of post-COVID relief and wanderlust—premature or not, remains to be seen—this unincorporated town of a hundred people living off the grid is seeing more and more people arrive in their rental cars and sprinter vans, with no idea what they are doing. The place has been "discovered," that loaded word with its grim historical legacy of people laying claim to lands they feel they deserve.

In 2020, Flannery Freund was working at the Polebridge Station, an isolated entrance to Glacier National Park, when record numbers of visitors often forced rangers to turn folks away because the park was too full. That year, visitors arriving at the main park entrances needed reserved tickets to be admitted, in addition to standard park passes. "Our visitation has increased over 200 percent since 2017," Freund explained, which is what compelled the park to create the new ticket system. That requirement forced some people, those "who bought their passes and planned their trips to come to Glacier, without realizing ticket entry was a thing, to drive to the non-ticketed entry stations." These entry stations include the one at Polebridge, on the west side, and Saint Mary, Two Medicine, and Many Glacier on the eastern side, all reachable from a state highway that runs through Blackfeet Nation, on the Blackfeet Indian Reservation. Throughout the entire 2020 tourist season, the Blackfeet Business Council, citing COVID-related concerns, decided not to open the Two Medicine, Saint Mary, and Many

Glacier roads. Polebridge was the only non-ticket-requiring option and tourists swarmed the place.

During the summer of 2021, as pandemic constraints lifted, many people, escaping cabin fever, headed west. "They'd been locked up for an entire winter and people from New Jersey, Texas, and New York" flooded the Polebridge gate, Freund said. "License plates I've never seen in the North Fork! We're not blaming it on any state or person, but every single parking lot, river access, hiking trail, was littered with toilet paper." It was, she said, "the first time ever in my life I had seen that." She characterized the people visiting Polebridge as primarily greenhorns, unfamiliar with remote western geography. "The type of visitor that was coming was very unprepared." They were vexed by the lack of cell phone service and minimal infrastructure, and they were clueless about the leave-no-trace ethic (the practice of packing in supplies and packing out every morsel of your own garbage and waste).

"Toilet paper everywhere—it was so maddening!" Freund continued. "Do you think it just disappears? What do you think happens when you use toilet paper, and you throw it on the ground?" The whole experience shocked her, as it did many residents. This park is an important portion of what's known as the Crown of the Continent Ecosystem, and the disregard by oblivious visitors left her dispirited. "It's one of the last intact ecosystems in the Lower 48…and they have no idea what that even means." She made this last comment not so much in judgment as with resignation.

Freund lives in a place where, for some, it's a vacation campground, and for others, it holds a far deeper meaning. Tourists can't be criticized for visiting—after all, that's why Glacier National Park was established. Teddy Roosevelt and other early preservationists imagined national parks set aside for leisure activities on what they deemed empty or "unpeopled" lands. This myth erases the generations who have lived in these places—communities that have congregated for thousands of years to hold ceremonies, hunt, build communities, raise families, and nurture, with each season, a relationship with the land. It is a space shared by animals, ancestors, and spirits. Chief Mountain, on the eastern border of Glacier Park, is the home of the Thunder Spirit. A great gray block that seems to thrust into the sky, this mountain has served as a significant landmark to many regional peoples who traveled the plains on horseback. Called Ninaistako in Blackfoot, its circumference spreads across both Glacier National Park and the Blackfoot Reservation—a reminder that on sacred lands, boundaries are arbitrary.

The North Fork headwaters and their forests provide abundant habitat to species that arrived long before the Pleistocene, tens of thousands of years ago. Those forests and waters are part of a complex of protected areas that includes Glacier National Park in the US, Waterton Lakes National Park in Canada, the Bob Marshall Wilderness, Flathead National Forest, and private and tribal lands, all interconnected to make up the Crown of the Continent Ecosystem. Wolverines, lynx, gray wolves, mountain lions, elk, deer, spruce grouse, pikas, bull trout, westslope cutthroat trout, and many other native creatures still make their living here. (The woodland caribou have vanished.) It is sacred land to the Blackfoot Confederacy—Niitsitapi—to the Salish-Pend d'Oreille and the Ktunaxa/Ksanka/Kootenai peoples. Their vision quests, ceremonial dances, and footpaths have long established bonds between the land and the people.

The road along the North Fork, leading to Polebridge and its park entrance, is unpaved and rough. Many visitors driving rental cars, according to Freund, have come with "no previous knowledge of gravel roads." The number one question she has heard is, "When will the roads become paved again?" People seem to assume that, just around the next bend, they'll get onto a nice two-lane blacktop rolling toward Kalispell. She would reply, "You have to turn around and go back exactly the way you just came." There *are* no paved roads. "People would get so mad!" she added. There were traffic jams that lasted up to four hours, composed of motorists with little to no idea how to navigate this extraordinary place, let alone appreciate it. "It's like, okay, then look at our water," she said of the nearby North Fork of the Flathead River. "Have you seen water like this before? No, you haven't. Why? Because there are no extractive industries, there's no ranching…It's 96 percent public land, 4 percent private land." She felt that this magnificent landscape was not only misunderstood but dishonored. People drove across gorgeous western terrain, arrived at an isolated outpost, complained about its remoteness, and tossed their garbage onto the vital ground.

"I don't know if you noticed that *Visit Montana* is now kind of changing their campaign to 'Recreate Responsibly' rather than 'Come Here,'" Freund mentioned. *Visit Montana* is more than a booster slogan; it's an entire campaign launched by the state's office of tourism. Indeed, the onslaught of visitors has compelled the Montana tourism industry to reexamine its strategy. In 2021, nearly 12.5 million tourists came to Montana, and while they spent about $5.15 billion, they also jammed roads, parking areas, river access sites, trailheads, and campgrounds. The crush of people put pressure on restaurants, hotels, and community services. In their wake, too many of these visitors left piles of trash, graffiti, and toilet-paper gardens where they relieved themselves, especially when they camped away from established campgrounds.

A 2022 study by the University of Montana Crown of the Continent Initiative and the Greater Yellowstone Initiative reported that 77 percent of those surveyed worried about the changing character of the state and the loss of habitat for fish and wildlife on public lands. A total of 76 percent were concerned about crowding at outdoor recreation areas, and 85 percent had serious concerns about development in open spaces. Sarah Lundstrum, of the National Parks Conservation Association, noted in a recent article that "there's an increasing tension between protecting park resources and the number of people coming to visit national parks. The question has become how do we protect park resources and a variety of experiences, including quiet backcountry solitude, in the face of ever-growing visitation?"

What makes things even worse is that national parks are experiencing the impacts of climate change faster than other areas. A 2018 UC Berkeley and the University of Wisconsin–Madison study found that "human-caused climate change has exposed US national parks"—all 417 of them—"to conditions hotter and drier than the rest of the nation…The analysis reveals that over the past century, average temperatures in national parks increased at twice the rate as the rest of the nation and yearly rainfall decreased more in national parks than in other regions of the country." Many western parks have become free-for-alls, overcrowded with people at the same time they are bearing the brunt of the climate crisis. And each year, more folks travel to the parks, consuming carbon and nature, treading lands they don't understand. The myth of the West as a cheap, rough-and-tumble playland is perilous in this region of extreme limits and incalculable value.

Back in 1885, when the federal government began to consider the establishment of more national parks—Yellowstone became the first in 1872—naturalist George Bird Grinnell visited Blackfeet land. On another trip, two years later, he noted, "Far away in northwestern Montana, hidden from view by clustering mountain peaks, lies an unmapped corner—the Crown of the Continent." Today, one glacier in the park, now quickly receding due to climate change, bears Grinnell's name. Freund told me that Jeff Mow, the recently retired superintendent of Glacier National Park, regularly shares a story of "people who hike to Grinnell Glacier to wait in line for this one specific rock that you walk out to and take a selfie…People were going to Grinnell Lake, hiking all the way in there for that very specific picture, and waiting in line." They were queuing to take a picture for social media—to create a post that for many, might outweigh the actual experience of being in one of the most exquisite and significant places in the world. To call that a misguided priority would be to err on the side of politeness.

American public lands include irreplaceable ecosystems for magnificent beasts. They encompass sacred sites within Native traditions. Yet they don't get the respect they deserve—even from some who are most insistent on their public ownership. Strewn toilet paper and big carbon footprints are left behind by tourists trudging miles for a trophy snap to post on Instagram. It's a commentary on America's focus and our disconnection from the land.

—   —   —

FRANCINE SPANG-WILLIS, OF NORTHERN CHEYENNE, PAWnee, and settler descent, is a stunning woman in so many ways. Having completed her master's degree in Native American Studies at Montana State University and oral history at Columbia University, Spang-Willis focuses on settler colonialism and, most recently, its implications for bison. She studied the Pablo Allard herd, buffalo bought by two men with Native mothers, Charles Allard and Michael Pablo, then let loose on Montana's Flathead Reservation in 1884. A measured and thoughtful person, Spang-Willis' observations are deeply considered—I like complicated issues, she told me.

In the first year of the COVID pandemic, Spang-Willis and I took to "walking the land," as she calls it—taking strolls on nearby trails with our dogs. We serve together on the board of WildEarth Guardians, and at one meeting in 2022, she asked me if I would give the land acknowledgement. This is an invocation given in advance of meetings or gatherings to honor the connectedness of lands to cultures currently and anciently grounded there. It is a statement of gratitude to the people who have interacted with and protected the land from time immemorial.

I had given acknowledgments in the past but had recently grown self-conscious, wondering if one spoken by a white person came across as more performative than heartfelt. It was Chris La Tray, a poet friend of mine and an enrolled member of the Little Shell Tribe of Chippewa Indians, who led me to these considerations. La Tray once described the typical land acknowledgement in his blog, *The Irritable Métis*, as a "brief paragraph someone Googled ten minutes before the event." He wondered, "Who are these acknowledgments for? The Indigenous people themselves? Then, why? To make us feel better about what we *used* to have, but don't anymore?" Such acknowledgments just aren't enough, he continued, suggesting other ways white people might consider the land, his land. "I don't think ass-hats from all over the country should be able to drive million-dollar truck-and-trailer/RVs with towed SUV/boat/mountain bikes/etc. combos THROUGH TRIBAL LANDS to get to vacation playgrounds without paying a hefty tax or toll," he wrote. "Put a gate at every access in or out, interstate, highway, or dirt road... Don't like it? Don't come here. Take your butt-ugly, three-story RV to Ohio and marinate your peeling, sun-burned Texas hide in one of their scummy, shallow, man-made lakes instead."

Curmudgeonly and bighearted with an edgy sense of humor, La Tray's own tribe was only recently recognized, meaning that the United States legally acknowledged a government-to-government relationship with the tribe and that the tribe exists politically in a domestic dependent nation status. He comes to this issue as a person whose very cultural existence, let alone tribal land, wasn't even acknowledged by American bureaucracy until the last couple of years. At the time he wrote this blog, the practice of land acknowledgement clearly rang

hollow to him. He has since revised that view, somewhat. Acknowledgment can act as an offering of "something akin to a prayer," which
appreciates the land and calls to "ancestors still lingering with the
land, that we might come together generationally and spiritually," he
has written, "to heal ourselves on what is a terribly bloody landscape
soaked in the sorrows of what has been done to so many people."
Though he has reconsidered the land acknowledgement, I doubt he has
done the same for the sunburned ass-hats.

Spang-Willis quite appreciates it when people, especially white
people, initiate the process of acknowledgment. "I think an important
point of White folks doing these acknowledgments is to consider the
sacrifice made for them to live on this land by the Indigenous peoples," she emailed me. (She also feels that "white" should be capital-
ized, as Black and Indigenous commonly are, because the white race
shouldn't be given the status of a default or neutral identity. She added:
"White folks need to own their race and everything that comes with
it," including the many benefits, as well as the baggage.)

Later, when I opened the WildEarth Guardians board meeting
with an acknowledgment, another board member, Dustin Martin, a
Navajo, shared a story about his relationship with the land. He's a
reflective and caring man who had recently completed a long trail run
from the Continental Divide through Chaco Canyon, an ultramarathon
that took him and other Indigenous runners three days to complete.
Fine-featured and ponytailed, with a beard and a pair of wire-rimmed
glasses, Martin leads a group called Wings of America, devoted to his
culture's tradition of running. "The point was to familiarize ourselves
with a landscape that is in question right now," Martin told us. "Our
Secretary of the Interior, Deb Haaland, is listening to comments about
the proposed withdrawal of lands from mineral leases in a ten-mile
radius around Chaco." Haaland herself, the first Indigenous cabinet
secretary, is a member of the Pueblo of Laguna. The Biden admin-

istration, in which she serves, has proposed a twenty-year ban on oil and gas drilling around Chaco Culture National Historical Park, a site of ancient pueblos and ceremonial sites in northwestern New Mexico that was home to thousands of people from 850-1250 AD. Martin sees that area not as acreage chopped by some private ownership and some federal boundaries, but as a living and connected cultural landscape that was shaped by the ancestors of his people.

"There are so many different groups fighting for the protection of Chaco in different ways," he explained. "WildEarth Guardians is really advocating for the recognition of what we call the greater Chaco landscape, not just a site or a historical marker or something with cultural significance, but the entire landscape." This is the point: Chaco is not a place of designations, photo ops, and consumption; it is a continuous story, one of people, wildlife, history, and land. "The way that you move through it, the way that you interact with it, there's something inherently valuable about that," he said. As he ran across the landscape over the course of three full days, "it became clear to me that just our right to move through a landscape, unimpeded on our feet, is a human right, especially for Indigenous people or people who consider themselves indigenous to the landscape. They should feel safe and free moving through the landscapes of their ancestors." This way of viewing and accessing lands, and moving freely across them, especially on foot, stands in sharp contrast to the Instagrammers at Grinnell Glacier. Acknowledging the land, its beauty, bounty, and sanctity, includes thanking the generations and generations of Native peoples who for centuries moved along its contours and curves. They too are part of the place, and the place is part of them.

A year earlier, Martin had told the board about plans made by Rio Tinto, a vast multinational mineral corporation, to mine Oak Flat, along what is known as Arizona's Copper Corridor. If this happened, he said, it would be the next Standing Rock—referring to the 2016 assemblage of thousands of people, known as water protectors, which included representatives from hundreds of federally recognized Native tribes. Together they stood in opposition to the Dakota Access Pipeline, on the Standing Rock Indian Reservation. Oak Flat is Apache sacred land, and Martin's point was that threats to mine it would galvanize another such protest. After his explanation, a white member of the board, who has known Martin for a while, asked him to say a prayer. He acquiesced, speaking in both English and Navajo. It was stirring and captured a regard and appreciation for the land that the current conservation movement lacks.

Over the next weeks, a few board members resigned, due to discomfort with Martin's prayer. Failing to understand the word *prayer* itself is not construed in Indigenous cultures as it is in a Judeo-Christian context, they decided Martin's words had violated a "secular" tone of the organization. They mistook the nature of what Martin had actually invoked. His prayer was not Judeo-Christian, nor was it recited in submission to a supreme power, or in reverence of dominion and subdual of earth. Rather it was an invocation of a relationship with place and all that it means to be connected to the land.

Nick Estes, a member of the Lower Brule Sioux Tribe and the author of *Our History Is the Future: Standing Rock Versus the Dakota Access Pipeline, and the Long Tradition of Indigenous Resistance*, wrote in his book that a prayer honors relationships between land, water, and the two-legged and "four-legged." The act of prayer is also an ongoing practice in the fight against colonialist extraction, desecration, and destructive expansion into Indigenous sacred space. This is what happened at Standing Rock, and the threats continue today on sacred lands. Oak Flat is still being contested.

The circumstances and misunderstandings around the board members' resignations were convulsive and painful, underlining the crucial need to better understand and heal our grave disconnections.

The idea of Indigenous belief being akin to organized religions with histories of missionizing and assimilation, is wrong, and it's a shame that those who resigned refused to appreciate. At the time, Martin had suggested the board read passages from N. Scott Momaday's *Earth Keeper: Reflections on the American Land* to better appreciate Indigenous ways of considering lands. In this book, Momaday, a member of the Kiowa Nation and a Pulitzer Prize–winning poet and novelist, now almost ninety years old, shares his tribe's stories about land, building upon his case for fighting the climate crisis.

A few months later in Santa Fe, I met with Momaday's daughter and caretaker, the filmmaker, activist, and actress Jill Momaday, on a shaded patio within the Counter Culture Café's courtyard. We talked over eggs and chilies about her daughter's upcoming wedding, her father's luminous career, and the history of her Kiowa people.

She was generous with her stories, and we fell into easy repartee. "Part of Indigenous life is that you honor everything," she said. "It's all sacred…There is no separation for the Native person. There's no separation with the earth." It makes sense then that *moving across land*—running, walking, riding—is part of being in relationship with it. Movement is a form of interacting with a place. It's building a rapport. It's learning character. In the documentary film *Return to Rainy Mountain*, about a trip she took with her father, she says, "I think of my Kiowa people. They are always on horseback and moving; traveling across the landscape, hunting, camping, telling stories…They migrated across these great mountains and plains following the buffalo thousands of years ago…We still have our spirits and we still hold this place and this landscape as holy ground."

Moving freely across the West has a long history. It brings tremendous joy and reaffirms the patterns of people who have lived here for millennia. (It also brings to mind the flow of those chasing Manifest Destiny.) But in reconsidering the impacts of car travel, despite the wonderful headiness of its "wind in your hair" freedom, those of us stalking adventures in distant locales need to understand our impact. Now more than ever, Jill believes, the words of her father and the messages of her people are essential. He writes in *Earth Keeper*, "It is good to be alive in this world. But on the immediate side there is the exhaust of countless machines, toxic and unavoidable. The planet is warming, and the northern ice is melting. Fires and floods wreak irresistible havoc. The forests are diminished and waste piles upon us. Thousands of species have been destroyed. Our own is at imminent risk. The earth and its inhabitants are in crisis, and at the center is a moral crisis. Man stands to repudiate his humanity." Given that thoughtless actions have dire consequences, we need to reevaluate our ways of interacting with land, take stock of our relationship to place, honor the ground we tread upon, and assess *how* we tread upon it. Extraction, overdevelopment, and ill-conceived federal management are all to blame for the mess we're in, but we also can't deny our own impacts on land. Turns out, the opposite of denial is *acknowledgment*.

— — —

WE SHARE HALF OF THE WEST WITH ALL OTHER AMERICANS because almost 50 percent of western lands are public. Yet 100 percent are traditional Native lands. These are places once traveled primarily on horseback and foot, but now more often by trucks, vans, and cars. Conservationists spend much time considering the impacts of mining, logging, and agricultural practices, and for good reason. But there's also industrial tourism, the very practice of consuming nature without acknowledging its significance and limits, further burdening a tired and misunderstood place. In addressing the strains that people put on western landscapes, we need to accept the full story.

Francine Spang-Willis gave a land acknowledgement to the board of WildEarth Guardians in the fall of 2022. She said:

As you might be aware, this beautiful and sacred landscape has a layered history. Millions of Indigenous humans had existed on it and engaged with it for thousands of years before it became known as the United States. Today millions of Indigenous peoples are still connected to it, including but not limited to the following Indigenous nations in Montana: Assiniboine and Sioux (Nakota, Dakota, Lakota), Blackfeet, Chippewa and Cree, Confederated Tribes of the Salish, Kootenai, Pend Oreille, Crow, Gros Ventre, Little Shell Band of Chippewa, Cree, Northern Cheyenne.

She continued to speak about "relationship" and "connection" to place, our responsibilities in caring for this earth, and the painful legacy of colonization and colonialism—the acts of settling land, then implementing plans and policies to subjugate peoples and exploit resources. Think of what our ancestors sacrificed for you, she asked. Consider the legacy of violence towards humans, wildlife, and land.

Of course, acknowledgment is only a step toward acts of reciprocity. First comes recognition. After this, there is a need for amends and ways to intentionally give back to the lands and Native peoples. Acknowledgment is only the beginning, a first step.

Over the course of our friendship, Spang-Willis has made me reconsider the West and see it more fully. It's a place where land and history are one, where waters are finite and precious, and where humans share space with all sorts of wild beasts. These are the homelands of numerous Native peoples. These forests, prairies, and deserts that have sheltered and fed peoples for millennia are now inhabited by an ever-burgeoning population with various desires. These lands have seen unimaginable violence. They have also heard ongoing prayer.

The West is more than a playground or storage site awaiting resource extraction. It is more than a second home or a selfie. It is a land of many cultures. It's a place of countless generations. A place where dancers in jingle dresses move to drums, thrilling pow-wow attendees. A place where rock walls hold messages drawn long ago. It's a land where wolves still den and nurture pups, despite vicious eradication programs. Where people run under high canyon walls and children swim in frigid snowmelt. Men have died in mines here under cruel conditions. Militias have gathered while book clubs read. This is a place where horses gallop, bears binge in their time of hyperphagia, and ponderosa pines topple in drought-desiccated soils. Glowing neon signs beckon from rain-soaked windows and pronghorn tangle and die in barbed wire. Here are reintroduced condors that nest in the cracks of desert rock walls and human families who struggle to secure homes. It's snow chains on passes, businesses closed for the season, and lariat loops that wildly fly toward the rear legs of racing calves. It's mile markers, mountain lions, and slag heaps. A rifle shot felling a twelve-point elk and AM radio blaring preachers and conservative rabble-rousers. This is a place of innumerable footprints of humans and beasts stamped in dust, mud, and snow. Where people live out on the landscape and need what that landscape offers. We must concede the history. We must recognize forebearers. We must honor the place as interconnected and whole, not chopped into rectilinear parcels by arbitrary boundaries or gutted for commodities. Actions without consequence, human dominion, inexhaustible abundance, and dualism—the idea that we are separate from nature—are myths bearing down on us. These must first be acknowledged before we begin to consider a better story for this place.

CHAPTER 11

A TOWN IN THE WILD

ESCALANTE, UTAH, IS SURROUNDED BY THE GRAND Staircase-Escalante National Monument (GSENM) and therefore lies smackdab in the middle of otherworldly splendor, a landscape of gulches, canyons, and soaring walls of red rock so incomprehensibly gorgeous that I'll refrain from further description. I couldn't possibly do it justice. Trust me. Encompassing 1,900,000 acres of such wonders, GSENM was recently returned to this size—its original acreage, as established in 1996 and restored with Biden's signature in 2021—after having been chopped in half by the Trump administration in 2017. Some locals resent the monument—the designation, not the land—but almost a million others, drawn annually from all over the world, beg to differ. The town of Escalante sits small and huddled within its expanse, an early outpost of the Latter-day Saints and their attempts to tame this wild, sprawling terrain. Town streets were carefully platted 130 years ago and fan out from Highway 12, the main drag. Original LDS settler homes, red brick with corniced roofs, stand on prim lots, leaving space on which horses graze sleepily and boisterous gardens bloom. But don't get too charmed by the place. Alluring as its historical architecture, its natural surroundings, and its small-town feel might be, you and I will probably never live there, and that suits many of the residents of Escalante just fine.

From Escalante to Bozeman and beyond, an illusion persists that people moving to the West will find an empty canvas. With an influx of folks looking to relocate, little towns nestled in striking, wild country often become suddenly transformed by recently arrived retirees, getaway artists, remote workers, and buyers of multiple homes. Communities get reshaped into forms that resemble the very places the interlopers have left behind. Characteristics once foreign, from exorbitant real estate prices to hipster breweries, and even paved roads, are sometimes jarring imports to old-timers. Our western myth museum displays the illusory belief, among all those others, that the West is unfettered and malleable—that it can and should be continuously overhauled and reformed by these enlightened and civilizing newcomers. There are benefits that sometimes do come with the outsiders, such as new economic opportunities, but at what cost?

Kandee DeGraw, an interpreter for the Dixie National Forest Interagency Visitor Center, lives in Escalante with her husband, Steve Henry. He's a backcountry ranger in Glen Canyon National Recreation Area, home to Lake Powell, a reservoir built in 1964 that is now, in the era of unimpeded development, the gridlock of water politics and withering drought, well on its way to becoming a dead pool. DeGraw and her husband share a small home that he rebuilt, with a giant backyard that empties into the enormity of the national monument. As a resident of Escalante for ten years, she comes from a large LDS family descended from Platte DeAlton Lyman, her great-great-grandfather, celebrated for his perilous journey from Escalante eastward toward the upper Colorado River to build homeland and broaden Mormon territory. In 1880, Lyman and others helped to open a tenuous wagon route for the Latter-day Saints along a thin ribbon of trail, dynamite-blasted and axe-chiseled into sandstone, through a slot in the rim of Glen Canyon and down to the river. It was a dicey passage, arduous to create and risky to follow, but made good on Brigham

Young's plan to settle eastern Utah, enacting the myth of Zion, LDS homeland. Known as Hole-in-the-Rock, it stands open still today, representing both a faith-promoting moment in Mormon history and a badge of honor for Platte Lyman's descendants, many of whom still live in the region.

Escalante has an unremarkable Main Street, which DeGraw considers a suitable sacrifice zone for tourists and would-be second homers, whom she does not want moving to her community and remaking it in the image of their fancy curb-and-gutter neighborhoods back home. She hopes that you will mind your own business if you visit, and stay close to the visitor amenities—but, with apologies to her, the whole town is really worth seeing. I was lucky enough to do that with a quick-witted and brutally honest tour guide: DeGraw herself.

Escalante is a testament to Mormon planning, architecture, and agriculture. If you can't convince someone to show you the place, as DeGraw did for me, grab a free map at the Ranch Dog Kitchen, a little joint owned by Susanne Stadler and her partner, Ted Levine. You might remember Levine, a former actor who now parks his Prius with a Bernie Sanders sticker in front of his café. He is memorable for his portrayal of Buffalo Bill in *The Silence of the Lambs*. The lotion-on-the-skin guy. But don't dwell too much on this when you visit his joint in Escalante. I recommend getting a Chicken in the Orchard sausage, plus homemade apple pie and an alcohol-free IPA to go. It's good to fortify yourself before touring town or, better still, venturing out into the monument.

On our stroll, DeGraw and I passed one yard sporting QAnon flags, a couple of homes spilling over with boxes and old furniture, a handful of newly renovated residences, some old orchards, and a few scurrying chickens. There were horses that I wanted to greet, but she said no, they bite. And why in the world do tourists always want to pet the horses? she asked. I laughed at the reminder: I *am* that tourist. We saw many big brick houses, striking examples of settler craftsmanship, sitting sadly empty. She explained that, as parents and grandparents die and leave their homes to multiple members of large LDS families, offspring are left to debate just what to do with them—and sometimes there's no consensus, just stalemate. The city council put a cap on vacation rentals in residential areas; only twenty-eight are allowed in such neighborhoods, though this does not include portions of town zoned for business. The city leaders don't want Escalante to become a soulless aggregation of investment properties or lack residences for people who want to relocate fully, raise families, and become a part of the community. The cap comes as a relief to people like DeGraw, given how popular her region has become. Without it, conceivably, every house in town could become a vacation rental.

One of the town's beauties is a grand old home across the street from DeGraw's that now belongs to a family unable to decide its fate. "They can't do Vrbo, which was kind of their idea initially," she told me. "There's six kids in the family and they can't find an agreement." Escalante's economic development director, Drew Parkin, a former Bureau of Land Management planner, has described this as a chronic dilemma with any number of old homes. "Families can't afford to remodel. They can't figure out what to do with houses, so they kind of just sit there," DeGraw told me. Of the home across the street, she said, "They'll come and have reunions every once in a while, but a lot of the homes need to be repaired. You have to restore them historically, which of course is super expensive." There are grants available, but they are modest and don't cover the hundreds of thousands of dollars necessary for historic renovation.

Escalante's Mayor Melani Torgersen, an impressive woman who's as candid as she is can-do, told me that of 693 residents of Escalante, roughly ten percent live in multigenerational households. She herself is from Kanab, about two hundred miles southwest. DeGraw is from

Monticello, the seat of San Juan County nearly three hundred miles east, in the lands that her great-grandfather settled. Her neighbor, the man across the street with a DON'T TREAD ON ME flag in his front yard, comes from a family with deep roots in Escalante. Next door, Lisbeth Louderback and Bruce Pavlik, an archaeologist and a botanist, respectively, came to Escalante from Salt Lake City, drawn by their interest in the area's unique varietal of potato, *Solanum jamesii*. This spurred the couple to launch the town's Wild Potato Days, a festival focusing on the first potato variety to be grown in North America, and a staple for the Zuni, Southern Paiute, Apache, Hopi, Kawaik, Tewa, Navajo, and Zia peoples. God bless a town that can celebrate its own potato. When Pavlik and Louderback put down stakes in Escalante, they brought value as well as their capital in a way DeGraw approves: creating a relationship with the town through an indigenous tuber, rather than, say, launching a campaign for a set of new streetlights or a Starbucks.

That endemic spud inspired early Latter-day Saints to name this place Potato Valley. It's a famous tuber in certain circles, but the town is better known for the national monument. Many in Escalante aren't crazy about this federal designation and the changes it brought to the community. Over the decades, the region has seen ever-increasing federal oversight of lands. Garfield County, in which Escalante is located, is 93 percent public lands, and the wind-and-water-sculpted sandstone arches, pinnacles, and canyons beckon to countless tourists every year, reminding locals that much of their own backyard belongs as much to outsiders as to them. Rural counties traditionally sustained themselves through resource extraction—logging, mining, ranching—but changing demographics, recreational trends, and emerging economic sectors have eclipsed these livelihoods.

Growing up in San Juan County, which constitutes the southeastern corner of Utah and was the end of the trail for many families on the Hole-in-the-Rock expedition, DeGraw and her five siblings were raised by a single mother. They came to adulthood among these lands, these trends, and these resentments. "We were very poor. I didn't know I was poor until I got older and looked around and was like, 'Why do they have a trampoline and we don't have a trampoline?'" We talked in her kitchen while her husband chopped vegetables for soup, drank a beer, and added occasionally to our rambling afternoon conversation. From the couple's kitchen window I could see huge pink and white sandstone domes, looming above the emerald green of a nearby irrigated field.

Although DeGraw and her family struggled financially, "we had a great childhood...My mom was a really fun parent. You know, she was playful and jokey, and she loved playing pranks even though she was working two, three jobs." The jobs included teaching PE at Monticello High (Go, Buckeroos!) for thirty years, and working with Latino and Native American clubs to organize their events and logistics on trips to Salt Lake City, nearly five hours north.

For fun, the family often visited a nearby slot canyon and swimming hole. DeGraw regrets that this pond is now in private hands and has been hammered by cows. When she was growing up, her mother would drive with a car full of kids to the spot, stretch out in the sun, and turn them all loose. "One of the things that would occupy us for hours was carving our names in the rock." She laughed at herself, knowing this is unacceptable nowadays. Still, she told me, it was something that everyone did, her brothers and sisters, parents, grandparents and great-grandparents. "Their names are all over the place out there. So, it wasn't something that was even thought of as bad," she said. Then, well aware of her responsibilities as an interpreter for the Forest Service, she added, "Of course it's a crime."

In addition to graffiti, people often collected relics found in ancient dwellings. "We would look for potsherds," DeGraw told me.

"If you found a ruin, you would plunder it. It was just what you did, and then you'd bring them home...The thought back then was, 'We can do whatever we want.'" She channeled the old sentiment, exclaiming, "This was our land. It was ours!" She laughed again, letting the half-guilty memories trail off.

There had long been laws protecting ancient pueblos and the items their inhabitants left behind; plundering them, as DeGraw said, is a felony. As those laws were better enforced, local white people grew more and more resentful as their hobby drew scrutiny. With increased federal oversight of artifacts, DeGraw explained, what people heard was, "Don't touch the pottery...This is special and you don't deserve it. You don't understand it. The way we love it is better than the way you love it."

DeGraw's work now involves educating visitors about the monument, the region's antiquities, and how to leave no trace in the backcountry. She is the person who enlightens visitors on protocols—a twist, given that previously this was generally handled by those outside the region, but she grew up in southwestern Utah herself. She appreciates protection laws pertaining to ancient dwellings and the environment, and she is happy in her own role preserving them. But she also believes that the highhanded tone of decades of enforcement efforts created animosity in many regional communities. Environmental laws such as those protecting wilderness attributes, and heritage protection laws protecting sacred sites from "pot-hunting," left locals piqued. "I think a lot of old-timers were like, 'What the fuck are you talking about?'" And things just got worse when Grand Staircase-Escalante National Monument was created in 1996. Part of the reason why DeGraw feels so protective of southern Utah is the way feds, researchers, biologists, and recreationists interacted with LDS families that had been here for generations. Self-righteous jackassery by the Johnnys-and-Janes-come-lately played out as condescension to locals, impeding the transformation to an agenda of protecting Indigenous history and staving off cultural erasure.

Though she has since left the Church of Jesus Christ of Latter-day Saints, DeGraw remains fiercely protective of the residents in little Utah towns. Before the influx of tourism and the money that comes with it, "you had the rich people, you had the poor, but most people were level." Now you have these communities with recreation-based economies, she said, and with that comes stratification. "You have the very wealthy and you have the servant class—the society fractures. There's not this level community anymore." People separate into factions and spend time with the like-minded, so that there are "certain people who would never deign to talk to the bishop." An LDS bishop sits high in the social strata in his community, but might be disregarded by outsiders. "They wouldn't invite people over to dinner who work at the gas station," DeGraw explained. "What kind of kills me is, 'I'm multicultural. I'm very into supporting other cultures.'" She laughed, channeling that superior attitude. "It's a totally different culture here. You have the opportunity to learn about this rich, old history in the West and instead you make fun of it." DeGraw has heard over and over again that Latter-day Saints are idiots or members of a cult. She noted the acute contradiction. "It's like, well, then you're not really multicultural are you?"

Regional Indian nations, including Ute Mountain Ute, Hopi, Navajo, Pueblo of Zuni, and Ute Indian Tribe, were eager to put an end to years of ongoing desecration of hallowed sites in the Bears Ears National Monument area that lies east of Escalante and Grand Staircase-Escalante National Monument. DeGraw understands why they and others wanted to stop the looting, the graffiti, and the desecration of gravesites. She also concedes that her culture has major baggage. "*Nobody* wants to admit that parts of their history are horrible! That their ancestors may have done terrible things," she told me. Then she cited a notion in early LDS writings, that Indigenous peoples might achieve not just assimilation but transformation if they converted to Mormonism. "I think they called it the gentling and the whitening of the West by converting and marrying," she said. "What's that quote?"

"It's *white and delightsome*," I offered. Latter-day Saints believed that, with conversion, Native people would become light-complected and subservient. I was aware of that belief, having written about LDS relations with Indigenous populations and their lands in my dissertation. LDS scripture contends that Native folk of the Americas descended from the *Book of Mormon* patriarch, Lehi. Progenitors of Lehi's sons, Nephi and Laman, separated into two tribes—the white Nephites, and the darker-skinned Lamanites, whom the church believes were the ancestors of Indigenous peoples. Joseph Smith offered conversion as a way to bring the true religion to Native Americans and thereby make them white Saints. Though the Church has long since abandoned this idea of religious conversion or adherence changing skin color, LDS people in southern Utah may have initially felt both drawn to and entitled to antiquities because of such early Church understandings.

There is a story that may have been familiar to LDS pioneers first settling in the area. In 1834, before their move to the Great Basin, Latter-day Saints were attacked by locals in Jackson County, Missouri. Prophet Joseph Smith led a militia to retaliate against the offending mobbers and on their march from Ohio to Jackson County, he and his soldiers came upon ancient burial mounds, presumably made by Nephites and Lamanites, and dug up human bones. *Ah, the prophet Onandagus Zelph!* Smith exclaimed upon seeing a vision. A Lamanite warrior who had fought in a great battle, Zelph, in spite of his transgressions, became "white and delightsome." These very bones, the prophet revealed, to the amazement of his men and the few women on the march, represented the remains of a converted Indian. Researchers later determined that the bones came from a prehistoric Hopewell burial site, but the story of Zelph, according to the fourth church president, "was known from the hill Cumorah or East sea to the Rocky mountains." In other words, across Mormondom. Zelph's bones at one time stood as evidence that Joseph Smith's revelations could be found in the ground, a tricky notion that might have led to digging that threatened Indigenous history and identity.

It wasn't only protecting ancient structures that galled locals in places such as Escalante; it was also environmental laws that impacted lands over which they felt proprietary. Growing up in the 1970s and '80s, DeGraw saw bumper stickers on cars and trucks in Monticello, complaining "WILDERNESS: A LAND OF NO USE." Wilderness designation and other legislated conservation measures were wildly unpopular, she said. Contempt grew over the federal presence, as did antipathy toward outsiders who valued the lands over the rural people and practices. Some folks brought with them self-righteousness that only served as salt in wounds. "*I'm educated,*" DeGraw said, mimicking these attitudes. "*I've studied this. This beauty really is for the people who understand it, not for you guys.*" Still, she is aware of the paradoxes. Her people were once the invaders, settling on Indigenous lands, and now those old invaders resent the new invaders, the tourists and federal agents who assert other uses for and valuations of these lands. "*Everyone* feels entitled to them," she said. "I kind of feel like everybody is a little wrong."

— — —

MOST PEOPLE COME TO ESCALANTE, NOT TO GO ON A walking tour of the town, as I did with DeGraw, but to see the stunning Grand Staircase-Escalante National Monument, with its petroglyphs and ancient dwellings, its essential habitat for wildlife, and its geological wonders. People who live in the area love this land, but some don't appreciate the monument designation. Six hundred and forty-eight bee species have been found within monument boundaries, and 125 species of plants live there, including some so resilient that they tolerate the 160-degree temperature that has been recorded on the surface of the sandstone terrain. It can get really hot and dry. With the stresses of ongoing drought, traditional uses within monument boundaries, such as livestock grazing, need to be monitored and managed so that wildlife can survive. This is an unwelcome notion for many ranchers with public land grazing permits. In 2001, when federal officials shortened the grazing season on the monument after a prolonged drought, a permittee and one-time Escalante resident, Mary Bulloch, refused to abide by the constraint. As a result, her animals were confiscated. Other regional ranchers, including Cliven Bundy, then enlisted the support of a sympathetic sheriff and forced the release of Bulloch's cattle in a precursor to the Battle of Bunkerville. Thirteen years later, Bundy fought against the confiscation of his own cows and many living in this area are sympathetic to his cause, though not necessarily his *modus operandi*.

In 2015, nearly twenty years after the monument was created, the county commissioners of Garfield County, of which Escalante is a part, issued an emergency declaration blaming the Grand Staircase-Escalante Monument for declining school enrollment. The unusual declaration was followed in 2017 by a resolution, passed in both the state house and senate and signed by Governor Gary Herbert, that stated, "For more than 20 years, the Grand Staircase has had a negative impact on the prosperity, development, economy, custom, culture, heritage, educational opportunities, health, and well-being of local communities." The monument status had effectively shot down the opportunity for coal mining on the Kaiparowits Plateau, which locals dreamed of since the 1970s. Before the monument designation, environmental advocates had kept the region protected from mass industrial extraction for decades, in spite of this large coal vein in the area. In Garfield County, the commissioners argued that since school enrollment was down 67 percent the monument designation must be responsible. But they didn't factor in demographics—the town's aging population (hence empty brick homes)—and dwindling opportunities for industry jobs long before Bill Clinton created the monument.

The state's resolution coincided in timing with a review of national monument boundaries by the Trump administration, at the behest of Utah's congressional delegation who echoed the economic concerns of rural politicians about monuments. But two years before the state resolution, an independent nonpartisan research organization called Headwaters Economics, based in Bozeman, issued a report with contrary findings: that "communities in Garfield and Kane counties, Utah, neighboring the Grand Staircase-Escalante National Monument (the Grand Staircase-Escalante Region) experienced strong growth after the designation of the monument, continuing previous growth trends. From 2001 to 2015, in the Grand Staircase-Escalante Region, population grew by 13 percent; jobs grew by 24 percent; real personal income grew by 32 percent; and real per capita income grew by 17 percent." It should be noted that some rural Utahns find the Headwaters report "grossly misleading," and don't buy it. The truth is, even the loss of imagined jobs due to the establishment of the monument, like in mining the Kaiparowits Plateau, has left people resentful. They feel robbed of opportunities for livelihoods that have helped put food on western tables since white settlement.

Headwaters' analysis bears out that protected public lands are good for western communities. They attract businesses whose employees find great appeal in backcountry activities. True, tourism brings jobs and dollars, but true also that it is seasonal, and while some local entrepreneurs thrive, service-industry jobs often provide marginal or inadequate income for a family with kids. What Headwaters recognized and what the numbers in their report reflected was that though the tourism industry is a mixed bag, other economic sectors, such as IT, health care, and manufacturing, for example, are drawn to western towns surrounded by public lands. Proximity to wilderness, they assert, can be a lure to many forms of business and their potential employees as long as an airport is within an hour drive. Of course, the closest one to Escalante is almost two and a half hours away.

The state's declaration, like Trump's subsequent move to reduce Grand Staircase-Escalante National Monument by nearly half in December 2017, reopened wounds in the community of Escalante. There were those who still felt indignant about Clinton having created the monument, and there were those who felt that the monument was being scapegoated. And there were others who saw value in the monument. Long-time resident Karen Munson was quoted in the *Salt Lake City Tribune*, saying, "I refuse to be labeled a victim because of the Grand Staircase." Referring to the county commission emergency declaration, she declared herself "unimpressed with their blaming our problems on the monument." Munson, a big-hearted former schoolteacher, helped me to understand the issues in and around her town. She ran the Escalante Home Center, a hardware store that she had opened with her husband so local folks wouldn't have to drive the 120 miles to Cedar City to buy hammers, duct tape, light bulbs, landscaping materials, wood screws, and other supplies. The store was thriving after the monument's designation. "We have exceeded every sales goal we set," she said. "We sold three hundred trees last year. The paint is just flying off the shelves."

Munson, in addition to selling durable equipment, is a philosopher and a gatherer of stories. Some of these she has published in a book, *In the Aisles: Tales From a Rural Utah Hardware Store*, a slim volume of vignettes featuring townsfolk, their circumstances, and life at the Escalante Home Center. This is how I first connected with her.

Hearing about the book, I emailed her and asked to buy a copy. She sent it a week later and I read it cover to cover. The town of Escalante has experienced great changes in recent decades, and those changes are personified by the people Munson has met. Her anecdotes include varied exchanges with newcomers and well-established locals; dinners at Hell's Backbone Grill, the celebrated restaurant in nearby Boulder; time with her beloved book club (which, she later told me, dissolved during the pandemic due to different fears and understandings of COVID, a sad counterpoint to the Ketchum group); and an acting lesson with Ted Levine, of Buffalo Bill fame.

On a sunny spring day, Munson and Mayor Melani Torgersen agreed to meet me at the Escalante Community Center, in an office tucked into a building erected atop the spot where the old school once stood. I talked with these two close friends about their beloved town, the monument, their families, and the need for steady leadership. Torgersen was tied up a bit that morning. She wears multiple hats in this little town and had to dash away to her duties, including her work at the community food pantry. Munson had a bit more time in her schedule before she was due back at the hardware store, from which she and her husband were soon to retire. The women told me of Torgersen's role in the Vrbo cap and more recently, her work on securing affordable housing for the town. The mayor is also focused on collaborating with experts to ensure the water supply, a dire concern in the West. "We have engineers helping us know exactly how much water is available and how many water meters we should give out. We have seven or eight springs, and water rights to additional springs. It's been a process," she said. Water rights in the West are not only coveted, they are byzantine. Escalante, with a cold, semi-arid climate, gets just over ten inches of precipitation a year, on average, including twenty-six inches of snow. Water is a precious commodity in the area. According to the women, the previous mayor had placed a moratorium on development because of concerns over water. That was bold, but long-term solutions might need to be more complex. "Melani has fought through all of these legal battles of getting these water rights with the springs," Munson said, "because there was massive paperwork where things weren't filed properly. She's been a phenomenal mayor. She's really transitioned the town into a place of stable but conservative growth." Munson felt that the previous leadership held the town back—the former mayor's moratorium caused a worrying decrease in growth and investment in development. Escalante residents want their town to remain vibrant, as one might imagine, but its remote location, its water limits, and the surrounding public lands keep opportunity for growth limited. Still, its remoteness is also its attraction.

There are now people clamoring to move to Escalante (the only property available when I visited was an old trailer, listed at over $300,000), but the town is not for everyone. It's remote and it's rural. The closest Costco is in St. George with a roundtrip of six hours. Munson believes it's usually the woman in a new couple who can't tolerate the town, because of its lack of amenities. "Amazon has been a godsend," she said. "But for someone who likes to shop or get her nails done once a week," Escalante is not the place. Even Munson had reservations about moving here, but then she met her husband Reed, who was raised in the town. She grew up LDS in Ogden in northern Utah, and in some ways, she had felt smug about her city roots when she first came. "I didn't expect to ever live here. I thought this was a hick town. I was really snobby in my attitude," Munson said. When she and Reed became engaged, she said to him, "Promise me we will never live in Escalante." He had just smiled, "because he didn't know what the future would hold, and he loved it here." Now, she said, "my opinion couldn't be more different. I've done a one-eighty. I love it here." While we talked, she misted up on a few occasions, telling me of raising her 10 children—a few of whom were adopted—of her years teaching, of getting to know and love old-timers, and learning to bake rolls, and make applesauce. It's clear that in spite of her initial skepticism, Karen Munson is right where she should be.

— — —

DESPITE WORKING FOR THE FEDERAL GOVERNMENT AND NO longer being part of the LDS Church, both Kandee DeGraw and her husband feel very much at home in Escalante. It was the LDS community that took care of DeGraw, who is now in remission, when she was struggling with cancer. Neighbors brought her food and prayerfully laid hands on her with LDS sacred consecrated oil. Her husband, with a longer history in town, has a child from a previous marriage here. "Having my daughter here was like a huge thing," he told me. Though his daughter has since moved away, everyone in town knows her and loves her because, in Escalante, children tend to bind people to the community. DeGraw and Henry may be seen as heathens, they joke, but they get along well with families who have lived here for generations, and even with the town's most devout. They are also on friendly terms with former mayor, Wade Barney, who heads the Escalante Guard.

Militia? I wondered. DeGraw assured me that "it's so much quieter and calmer" than you might expect. I later talked to one member of the Guard, AJ Martel, a thirtyish accountant, with dark, closely cropped hair and a tiny widow's peak. We met in a big, empty dining room at the Canyon Country Lodge, which he had reserved with the owners. He is a keen and intentional man, with an engaging smile that tightens a bit when he makes serious points. We talked about his family, his involvement in the community, and LDS perspectives on land. The conversation turned to cows, the regional hot potato in a place known for its regional potato. Are there places that should be off limits to cows, I asked, given periods of extended drought? Allotments that should be retired entirely? Sharing views on public land use, he explained the conviction, held by the Bundy family and others, that grazing on public lands was a right, as much as it is a permitted trans-actional agreement with the government. This is a bone of contention and of ongoing debate at the root of many public land battles—grazing permits as rights or privileges.

I couldn't help but think that he seemed an unlikely member of the Guard, which he told me wasn't really a militia. In fact, he wasn't very comfortable with guns, having not grown up with them. His wife, he joked, was the hunter in the family. He joined the Guard when it formed in 2020, because of his concern about the safety of Escalante during that chaotic year. The Guard started, he explained, after a local Black Lives Matter protest, where he'd recognized few, if any, of the participants. This left him and other residents wondering if infiltrators were behind the event, as they'd heard had happened in other places.

Perhaps there were out-of-towners at the Escalante rally, but it was also attended by locals. Among the marchers was Susanne Stadler, co-owner of the Ranch Dog Kitchen, the Main Street cafe with the maps and the pie. She explained to the *Wayne and Garfield County Insider* why she chose to participate. "To me, 'liberty and jus-tice for all' is what America stands for." After talking to Martel, I feel he would agree with Stadler on this issue, but on the day of the protest, these two residents were viewing matters from different angles. While George Floyd's death brought many people together, fears of Antifa invasion seeded by endless clips of serious though limited discord in Seattle and Portland, brought others out to defend their towns.

The Guard is currently focused on emergency planning. Prepared-ness is an LDS value and Escalante, one of the most remote towns in the lower 48, is susceptible to both floods and earthquakes. Though members do not consider themselves militia, other groups across the country often use the idea of community service as a recruiting tool. Still the Escalante Guard really does seem quieter and calmer, as DeGraw described them, than other such groups I've encountered. They've had a couple of hotheads show up at meetings, Martel told me, but so far leaders have thus far kept them at bay. All the same, the Guard's formation underlines the anxiety that many western communities have felt in the last few years, and they've taken it upon themselves to organize in an age of disquiet.

Toward the end of our parley, the conversation became lighter. Suddenly Martel, with a grin on his face, recited a line from a poem about a town called Pocketville. "Way down south in Pocketville, where Duncan dug his ditch uphill..." I laughed and asked him about the verse. Pocketville—wasn't that what they used to call the town of Virgin? It is, he responded in surprise. Virgin is where his wife is from, a little place twenty miles west of Zion National Park, at a low point or "pocket" along the Virgin River. Settled by LDS homesteaders in 1857, its population is still fewer than seven hundred residents. The ditch refers to early Mormon irrigation efforts in an area once known for its gorgeous orchards, but from that low pocket along the river, water *couldn't* flow uphill to the fruit trees. It seems that Duncan's ditch was foolishly plotted along such a slope, destined to have gravity stop the flow of water.

His wife's experience being raised there, Martel added, was what convinced them to opt for "rural living" to raise their family. In Escalante, they have chosen a place in a geography of ancient dwellings and Native sacred land; longtime livestock operations; recreational paradise and entitled tourists; kindhearted neighbors and community protectors; LDS settlements; wildlife habitat; and shared public land—the legitimacy of all these claims depending on your perspective. Martel himself is a city boy, from Orem, Utah, but he felt the draw of a small town after hearing stories and poetry from his wife's childhood.

When he quoted the Pocketville poem to me, it was an icebreaker moment. Though Martel and I had spent three hours talking about the issues polarizing America and the West—from his concern over the erosion of rights and his distrust over conservation groups to his lack of confidence in the federal government—we ended the discussion in a shared delight over an engineering error by a bungling homesteader. An uphill irrigation channel? There was an aptness to that. Like Duncan's ditch, our encounter was a bit of an uphill trek—but we were blessed, and the conversation flowed against the gravity of differing perspectives.

CHAPTER 12

THE LIE OF THE
IRRECONCILABLE OTHER

W HAT I HAVE ASKED *YOU* TO DO OVER THESE
pages is to walk with me through a myth museum. Gaze
upon its main diorama: The Cowboy, Free Land. Peek
at its oddities: A *Guyasticutus*, An Algal River. Consider its anach-
ronisms: Frontier Individualism, Wild West, Salubrious West, Blank
Slate. But it's not just the displays that should be our focus. It's the
stories of those who are browsing them.

So as we approach the end of our tour, just before you exit through
the gift shop, let me usher you into our theater. Take a seat, my friend.
We are going to watch a western, America's favorite. And this genre,
the western, is the reason so many myths about America west of the
Great Plains proliferate the world over. From *My Pal Trigger* to *The
Power of the Dog,* from *Smoke Signals* to *Django Unchained,* west-
erns have taken themes such as I've discussed and made them loom
large. The way we look at the West has been created, in part, both from
and for our entertainment. It's weird to consider. Hollywood itself is
not really the West, but it has played an inordinate role in how the
region appears in our minds.

Then again, not every western film is a Hollywood construct.
Some are determinedly independent. The one that I want to leave you

pondering is unique in its field, in that it doesn't perpetuate myths, it busts them. If Steven Seagal's *The Patriot* was one of the worst film portrayals of the West, Jim Jarmusch's *Dead Man* is one of the best.

This movie opens with a train moving over endless miles, the camera panning across the pistons of the locomotive's driving wheels—innovations of the Industrial Revolution—and then the faces of weary travelers, jarred along in a passenger carriage. Hours pass, and more hours, as the train presses westward and the individual identities, and the general character, of its passengers change. Seats filled with easterners give way to mountain men dressed in the animal skins of the fur traders who come alert to shoot bison from the carriage windows. The journey unrolls like a frieze of dark obsessions leading toward dire modern repercussions. They are the subtext. Cross-country travel is achieved through coal-dependent technology, the first wave of the Industrial Revolution and foundational to climate change; wanton treatment of Indigenous peoples during the "winning" of the West undergirds ongoing chronic abuses; gun violence and vigilante justice, such as the movie portrays, lie beneath current acts of western and national insurrection; and a disregarding and ruthless wealthy class, the barons of western bonanzas, have their counterparts in Tim Blixseth and other moguls who drive today's land rush. *Dead Man* also depicts ongoing Native resistance in the fight for homeland and identity, amid white "progress" and the squalor and anguish it has caused.

The lead character, an initially naïve easterner named William Blake, is played by Johnny Depp. Blake's companion for much of the movie is a Native man known as Nobody, memorably portrayed by Gary Farmer. These two go up against an assortment of villains. It's a story first of alienation, and finally of alliance, as Blake and Nobody share fates deeply intertwined. Neither quite understands the other, but they slowly build rapport amid the brutalities of the western frontier. Nobody, a Blackfeet-Crow, grew up as a hostage kidnapped by British infantry, and later trotted around Europe with a circus. He thinks Blake is "a stupid fucking white man," but also confuses him with the famous English poet. He's right about the stupid but wrong about the poetry: Depp's Blake isn't *that* William Blake. Nobody's recitations from some of the poems in *Auguries of Innocence* initially cause Depp's Blake his own confusion, since he's ignorant of his namesake. Nobody's Native perspectives, a blend of Indigenous Plains and northwest traditions, are also befuddling to Blake. At one point, he yells at Nobody, "I have not understood one single word since I've met you—not one single word!"

Yet they create a relationship, despite so little shared background, that does honor to both of their characters. Blake learns to better navigate his circumstances, and even to appreciate some of his namesake's poetry. His emerging consciousness comes from listening to someone who has different ways of seeing. Of course, Blake and Nobody kill bad guys, sit around campfires, and ride horses through wild country—it's a western, after all—but they gradually form a bond essential to them both. It's this unlikely alliance that brings me to my last fiction, the idea of the irreconcilable other. Although not a myth in the sense of the others we have considered, it's a falsehood that is keeping us paralyzed within the current political climate.

— — —

MIKE SATZ FOUNDED THE IDAHO 97 PROJECT, A BACKHAND reference to that militia group who call themselves the Real Three Percenters Idaho. A corporate lawyer in Boise, Satz believes that the only way to combat the intense polarization in his state is to engage in conversation. Although Idaho has a history of extremism, things have changed drastically in the last ten years, as Satz explained to me over the phone. An influx of people, the many residents new to his

state, have brought with them "their confrontational politics," as he
puts it, "evangelical nationalism," and "a moral superiority" that justi-
fies "telling people what to do." But it's far worse than just that. These
archconservatives, many of whom are from out of state, have taken
over county commissions, city councils, and school boards. According
to journalist David Neiwert, who has long covered western militia and
radical influences in the Pacific Northwest, "A steady deluge of 'white
flight' newcomers from more populous states—particularly California—who see Idaho as a far-right political refuge have gradually
turned the state into a haven for extremist politics, with an unmistak-
ably bigoted, menacing, and violent ethos."

According to Satz and his colleague Alicia Abbott in Sandpoint,
people don't realize what is happening to politics in their state. It's
really troubling, says Satz, "just how low-information voters really
are." And that's not just Republicans, whose party has been high-
jacked. "Democrats are part of the problem, too," in their ineffec-
tiveness in offering solid platforms and winning elections. It's true
that Idaho's Democratic party has languished in recent years as rural
and urban divides widened and the working class felt overlooked.
This left room for archconservatives, yelling about "woke mobs"
and "cancel culture," many from out of state, to stir up discontents,
resentments, and add to ongoing disconnection. The result is the
absolute dominance of extreme rightwing politics and an ongoing
erosion of women's rights, voter rights, and LGBTQ protections. It
also means bounties on wolves, deep cuts in education funding, and
the vilification of any political position that isn't in lockstep with
orthodox far-right ideology. According to the Idaho Freedom Foundation, boosters for these ideas are succeeding. Even when their own
endorsements are unsuccessful, such as Ammon Bundy for governor,
the IFF pushes other Republicans, who fear the Foundation's power
and a loss of their own, ever farther right. The same trend is happening in Wyoming and Montana, where politics also careen ever more

extreme. Satz laments the collapse of civility and the heightened partisanship from coordinated campaigns to deceive voters and bully moderates. Many voters, he told me, are simply receiving "misinformation, disinformation, and angry information."

Alicia Abbott has another way of describing it. "I call it a shit sandwich. They give them a positive, they sneak the fear in, they give them a positive. Then they feed it to them." This is the tactic for making policies ever more extreme—from taxes (being slashed), to gun laws (or lack of them), to book bans, to defunding education, to talk of outlawing COVID vaccines. Abbott acknowledges that only a slim percentage of the population in her state are actually the kind of people who hate other races or truly want to kill people, but she notes that anti-government radicals have used "manipulation campaigns" to control the narrative. "People come here for the prepping and the homesteading aesthetic," she said, but "they don't realize that they're doing this alongside people who, like, want to blow up Planned Parenthood." It's groups such as the IFF that bundle these people together, telling them that Democrats are socialists, communists, godless, and to be feared. This creates the dread that unifies such people with one another, isolates them from those who see the world differently, and pushes them into the arms of extremists. When people don't talk to each another across such divides, fanatics control the narrative.

Satz believes that it's possible to pull Idaho back from the precipice. When he's out talking to rural people, he finds agreement on 90 percent of priorities and values. The trick is to engage in real conversation, establishing common ground. This is a remarkable observation, given that Satz is a Jewish Black man working in a state where a growing number of residents dream of a white Christian homeland. Combating divisiveness and challenging the falsehoods driven by news outlets and social media require communication, connection, and trust. Satz and Abbott believe it's possible.

We have a choice. There are those who want us to take to the

streets—think of *High Noon* and quick draws—and others who want
to build rapport, work together, and look for common values. It's clear
that societies go through convulsions at various moments in history,
and perhaps that's where we are. At a time when civil war is being
discussed as commonly as fuel prices; when anti-Semitism is becoming dangerously overt; and when a white supremacist and Holocaust
denier is invited to dine with an ex-president at his fancy Florida
resort, it certainly feels terrifying. But let me note that, in researching
this book and hearing so many perspectives, I've encountered mostly
agreeable comradery. No one likes being misunderstood, and most of
us do not like being at odds with others. I've come to understand that
most Americans feel that they are part of an "exhausted majority." We
are tired of being told to hate one another by a minority.

A myth is a canonized story, but we each have our own stories.
The key is to respect the variousness and individual value of these.
There are fragments of truth in many stories, and the more we listen
to one another, and hear these truths, the more we will understand one
another and the world in ways that get beyond myth's blur.

—   —   —

SATZ, ABBOTT, AND GREG CARR DON'T KNOW ONE ANOTHER,
at least not yet, though common concerns may bring them together.
Carr is an Idahoan from a multigenerational Idaho family, who came
into serious money before his fortieth birthday. He made $800 million
from the sale of a technology company he cofounded that facilitated
the then-revolutionary capacity to link telephones and computers. He
now splits his time between Idaho and Mozambique, donating large
portions of his fortune and his time to beloved causes through his Carr
Foundation. His generosity comes in many forms, including devotion
to his extended family, a lifelong crusade for human rights, and exten-

sive conservation pursuits. For two decades he has worked to restore Gorongosa National Park in central Mozambique, a protected area that was neglected and devastated during the country's sixteen-year civil war. In addition to his work in Africa and philanthropy elsewhere, Carr has been a benefactor in his home state, funding the renovation of Ernest and Mary Hemingway's home in Ketchum to accommodate writers, and the Museum of Idaho, right next to his Idaho Falls office. He also bought the former Aryan Nations headquarters in Hayden, Idaho, up in the Panhandle, where a former aerospace engineer and radical ideologue named Richard Butler presided over a compound of neo-Nazis. In 1998, members of Butler's group attacked a mother and her son after their car backfired near the compound. The Southern Poverty Law Center sued on behalf of the victims and won a $6.3 million settlement, forcing Butler to sell the property. Carr bought it, then donated it to North Idaho College to be rechristened a peace park. Since then, the college has sold the place, promising to create an endowment for "human rights education," though given that a majority of the college trustees are cronies of Idaho Freedom Foundation Chair Brent Regan, success of such a program seems doubtful going forward.

On a sweltering day in the summer of 2021, I swung by Carr's office in Idaho Falls. Almost sixty, Carr is youthful and fit, and though his sandy hair is flecked with gray, his energy and optimism belie his age. Over salad and soda in the beautifully renovated, sparsely furnished old house, we discussed his latest project. Idaho Listens is an in-person forum organized through Boise State University and tailored to bring people from various walks of life together. "I don't want to oversimplify, but let's just say some of my progressive friends in the East probably don't understand how it's possible to be a conservative and a good person at the same time," he explained. The idea is to get people to relate to those with different perspectives. "There seems to be a gap in this country," he said, "where people who lean progressive and people who lean conservative just simply cannot possibly understand how the other person thinks. We've stopped talking and all we do is shout now, and scream, and call names, and worse."

"I've seen violence," Carr added. By now, of course, violence is commonplace. Shootings at Black Lives Matter protests, churches, synagogues, Club Q in Colorado Springs. Many of us also watched in horror as supercharged polarization and insidiously and intentionally disseminated misinformation led to the storming of the US Capitol on January 6, 2021.

Being enthusiastic, and wealthy, Carr decided he would sponsor a series of conversations between people to build better understanding. "I contacted the president of Boise State University and contacted various Republican legislators in this state," he told me. "I said, 'We all ought to get together and talk…We'll call it Idaho Listens.'" The program involves letting people share their experiences with others who might lack certain perspectives. "Just give them a chance to explain their life." This man, who invented some of the technology that allows us to be plugged into a 24/7 news cycle via our phones, is now championing a far greater communications need: face-to-face discourse.

Carr believes it isn't too late to see major cultural shifts in the West, or in the country. We've waged big battles before, and we'll do it again. "Somebody had to fight for women to get the vote," he pointed out. The country's civil rights movement was an epic effort, and the passing of the Civil Rights Act in 1964 was an epic victory. "We can make change. We just need to work at it and believe that it's possible. But first, we need to engage people, to help them to see different perspectives." How? "You begin by listening."

I later live-streamed the inaugural session of Idaho Listens, watching twelve people tell their stories to an audience who had been asked to refrain from clapping and to "listen reverently." A Korean American woman talked about her fear of being targeted over COVID-19-related racism, and spoke of her own bias, which she recognized one day upon encountering a kind white family on a hiking trail. Another woman who had immigrated from Mexico as a child, shared the anxiety she felt as a young girl ordering off a restaurant menu in her newly acquired English. A Syrian man, now an American citizen, told of a painful experience when confronted by a woman, his Uber passenger, who told him that since he wasn't born in America, he shouldn't be here. He had been in the US for thirteen years, and asked the audience: When does a refugee stop being a refugee? A Jewish woman, a veteran, single mom, and rape survivor, asked the audience to stop defining others by labels, but with our common humanity. "We share in this human essence...I am bone and flesh and filament. I plead. I think. I hurt. I weep. And so do you." Bart Davis, a Latter-day Saint who had served as a Republican member of the Idaho state legislature and as United States attorney for the District of Idaho, talked about the murder of his son. Although he didn't go into detail at the event, I later learned that another student, Vincent Craig Olsen, shot Cameron Davis in 2003, after a bout of heavy drinking. Davis and Olsen had been students at Boise State and both had been Eagle Scouts and Latter-day Saints. They'd also had brushes with the law. In fact, Bart Davis admitted that decades after Cameron's death, he still remembers his son's probation officer's phone number. As he told the audience, he was a happily married statesman, elder, and successful lawyer who had a troubled son that was murdered. People make assumptions about others, Davis said, but we can't really know one another without hearing each other's stories. "I frequently learn by listening," he said, pointing out that "there's a difference between listening to repudiate, listening to agree, and listening to understand. Listening doesn't always lead to agreement, but it often leads to understanding and frequently to respect."

Rebecca Miles is a member of the Nez Perce Tribe who recently celebrated her fiftieth birthday. She spoke of visiting a concentration camp in Poland, guided by a man who felt a deep obligation to tell its story. She was overcome when she walked into the gas chambers where millions and millions of Jews and Poles were murdered, she said, tearing up. "I thought of my own history and of my ancestors… the similar piles of bodies of my people." She told the audience, "They were often proudly piled in similar fashion in an effort to tame the West." Her grandfather, she said, had been sent to the Idaho state penitentiary for a murder he didn't commit. He served time and was later exonerated, although no one bothered to tell him this until years later. "I never knew him to have enemies, and even if he did, he did not pass them on to his next generation. He was a true statesman, a man of the highest degree of integrity and ethics. All he wanted to do was live in peace and love life." She continued, her voice quiet yet strong, "I realized we are all simply wanting the same thing—to be able to raise our families as we choose in a loving and safe environment and to be able to thrive and celebrate life. All living things on earth require two things to live, oxygen and water. Yet in today's world we're going out of our way finding our differences."

— — —

FRANCINE SPANG-WILLIS IS A DESCENDANT OF PAWNEE Woman and Morning Star, also known as the great Chief Dull Knife, who secured the land of the Northern Cheyenne for his people. Francine's Cheyenne name translates to Appearing Flying Woman. As an oral historian, she thinks a lot about people's stories. When someone tells you a story, she said to me, you are given part of it, and you have a responsibility to understand why they are sharing it with you and what they want you to do with it.

And I've taken her words to heart. So many people have honored me with stories, and it is now my responsibility to care for each one. Every person I spoke with while researching this book opened my understanding wider when they shared their knowledge. The act of being in genuine discussion helps us reflect on our differing convictions in a way wholly distinct from the facile interchanges of social media. This is not to say we will agree with one another, but when in relationship with one another, we recognize our shared humanity. Fractured connections created havoc and allow people to work mischief upon us—from planting misinformation to fomenting hate. If we don't engage in listening, we will only ever become more complacent in our sense of rightness, and more confident of the faults of others. As humans, we are social beings. Ironically, "social media" have eroded our ability and inclination to be effective communicators. Those conduits of glib exchanges often make us less civil, less compassionate, and less engaged.

Jonathan Haidt, in his book *The Righteous Mind: Why Good People are Divided by Politics and Religion*, explains that all of us are intuitive in our thinking, at least at first. Our "truths" come from an emotional response. When we hear information, we immediately work to verify our feelings about a statistic, or a news story, or a podcast, with arguments. This he calls the "inner lawyer." For example, a reaction to climate change news or vaccine news comes from instinct, first, around which our inner lawyer builds a case. Haidt calls this process "confirmatory rather than exploratory." This is how we assess what is "real," working to support gut feelings through internal validation. But we temper this process, Haidt offers, when engaged in discussion. Dialogue challenges hasty reactions and smug complacency. "When people know in advance that they'll have to explain themselves, they think more systematically and self-critically. They are less likely to jump to premature conclusions and more likely to revise their beliefs in response to evidence." Discourse with someone who differs from us, if done without anger, allows for thinking critically. It also allows for the shattering of misperceptions and creates opportunities for relationship building. I talked with a conservative man in a very rural corner of the West who told me that if he had never met me, he'd have been scared of me. Fear comes from the unknown. It's time to get to know our neighbors.

In a world of mounting polarization and factionalism, we are primed to become ever more truculent when we are frightened of others. Partisan politics pressures us to steer clear from those who see the world differently. In early 2023, Representative Marjorie Taylor Green called for a national divorce between red states and blue states. Leaders like her benefit from our factions. Their platforms are aimed at division. Politicians who ask Americans to hate one another based on our politics do not have our best interests at heart. Authoritarianism eschews investigation or inquisitiveness, demanding only obedience. An open mind is perceived as a threat to narrow, dictatorial points of view. This applies in our current political climate to folks on both the right and the left.

Journalist, writer, and Idahoan Anne Helen Petersen, who has worked on stories from Black Lives Matter rallies to the Bundy rebellions, once diagnosed this problem with the observation, "It's not enough for someone to be conservative, or liberal—they have to be your very specific strain of conservative or liberal. And those who are not, aren't just different: they're dangerous." When people in power demand absolute fidelity to a system of belief, nuance and understanding endanger the brittle and coerced worldview. There's a reason why many politicians reduce issues to slogans and turn the slogans into cudgels. They want us to be reactionary and angry, rather than in conversation. Relationship-building allows us to confront falsehoods and myth, returning power to communities and building bridges among neighbors.

The Glendive Dinosaur and Fossil Museum's purpose is to disparage the idea of evolution. To challenge the biblical account—for instance, by believing in evolution—is to reject not just a scripture or the faith it supports but also the philosophy, the culture, and even the sense of identity that comes with fundamentalist Christianity. Inquiry leads to skepticism and reconsideration. Embracing beliefs without exploration shuts down curiosity, discourse, independence, and, finally, relationships. All-or-nothing thinking leaves ideas, and the people who hold them, unexamined, ignored, or at worse, reviled, creating an environment suited to manipulation, control, and supremacy.

This is something else interesting about denying the theory of evolution in favor of religious narratives: to eschew evolution is to deny that species, including humans, continually adapt in order to better navigate the world. That myth would stop our progress and end our story. Thank goodness evolution is real.

— — —

THE WEST IS A REMARKABLE PLACE, TESSELLATED WITH many facets, like snakeskin, or honeycomb, or stained glass. In this place, we live together, fitted into neighborhoods, towns, and states, settled within mountain ranges, watersheds, prairies, deserts, and badlands. Our lives proceed below the flight paths of sandhill cranes, along the hunting grounds of wolves, beside rivers of trout, salmon, grayling, and paddlefish. Under giant skies, we inhabit this terrain together, though we view it in ways as diverse as the land itself.

This is a shared place, made of stories laid atop one another. Some are dangerous and lethal obsessions; some are the unbearable moans of broken hearts; some are narratives of decency, bravery, and beauty; some are tales of the haves and have-nots. We are lucky to live here, but we must understand the great perils and responsibilities that come with inhabiting a museum of myths. Western myths are branded onto the hide of the nation: belief in ceaseless expansion, American individualism, unending abundance, and unbridled liberty. Metastasis of these mythologies and their regrettable confusions and consequences is ongoing. To stop their runaway progress requires a thorough reflection upon biases, assumptions, complacencies, and patterns. This takes paying attention, listening, understanding the culture itself and the varied voices within it by investing our time and energy in healthy modes of communication.

To successfully sort through the myriad realities here in the West, we need to understand why certain ideas are scary to some people. Social media poisons us against one another and turns us into holier-than-thou dolts. As Jonathan Haidt writes, these "platforms were almost perfectly designed to bring out our most moralistic and least reflective selves." He continues in his criticism, "Facebook, Twitter, YouTube, and a few other large platforms unwittingly dissolved the mortar of trust, belief in institutions, and shared stories that had held a large and diverse secular democracy together…Platforms like Twitter devolve into the Wild West, with no accountability for vigilantes."

So here we are, two decades into the twenty-first century: back in the Wild West. Some of us literally living here; all of us, across America, here in Haidt's metaphorical sense. The Wild West implies lawlessness. The expression itself is, of course, another instance of mythic labeling, as you've read about here. But what we are facing today, the sum of our new realities, is truly wild. Out here in the geographical West we are challenged by drought, fire, environmental and cultural pressures from the wealthy, politicians bowing to extremism, growing inequities, and fracturing communities. Also, not least of all, the people deluded by Wild West fantasies, who put our communities, our lands, and our wildlife at risk. Some of these myths are crushing us. If we are ever going to tackle this whole pile of issues and challenges that impact our beloved West and the United States, it's going to take healthy communities and trusting relationships. Politics, technology, industry, and reforms are not solving our problems. As people lose faith in institutions, and our democracy hangs in the balance, we need to engage with one another, build rapport, act with compassion, and listen.

—   —   —

RAY AND RESA ROETHLE LIVE DOWN A QUIET COUNTY ROUTE outside Glendive, Montana, among family farms watered by the wide and mighty Yellowstone River. I sat down with them over coffee in their kitchen on a sunny summer day. Ray and Resa had left Bozeman and moved to a tidy little farm in eastern Montana. The Roethles don't have animals anymore. Their horses had to be put down a few years ago because the animals were caught in an awful storm that pummeled them with softball-size hail. It broke their hearts. Both have grown ever more worried about politics and polarization, and they don't have a lot of hope. We didn't agree on politics, but we really liked one another. We talked over coffee about how Bozeman has changed, about growing up in this town when its roads weren't yet paved, about the sky-high housing prices of today. I asked if they were hopeful about anything. They laughed, an uneasy sort of laugh, and said they really weren't. This was something, something saddening, I heard a lot in my discussions. Me, on the other hand, I've grown more hopeful. I'm not sure what has happened to us as a region, a nation, a world, but I know that sitting with Ray and Resa Roethle, in some ways so very different from me, made me happy—just to be in their company. And with the happiness came hope.

Writer Chris La Tray, the irritable but wise Métis, said it well when he gave me the following example. "Look at my neighbor across the street. He's got Trump stickers and I see him carrying his guns in and out of his house to his car to go to the shooting range. It's easy to judge the guy for that. But then I remember a couple years ago, when this other neighbor, who has since moved, got her power shut off. She wasn't going to be able to pay her bill until Monday and this is like a Friday evening, and the Trump guy's wife comes over." She asked La Tray if he had any long extension cords. Extension cords? "We're going to run power to her house," the woman said. "So that's what we did." He continued, "I see the dude out with his dogs, and I can tell he loves his dogs, and his dogs love him, right? So, I'm thinking we have more in common than not! When did we decide," La Tray asked, "that Fox-News–inflamed garbage opinions are going to matter more between us than all of this other stuff? I think we have looney tunes, but for the most part, I think we all have way more in common than we don't."

— — —

I STARTED RESEARCHING THIS BOOK BY ASKING MYSELF, "Who cares what people believe?" and have found that the answer is complicated, because it really does matter. People's values, whether religious or political, become their truths. I feel all the more strongly now, at the end of this project, that dialogue is a way to sort some of this out—the confusions, the facts, the manipulations, and the nuances. I'm not saying everyone should be listened to—there are real bad guys out there who do not deserve the time of day—but I do believe that we will not move beyond our entrenched positions unless we spend time with those who do not see eye to eye with us. It's crucial to hear people from their own mouths, not from memes. Social media can make us stupid, lazy, and stunted. In our current situation, some politicians pit us against each other; corporate media profits off of us; QAnon and other forms of nonsense take us hostage; communities fall victim to ugly influences; and our country stays vulnerable to authoritarianism. We have so much in common as humans, as westerners, as Americans. We face the same problems—fire, drought, floods, housing prices, the influx of the monied buying up this place, and increasing radicalization. We also walk among the same myths. La Tray's question is apt: When did we chuck our common sense and neighborliness for nonstop inflamed, divisive, and disembodied bombast?

Americans, like me, living west of the 100th meridian may live in a western myth museum, though we ourselves are not displays. We are not fixed. We are not stuffed, mute, or unmoving. We are able to communicate and take action. Myths can be examined, understood, but never quite sidestepped in a place steeped in them. We live with them. Truths can be found in the stories and perspectives of others. Falsehoods can be challenged with civil debate while rapport can be created among those with differing ideas. As I've watched what has been happening—politics mired in partisan gridlock, amoral political candidates winning primaries, social media platforms pandering to the grubbiest of trolls, education programs bereft of funding and support—I've felt discouraged. But we can't count on righting any of this if we remain politically and culturally isolated. In building connections, and confronting our own blind sides, we might escape the boundaries foisted on us by those who like us sequestered and spitting mad. We're in this together as westerners and as Americans, no matter our political views. In the midst of innumerable concerns, we have no choice but to face them together. No, we didn't step aboard Noah's ark 6,000 years ago. But nonetheless, here we all are, stuck in the same boat. To keep afloat, we're going to need one another.

Coda

I SPOKE TO SO MANY PEOPLE WHILE RESEARCHING THIS book, and I want you to hear from some of the folks who have challenged my thinking and deepened my understanding about the West. There is no "last word" to be had—not by me, not by anyone. So instead of leaving you with *the end*, I am inviting you into community. We will find our way in conversation or over a meal, one relationship at a time, each one an opportunity to create our future.

CHARLIE CRAWFORD AND CHELSIA RICE ESTABLISHED A haven that has become essential to the community of Helena, Montana. Over wine and charcuterie in the upstairs floor of their business, I came to understand the role their inclusive bookstore, the Montana Book Company, played during the crushing isolation of pandemic. It is truly a place of intersects. If you visit, which I wholeheartedly recommend, you might meet a rancher, a retired police officer, a real estate broker, the director of an environmental organization, a working mom, or even a logger-cum-writer who occasionally skydives with Russian cosmonauts. The first time I visited their store, I met all of the above.

Crawford and Rice both feel the obligation to put themselves on the line for causes they believe in, especially social justice and the

LGBTQ community. "You gotta get up, you gotta be here, you gotta keep doing this. People are counting on you," Crawford said. The bookstore serves as a refuge for queer kids, especially those whose parents aren't supportive of them. Crawford knows this pain firsthand, having gone through this lack of acceptance with their own family. The couple is very open with their activism—above their shelves of books hang rainbow flags and Black Lives Matter banners. "I'm just like waiting for someone to throw a big brick through the window," Crawford told me. In 2021, after reading signs posted in their window—one welcoming all races, religions, and sexual orientations and another asking that people wear their masks—an older man yanked open the front door and yelled, "You are the most intolerant tolerant bookstore ever!"

Former Montana governor Steve Bullock shops at their bookstore and so does the current governor Greg Gianforte's wife, Susan. As you may recall, the Gianforte Foundation helped to fund the Glendive Dinosaur and Fossil Museum and supports other causes such as Grace Bible Church and the Alliance Defending Freedom, both with strong anti-LGBTQ positions. He also just signed a law banning medical gender-affirming care for transgender youth. "I really don't know why she shops here," Rice said. "I'll ask her next time she comes in!" she added. That's a conversation I'd like to hear.

MICHAEL CANTRELL-SMITH WAS RAISED BY A SINGLE MOM who depended on the Loon Lake Food Bank and Resource Center in Washington, where he now works. Growing up, after an accident "broke every bone" in his father's body and resulted in an addiction to painkillers, Cantrell-Smith and his mom were left to fend for themselves. He still lives with her and now his stepfather. At twenty-six years old, Cantrell-Smith is a kind man with long, light brown hair and a love for transcendentalism and the writings of Ralph Waldo Emerson. During the first year of the pandemic, he served as a lifeline to his community, becoming the only other person many interacted with. The food pantry building was closed to the public, but services continued as folks queued up in cars outside, awaiting supplies. Having grown up here, he knows almost everyone and took time to check in with the clients as they sat in their vehicles. His supervisor finally asked him to keep conversations brief amid lines of traffic. As the largest food pantry in Stevens County, the facility stayed busy—those in need doubled during 2020. "We never ran out of toilet paper," Cantrell-Smith bragged. Volunteers, many of whom I was able to watch in action as they filled boxes with bread, meat, fruit, and dairy, are a tight-knit group. They work together a couple of days a week in the close quarters of their warehouse. All keep to topics that don't ruffle feathers. "I couldn't tell you who's a Democrat or Republican," Cantrell-Smith told me. His coworkers got along just fine during the early years of the second decade of the twenty-first century. They focused not on polarized politics, but a community in need.

ANGELINA GONZÁLEZ-ALLER, A QUICK-WITTED BEAUTY WITH a PhD in political science and government, currently helms the Montana Human Rights Network. She grew up in New Mexico, and talks a mile a minute, pivoting between quips and incisive observation. One evening in 2021, we sat in my backyard and talked about her work in conservation and justice and my own research for this book. We both agreed in a need to better engage with rural people in the West. She comes from a family of many conservatives she doesn't always agree with, but she knows that no matter what, political divisiveness would never stop them from coming to her aid. "If I ever broke down in, say, Boise at three a.m.," she told me, "they'd drive all night to help out and never ask for a thing in return. My liberal friends might come get me," she said with a laugh, "but then they'd send me their Venmo account."

LIL ERICKSON FOUNDED THE WESTERN SUSTAINABILITY Exchange in 1994 to educate ranchers on working in balance with nature "to leave a healthier landscape for future generations." She invited me on a tour of the Crazy D Ranch north of Big Timber, Montana, where we spent an afternoon walking a windswept property with a stunning view of the Crazy Mountains. Hilary Zaranek-Anderson, ranch co-manager along with her husband, discussed their mission to a group of about twenty of us, explaining that the ranch had been devoted exclusively to beef production until she realized that this approach was "really contradictory to a nature-first approach." By that, she meant raising cows in ways that deplete natural systems wasn't doing the land any favors. "We had to flip our paradigm to 'how are we going to adjust ourselves to serve the land? As opposed to 'how is the land going to serve us?'"

Zaranek-Anderson and her husband, Andrew Anderson, turned to beetles and beavers. Teaming with the University of Guelph, in Canada, they're working to create a library of bugs. According to the Western Sustainability Exchange website, as "bugs are cataloged, [the ranch team] will set up traps and monitor the insect activity before, during, and after the cattle graze, which will tell them if they are increasing or decreasing bug species throughout the grazing season." There is an imbalance of dung beetle species on the property, curbing healthy soil production, and the managers are trying to figure out why. They've stopped using "pour-on and other pesticides."

The Andersons are also paying close attention to beavers. As drought bears down on the West, protecting water sources is imperative. Until recently, beavers were trapped on the property but now the animals have reestablished themselves and their dams are creating wetlands as waters spill from the creek. "When we came here three years ago, there was not a single piece of wood in the creek, not a single sign of beaver except for some old chewing," Zaranek-Anderson told us. Now that the population has returned, "the amount of water that we're capturing and holding is so exciting."

Joining us on the tour that day was a ranch manager for the new Yellowstone Club property, whose investors recently purchased the nearby Crazy Mountain Ranch. It remains to be seen if their new property will be managed with "nature first," rather than luxury first. The acquisition is extremely controversial in the area and for good reason with their track record in the Spanish Peaks. Serving the land has hardly been the mission for their exclusive gated compound outside Yellowstone National Park nor has creating ties with surrounding communities. So far, they've promised folks around the Crazy Mountains that heli-skiing and subdivision, two of the locals' greatest fears, will not happen. The holding company behind the purchase, Cross-Harbor, has said they will operate as a ranch and a resort—no permanent residents, only visiting Club members. It was encouraging to have the manger join us on the tour, but will we be seeing lip service or any sort of paradigm shift? I'm eager to hear Lil Erickson's take when I next catch up with her—the impact of the rich on the Crazies remains to be seen.

I VISITED WITH JERRY AND LINDA WERNICK IN A LIVING ROOM looking out on their land a stone's throw from the Canadian border. It's remote and hard to find unless you know where you're going. The property is crisscrossed by trails that wind through giant pines connecting greenhouses to a main residence. The couple lives off the grid in this corner of northern Montana; their house, where they raised a family, is hand built. Practicing Seventh-day Adventists, the couple ran Tamarack Springs Academy for decades, teaching kids a religiously infused curriculum. They're now retired. Both are vegetarians and grow most of their own food after turning their old school rooms into hothouses big enough even for fruit trees. Olives, figs, and lemons drag at the branches in their indoor orchards. On my first visit there, I ate the best apricot I'd ever tasted.

Sitting together, the three of us discussed everything from vaccines (both are inoculated—their daughter, a doctor, advised them to protect themselves) to the origins of the earth (both put the age at around six thousand years). Although the Wernicks' property is situated in a forested region seeing an ever-increasing number of fires, including one in 2018 that threatened their own land, Jerry expressed skepticism about climate change. "I know if you ask most environmentalists, it's settled the science." But he thinks that carbon and methane are too often blamed for climate change when "actually, the greenhouse effect is caused mostly by water vapor." Urban living—from the cutting of trees to the paving of streets—is to blame for increasing temperatures, he contended. Indeed, urban spaces sometimes measure ten degrees hotter than rural counterparts and create heat islands, but urban living can actually make a smaller carbon footprint. Some people mistakenly believe water vapor is the main driver of earth's current warming since it's the most abundant greenhouse gas and it is increasing. But increased water vapor doesn't cause global warming; it's a consequence of it because increased water vapor in the atmosphere amplifies the warming caused by other greenhouse gases. Spending so much time in greenhouses, Jerry must certainly know the impact of heat on water. Still, it seems that his way of understanding rising temperatures must, to him, justify his lifestyle choice—far away from urban ills in an Edenic off-the-grid compound, growing fruit trees in old classrooms of a now-shuttered religious school.

JIM THOMAS INVITED ME TO HIS CABIN OUTSIDE HELENA, Montana, at the end of a dirt road, where he lives with Patty Butterfield. They share the place with a horse, two dogs, a cat, and hundreds of swallows nesting in their barn. After thirty-year marriages to other people ended, they met on Match.com. Thomas first contacted me on social media to make sure I was safe after he read some of the work I've done on militia. He still checks in periodically via DM. It was smoky the day I hung out with him on his porch, on his property surrounded by public land. Dogs get abandoned out here all of the time, he lamented—his place is the last bit of private acreage before everything becomes national forest. We talked about his career as a cop, his childhood in Alabama, and his experience as a young man running with the bulls in Pamplona. Butterfield came out to greet me wearing a Blitzen Trapper T-shirt, a favorite band of hers, long silver hair about her shoulders. Both are over six feet tall.

Thomas moved to Montana in 1981 after participating in military training exercises here that included jumping out of a C-130 cargo plane. "We were doing stuff on dams, how to blow-up, how to defend, stuff like that." It was the state's beauty and libertarian culture that beckoned, though the latter no longer appeals. "I was all into it...I guess when you're young and you're healthy and you're cocky and arrogant, that philosophy kind of makes sense," he said. "Your rugged-individualism-type stuff. But it's not real. You get sick, I mean." He told me that Gofundme.com was a national safety net for health care—a third of their campaigns are for raising money for medical expenses. In other words, libertarianism has its shortcomings.

A buddy talked Thomas into being a police officer and he served for twenty years, finally retiring as a captain. He then worked on the nearby Grady Ranch, haying and moving cows. There are wolves in the area but Thomas said that they aren't an issue—he's only heard of one wolf killing livestock since he'd lived out here. We talked about the campaign to defund the police and racism in the force, two topics that were flooding social media and making headlines. He worries about racism that he sees. After Barack Obama was elected, "I thought it was going away, but it isn't," he said quietly. As far as the death of George Floyd and calls to defund the police, he thinks the phrase is tricky, but that the concept is worth consideration. Funding could be funneled from law enforcement budgets to mental health programs, he offered.

Thomas knows there are problems with policing in America. "Look at the data, from the traffic stops, all the way through—the arrest, the detainment, the courts, the judiciary, and then into corrections, then out of correction probation…People of color are treated differently than white people are treated. It's factual—the data, Department of Justice, has the information." His nephew thinks racism is no longer an issue in America. "I'm like, 'Buddy, you don't know what you're talking about!'" While they were discussing the matter a while back, his nephew said something that stuck with him. "I will always remember. When we were arguing about politics he said, 'Uncle Jim, you need to quit hiding behind the facts.'" He laughed and shook his head.

DAVE STRICKLAN WANTS TO ESTABLISH A NEW NATIONAL preserve. The site is near Arco, the little LDS town where he grew up, in eastern Idaho. I bounced along with him on dirt roads in his bright red Jeep as he gave me a tour. Our first stop was a canyon beyond a cattle gate, where he pointed out ash on a rock wall from an ancient cooking fire.

With the establishment of this preserve, Stricklan, working with the Sagebrush Habitat Conservation Fund, wants to retire all of the public grazing allotments in the area. He feels confident that he can talk the folks who have leases into a compensated withdrawal. He's known these ranchers all his life. They went to high school together. "I've dated all their wives," he told me, chuckling. Stricklan explained the many reasons grazing is problematic in this ecosystem. Extermination of wild predators is part of the price of public lands grazing. So is the befouling of springs and wetlands, invasive species in overgrazed areas, and destructive impacts on insect populations. He also mentioned the pressures put on sage grouse, a bird species that many environmental organizations throughout the West are worried about.

The greater sage grouse is a marvelous critter with a spiky set of brown and white tail feathers. Every spring, males gather in groups called leks, to dance for the females. Inflating two air sacs on their torsos, the randy fellas lurch upward, push their bulging chests out, and warble their songs. When females take notice, it's business time. But despite this annual bacchanal, grouse numbers have plummeted. Under threat from climate change, oil and gas development, and grazing, their population numbers have decreased an estimated 95 percent in the states they inhabit, including Washington, Oregon, Nevada, Wyoming, Idaho, Montana, eastern California, Utah, Colorado, North and South Dakota, and Nebraska. Federal conservation regulations targeting grazing practices to protect these ground dwellers chafe western ranchers. That's one of the reasons Stricklan is working to establish this protected area and restrict grazing.

Cattle, he explained, remove the grass cover and the understory cover, so that there isn't protection for either the birds or their food. Grouse nibble sagebrush and the bugs that tangle in limbs. "If there aren't small insects for the chicks to eat in the first week of their life," they can starve. In grazing operations, water is diverted to cattle rather than native species. "After sage grouse fledge, the offspring need wet meadows in the sagebrush," he told me. Insects do as well. But with cattle operations in the arid West, all of the water available, either running water or whatever is captured, goes to livestock. Seeps dry up, leaving birds and insects on parched lands. "It's a habitat thing," he explained. Cows compete for moisture in this place that receives little rain, and wildlife suffers.

Since my tour, Strickland told me he's making progress on his plan and is in partnership with Rewilding Europe and the American Museum of Natural History. He urged me to come back and stay in guest cabins they are acquiring. He also sent me a sneak peek of a video in development. The footage included elk herds, bighorn sheep, a lazuli bunting, wolf tracks in fresh snow, two burrowing owls, and a handsome sage grouse, resplendent in his feathered ruff. Hello ladies!

TRAVIS MCADAM AND CHERILYN DEVRIES OF THE MONTANA Human Rights Network told me about their work in tracking white supremacy, militia maneuvering, and countering hate. We compared notes in my backyard, swapping stories and exchanging jokes—both are incredibly funny despite their challenging work. DeVries has been helpful to me over the last years on how to discuss threats of radicalization. She's a great resource and has become a pal.

McAdam, who has researched extremism in Montana since the 1990s, is a bona fide authority. When I asked him about outsiders bringing radical ideologies to communities in the West, he explained, "It's interesting to think about why people move here. I think you have absolutely either the conscious or subconscious white flight mentality from places like California. Those folks move up here. They have money, they buy land. They build big houses. When you look at the American Redoubt, it's basically the most recent relocation strategy for this area of the country." He went on to talk about the roots of white nationalism in the region, telling me that when he gives presentations on radicalization, he starts "with Richard Butler moving up from California starting the Aryan Nations compound in the '70s. You get the whole NW Territorial Imperative [a separatist movement in the 1970s-1980s spearheaded by neo-Nazis and white nationalists] thing that's very much just a blatant white Aryan homeland, a white ethnostate idea, that sort of mutates over time and obviously strategically doesn't work."

He described the recruiting process in this movement, using the Kalispell Pioneer Little Europe as an example. "A lot of the people are drawn in" by the ideology perpetuated by white supremacists, resulting in "a kind of a mix. Some people do have money and resources, but you also literally have people who exist at such a basic level that they read something one day and they can literally throw everything that they own in their vehicle and drive up," he said. Kalispell Pioneer Little Europe was one such iteration of white homeland conceived in the 2000s by April Gaede, a neo-Nazi who grew up on a ranch in Fresno, California, with a dad who branded his cows with swastikas. Gaede moved to Montana in 2006 and worked for years to attract white, ideologically aligned people to the Flathead Valley. In comments with filmmaker Louis Theroux in 2003, she said, "I find other races annoying...I don't like their chattering in other languages, I don't like the way they look. I mean, 99 percent of them, they're just not pretty. I don't want to be around them. I don't like the fact they seem to make everything just dirty and messy wherever they are...I want to be around all white people."

According to McAdams, Gaede's vision didn't really pan out. "She came to the conclusion like, 'Huh, I'm not really attracting a real high-caliber type of person,'" he said, acutely aware of the irony. Even she was "kind of shocked," he said, by the people who showed up. Like David Joseph Lenio. Recruited in 2015, he tweeted he wanted to murder a rabbi and kill one hundred schoolchildren "until cops take me out." On his Facebook page he wrote, "Seriously I think it would b [sic] hilarious if someone beat the sandy hoax school shooting spree high score in kalispell Montana cuz I'm too poor." He was arrested but the Flathead County prosecutor didn't try the case. High caliber indeed.

McAdam told me that Gaede is no longer active in the movement. She still lives in Kalispell as do her daughters, Dresdan, Lynx, and Lamb. The latter two are twins who saw brief fame in the 2000s with their singing group Prussian Blue, named after the color of the pesticide used in gas chambers in concentration camps. In a follow-up interview with documentarian Theroux in 2020, the women, now in their thirties, call themselves pot-smoking, liberal hippies who have renounced their years as young white supremacists and Holocaust deniers. They still live in Kalispell, as does their mother.

IN THE LAST COUPLE OF YEARS, MY PALS JON COLEMAN AND Ixtla Vaughan have moved to Stevens County, Washington. Vaughan's stepfather, Gary Hemingway (no relation to the writer), whom everyone calls Gar, and her mom, Carol, retired here years ago after careers as public defenders in Spokane. They now live in a large wooden home with plenty of bedrooms for visiting friends, children, and great-grandchildren. Together the family shares one hundred acres just up from Mike Pickering's place, a neighbor who grew up nearby and knows everyone around, their family histories, and the best places to hunt, fish, and go berry-picking.

On one visit in 2021, when Vaughan was at her office—she's a graphic designer who works remotely for the company Pacifica Beauty—I chatted with Pickering and Coleman about soaring temperatures, which that year had reached 113. "Yeah. I mean it was like five or six days I think over 100 and that's so unusual," Pickering said. We went on to discuss recent wolf activity, which Pickering is lukewarm about. They are reestablishing themselves in the area, much to the chagrin of many locals. Pickering worries about impacts on game animal populations and is a bit piqued that the canids can't be easily watched. "It's not like you can view a nocturnal animal, you know, like at state parks or Yellowstone." (Wolves are active at night, but are actually crepuscular, meaning most active at dawn and dusk.)

Pickering is a solid, good-natured man, who first eyed me suspiciously from his truck while I fussed over Wiley, the Hemingways' dog, on a lonely dirt road by the family's property. He later confessed he'd thought that I might be trying to steal the darling, furry rogue. For twenty-five years, he's worked for Avista, a utility company providing electricity and natural gas in Oregon, Idaho, and eastern Washington. Coleman has worked for the US Census Bureau. They both told me about people who become murderous when these men try to do their jobs. Pickering checks meters and Coleman surveyed door-to-door. At one point, Coleman arrived at a property and noticed a sign on the fence that read, "I have the right to uphold the Constitution of the Second Amendment." The sign indicated this guy would "do anything to uphold the Constitution, so I snapped photos on my phone of the Constitution," Coleman said. "The census is one of the primary things in the writing [in the Constitution]. I was already prepared" when he went to the man's door to ask him census questions. (The US Constitution sanctions Congress to hold a census in "such manner as they shall by Law direct" (Article I, Section 2).) When Coleman tried to make his case that the census was a part of this man's beloved Constitution, it made no difference. "He pretty much started off with get off my property and I'm going to get my gun. I tried to explain to him that by completing the census, roads, schools, and other public services... would benefit him and his family. He was pretty angry the moment I got there." Stevens County, a central American Redoubt stronghold, is full of people who do not want others in their business, nor do they want anyone contradicting their understanding of rights or reality, no matter what the Constitution says. And many do not want anyone working for the government on their properties.

DUVAL EULAND, ONE OF TWO BLACK MEN LIVING IN FOR-syth, Montana, moved out west because he fell in love with the mountains. When he arrived in the town of Forsyth on the Yellowstone River, home to about 1,600 folks, he felt embraced by the tiny community. He works for a fiber optics company and is a proud father of two girls. Euland showed me one daughter's college acceptance letter when I met with him in the lobby of an apartment building across the street from a favorite haunt, the Joseph Café. Topped by a camo bucket hat with a Louisiana State logo, Euland told me how he got from the South to the West. "Three years ago, I went to Grand Teton, you know, Yellowstone, things of this nature, way, way different than the city." He said he'd "tried to move to Portland, Oregon, find a job and just connect with the outdoors." That didn't work out and he kept looking.

When pandemic hit, the West also appealed because of the low COVID numbers. "In my mind, I was thinking more or less, the rural area is not as affected as the big city. But, I knew that coming here…I guess the mentality towards COVID probably wasn't what I would like it to be," he said, referring to the skepticism that affected many people in rural communities and kept vaccine rates way down. "I was vaccinated, fully vaccinated," he said, but "I was the only one at work wearing a mask. That's what my daughters, they're [sic] afraid of… they're like, 'Oh, God, you're going to this place.'" In addition to COVID considerations, his girls worried that Montana was only 0.5 percent Black. "Listen, so I've lived all over the world, you know. You're not going to escape, if that's your fear of white people. I grew up kind of like…Black people have fucked me over and I've had a couple of things where white people have tried the same."

When Black Lives Matter rallies were making daily headlines, one guy approached Euland in a grocery store and asked him to explain the violence he was seeing on his nightly news. This irked Euland. "Forsyth only got like one Black person here," before he moved there. "So, why would the people be aggravated or fearful of Black people...I mean, where are they getting this information from? Are they getting it from news?" he asked me rhetorically. We both knew the answer. "I don't know what they're fearful of, but when I talk about the guy at the IGA," he said, that man was ready for agitators who might find their way into rural Montana. He told Euland that "A bunch of people here in Forsyth have guns" and "we're not going to let anybody overtake us." Euland was left incredulous. That all said, the town has been a good place to be, he told me, and the people he worked with have been welcoming. But he couldn't believe that anyone in their right mind would fear Antifa in this little white rural town.

"DID I TELL YOU I GOT MY LEG CUT OFF ON CHRISTMAS?" Vincent Easley asked me when we last spoke on the phone. Easley, who runs Real Liberty Media, is an ardent supporter of the Bundy family who has an enviable gift of gab. Incarcerated at the age of fifteen for armed robbery, he's not had an easy life, but over the decades he's found exhilaration in exploring the West and in telling stories of the Patriot movement on his podcast, A Ponder/Gander. His leg was amputated due to an infection and diabetes, he told me, but he's hardly slowed down. After our first conversation, he sent me a video of him dancing on one leg as Ram Jam sang "Oh Black Betty" from his truck speaker. Easley has great sympathy for rebels, no love for the government and he is open, considered, smart, and delightful to talk with. He also has a penchant for weed. I'm not sure we will see eye to eye on grazing, public lands, or what constitutes lawlessness, but I really enjoy keeping in touch with him. We've talked about many topics on which we find common ground. His irrepressible joy always brings a smile to my face and I'm very happy we're friends.

JENELLE JOHNSON HAS A LONG HISTORY IN BIG SKY, MONtana. As a visitor in the early 1990s, she became a full-time resident in 2014 with her husband, Fred. He started skiing there when founder and former newscaster Chet Huntley was still alive—he died in 1974. Huntley once predicted the resort would one day be "the greatest thing that ever happened to Montana…bigger and better than Aspen, Vail, Sun Valley." Well, *the greatest thing?* I guess it depends on whom you ask.

The two of us had breakfast together in the Town Center, a "Main Street" type of development in a resort that was never a town before it became a ski destination, just home to a few loggers and ranchers on checkerboarded lands. While I gobbled my piece of avocado toast in its entirety, Johnson carefully carved a circle in the middle, eating the inside, and leaving the rest. A slight woman, who is both engaging and warm, she loves this place but has enormous concerns about its growth. Serving on the Gallatin River Task Force, pollution is a major worry for her, as is community planning in the case of an emergency. As of now, there is no fire plan in a place surrounded by forest with only two routes of escape—US 191, to Four Corners of Yellowstone National Park, and Jack Creek Road, to Ennis. She said, "I mean we're all concerned if there's a big wildfire that comes through this area—there is no evacuation plan. They're working on it but how are we all gonna get out of here? God forbid the road gets shut down…I mean people are really concerned about safety." If a fire burned near the resort, traffic from tourists, workers, and residents of Big Sky and the Yellowstone Club, could clog routes as people rushed to evacuate. Currently there isn't a designated shelter in town.

The issue is particularly scary. In the summer of 2021, a million acres burned down in Montana, though when we met, in 2022, the fire season had been a quiet one. Still, the danger is a real worry in a community so vulnerable to fire as well as to economic inequality. "There are about sixty people living in the Big Sky who are living out of a car or a vehicle or camping," she told me. "We had a situation last summer where somebody was camping near the South Fork on Gray Drake," a place near her home. "A fire was started and we thought the whole neighborhood was gonna go up in flames." She continued, "there was somebody who was camping," and "set up a campsite in an open space. They had set up snowboarding rails [and] they had a bonfire area and a campsite." A police sergeant discovered the bonfire and asked the people camped there to find another spot. "You know people don't intend to start a fire, [they] don't understand. I mean, fire is so dangerous."

She went on to tell me about her experience in Big Sky and the influx of people. Lift lines have gotten longer on the mountains and development has exploded. Still, she says, tourists are friendly. "I was riding a chairlift the other day with a guy who was staying here for the winter from California and, you know, he just he [sic] wanted to make sure that that he fit in…He was kind of concerned that people were going to see his California license plate," she explained, then treat him with scorn.

"But I haven't really encountered people that are mean [to out-of-staters]," she told me, maybe because there aren't really any locals since so many folks moved here from other places. Big Sky was never a town before Huntley's dream, so there isn't a population that has long ties to the area. And so many towns in Montana are filling with newcomers, so it really isn't unique to Big Sky.

The Johnsons have lived all over the world, from Singapore to Moscow. "We were expats when we moved to Big Sky," she said. "Everybody was welcoming and adventurous…We sort of felt like we were expatriates again, which was kind of fun." In spite of being an outsider, she is very invested in the place and strives to create community. In addition to serving on the Gallatin River Task Force, when she's not skiing, hiking, or traveling, she also serves on her homeowner's association board and volunteers for the Big Sky Community Organization and the Arts Council of Big Sky. She loves it here and in spite of the concerns over safety and pressures on the Gallatin River, she's very glad to call Big Sky home.

IN 2020, WRITER REBECCA STANFEL MOVED OUT OF HER OWN house for months to avoid COVID. Her husband, Jay, a lawyer, and her son, Andrew, a high school student, had to be out in the world, and she had to isolate. She had moved back home when we connected in her living room in August of 2021 to talk over her circumstances. "I was diagnosed seventeen years ago with an inflammatory disease called sarcoidosis. I was thirty-four and it just kind of hopscotched through my body and it now is in my heart. It was in my brain," she explained. "I went, I don't know, how many years of chemo? Five? Seven? Months in the hospital." But in the years just prior to pandemic, Stanfel had improved. "In the strange way that immune diseases work, I've been feeling a lot better. I'm still on pretty heavy immunosuppressants though," she said. "I had these periods of a couple years of getting better and being able to return to things I love, hiking, backpacking. I wept when I was able to get back on top of Mount Helena." When COVID hit, her specialist told her a case could be a major threat to her health. He recommended that either "you, your son, and husband not leave the house, or you need to create a space separately."

During 2020-2021, she watched while people bucked protocols. Protests over the state's mask mandate, as well as the anti-vaxxers, conspiracy theorists, and COVID deniers were both weird and scary.

To see "this radicalization happen around these issues that seem so common sense" was exhausting to her. "The capitol is like a couple miles from here and they're burning masks over there. Parents last year were storming the stadium where the football team played...I mean it just doesn't feel like the Helena I've lived in for nearly a quarter of a century!"

She was one of the first in the state to be vaccinated but wasn't sure if it would work. She finally did get COVID a year after we met. The day she tested positive, Stanfel later told me, she was treated with monoclonal antibodies and recovered. In the meantime, she has become quite active with the Montana Jewish Project. She joked that she's bumping into some of the same folks I write about—antisemites and trolls. Hate and COVID conspiracy theories have oddly braided together in extremist culture. Her organization had just bought the Temple Emanu-El, the first synagogue in Montana, built in 1891. In the days of the gold rush in Montana's Last Chance Gulch, the Jewish community in Helena had been well-established. Montana's governor laid the cornerstone of the synagogue with the Hebrew date 5651 during a huge celebration attended by a crowd of Jews and non-Jews from around the northwest. The temple was sold during the Depression, but thanks to Stanfel and her organization, it now is back in the hands of a growing Jewish community in Helena. In 2022, for the first time in ninety years, the menorah was lit at Temple Emanu-El.

JON MARVEL, FOUNDER OF THE WESTERN WATERSHEDS Project, told me about grazing allotments that he helped retire and half-playfully admonished me for being too sympathetic to ranchers. I sat down with him and one of his organization's longtime supporters, my dear friend, Ann Down. A few months later, Jon and his wife Stefanie came to see me give an atrocious talk (I froze mid-way through—sorry everyone!) in Stanley, Idaho, where they live, then we all shared dinner at the gorgeous Red Fish Lake Lodge. He's one of the funniest humans I know, having charmed me thirty years ago when I met him at the Teller Wildlife Refuge in the Bitterroot Valley at a big fundraiser for a regional conservation group. He's also pretty ruthless in his campaigns against public land grazing. *Range Magazine* called his tactics "scorched earth and uncompromising," but I can assure you, when he wants to be, he is generous, warm, and a really good dancer.

I HEARD FROM CRAIG SMART ONE AFTERNOON IN 2021 AT Glendive's Beer Jug, across the street from the old train depot where he used to work. He never expected to end up here in this town. As a student at the University of Missouri, drinking beers and "smoking left-handed cigarettes," he really had no idea on a direction. He recalled taking one class in fashion merchandising, thinking he'd skate. Just days before his final project was due—he'd decided to sew a pair of coveralls—he turned to a few smitten gals to help him. "I wasn't Brad Pitt or anything, but I did okay," he told me. He passed the class thanks to them. Still, and to his father's dismay, Smart was offered a job on the railroad before he graduated from Mizzou. "I got a phone call that said, 'Be here on Monday morning.' So I took a 1973 Opel GT and traded that in for a '73 Dodge pickup. I had a twenty-five-dollar camper shell. I had three shotguns. One .22 rifle. Five or six frying pans, my clothes, and add a black-and-white TV about as big as my head. I moved out here and I thought I'll be under six months—a year. Then I'll go back to college."

But he was wrong. He stayed in Glendive. "This has been a great existence. I raised three great kids here. They have a public education here. They all came out with flying colors. They all graduated. They were all on the honor roll. They all three maintain pretty good jobs.

They're semi-successful, have semi-normal friends, and all three will be married as of the twenty-second of next month. I can't imagine raising a family anywhere else but here and I'm not saying that because you're asking questions. I would say that to anybody." We walked out of the cool dim of the bar and into the bright midday sun, and I bid farewell to this man living a good life in a good place. Then I got in my car and headed back to my own well-loved home.

Acknowledgments

So many people have helped with bringing this book into the world. My husband has patiently read through draft after draft offering endless counsel—he is truly an angel and I am so lucky to share my life with him. My dad, Gene Gaines, whom I adore, read it twice and helped me square up wobbly bits. Kirsten Johanna Allen, my cherished editor, was so kind to me during my most nervous moments, reading the manuscript more times than she bargained for because of my endless additions and edits. Also, Will Neville-Rehbehn, thank you from the bottom of my heart for your support and confidence. Lynda Sexson, a dear, wise friend and former advisor/professor at Montana State University, sat down with me twice a week in 2022 so we could read our projects to one another—she helped me immeasurably. Marta Tarbell, my funny, brutally honest former editor from the *Telluride Times Tribune* days gave me incredible advice on direction and content. Rebecca Watters, the brilliant biologist and great pal, offered so much helpful feedback and edits. Don Snow, another wonderful former professor, gave me amazing suggestions on framing mythology and made this book better.

I can't thank Sean Beckett and Julie Dahinden enough. They were my sounding boards, stalwart friends, and some favorite diversions during the bumpy years of the early 2020s. I am so blessed to have these two in my life and I treasure them. This goes as well for Ixtla Vaughn, Gary and Carole Hemingway, Jon Coleman, Robin Chopus and Ann Down for being beloved friends and offering generous room, board, and laughter. Blake Spaulding and Maggie McGuane were there at all hours of the night to check in—thank God! A heartfelt tip of the hat to my crew: Katie Gaines Madison, Lily and Mae Madison, Amy Stix, Claire Sands Baker, Gigi Aelbers, Faye Nelson, Lynn Donaldson, Ryan Newcomb, Danielle Girard, Suzanne Truman, Sebastian Suhl, Sabrina Lee, Doug and Andrea Peacock, Cora Neuman, Kristi Chester Vance, Cara Wilder, Judith Heilman, Gilly Lyons, Kirsten Leonard, and Hannah Stebbins. Thank you Scout Invie, Gray Buck-Cockayne, Kathleen Metcalf, Michaela Bown, Erin Sells, and Anne Terashima for helping to midwife this project! You are the best team ever!

Austin Schoenkopf graciously read chapters and workshopped my introduction with the fabulous Montana State University history graduate students. Peggy Grove, Martha Williams, Jenny Emery Davidson, Carter Hedberg, and the Ketchum Community Library made my stay at the Ernest and Mary Hemingway House residency a once in a lifetime experience. Shout outs to all my friends in Blaine County, Idaho—Greg Carr, Clare Swanger, Melinda and Dick Springs, Jeannie Cassell, Jorjan Sarich, Bob Probasco, Sharon Bockemohle, Mardi Shepard, Ingrid Gladics, Patti Lindberg, Mike and Elaine Phillips, and Julie Driver. I also want to thank Jim Grossman, who spent hours on the phone with me telling me so many stories about his home in Ketchum—you are missed.

I'm grateful to Kathleen McLaughlin, Ryan Busse, Jennifer Hilldebrandt, Chris La Tray, Hampton Sides, Beto O'Rourke, Don Snow, and Tim Cahill for reading this book and sharing your supportive words! I participated in two workshops while writing and want to thank Amy Irvine and Russell Roland for their immeasurable talent, wisdom, and encouragement. Thank you for the careful feedback from other participants: Danielle Tatsakron, Dee Metrick, J Clemens Conjure, Karen Osborne, Kate Clemm, Linda Wastilla, Peggy O'Neill Jones, Robert Hall, Suzette Roth-Jacobs, Ellen Metrick, Cara Long, Harry Greene, David Perry, Tracy Ross, Adam Sowards, Caroline Van Hemert, and Shannon Walton.

Grateful also to those who set me straight and gave me wonderful insight: Tasha Adams, Karen Munson, JT Martel, Francine Spang-Willis, Alvin Hoff, Lance Kafell, Scott Bosse, Roger Lang, Linda Owens, Gregory Graf and the lovely Andrea, and Konchog Norbu. Thank you to Leah Sotille, Tay Wiles, Daniel Walters, Shaun Vestal, Rocky Barker, Nick Bowlin, David Neiwert, Todd Wilkinson, Scott McMillion, Heath Druzin, Nick Eaton, Carl Segerstrom, Ian Max Stevenson, Anne Helen Petersen, Sam Benson, Brian Maffly, Chris D'Angelo, Tony Bynum, Lisa Rein, and Kelly Weill, James Pogue, and Antonia Hitchens for all of your insightful journalism—it's been invaluable. Also thank you A9 Collective, Southern Poverty Law Center, Mark Pitcavage, Devin Burghart, Travis McAdam, Cherilyn DeVries, and Korihor of the Deseret for your essential research!

Nothing but gratitude to those I interviewed and helped my process: David Madison, Patti Gaines, Catherine Gaines, Nancy Holland, Alexis Bonofsky, Gloria Theide, Mike Pickering, JeNelle Johnson, Charlie Crawford, Chelsia Rice, Vincent Easley, Eric Heidle, Tim Lehman, Mark Mathis, Nick Cooper, Sheryl Wright, Andrew Finstuen, Sarah Rushing, Patty Butterfield, Jim Thomas, Bart Davis, CMarie Fuhrman, Dustin Martin, John Horning, Cathy Bailey, Valerie Hemingway, Susan Brewer, Justin Fonda, Thomas McGuane, Steve and Marylou Osman, Bruce Comer and Helen Lee Comer, Gerry and Inessa Wheeler, Peter Schoenburg, Angelina Gonzalez-Aller, Gay Dillingham, Anne Butterfield, Craig Heacock, Dena Hoff, Mimi Hoff, Krista Hazel, Jay Pounder, Erik and Jamie Kalsta, Terry Sayles, Bill Symes, Robert Canen, Dena Hoff, Roger Lang, Steve Primm, Tanya

Rosen, Lisa Kalfell, Russ Schwartz, Jim and Becky Hicks, Teresa Hicks, Cathy Bailey, Thermos, Nicolas Sironka, Tuk Van Kraska, Simon Allen, Jon and Stefanie Marvel, Dave Strickland, Mike Bugenstein, Dale Galland, Flannery Freund, Jill Momaday, Kandee Degraw, Steve Henry, Duval Euland, Melani Torgersen, Alicia Abbott, Mike Satz, Shelby Rognstad, Beth Rembold, Jerry and Linda Wernick, Lil Erickson, Lisa Lenard, Michael Cantrell-Smith, Craig Smart, Rebecca Stanfel, and Rattlesnake Rita. I spent time also with many wonderful people who didn't get into the book but were generous with their time and stories: Ozzie Knezovich, Anita Tigert, Sharon Bockemohle, Tom Butts, Anna Demetriades, Tim McWilliams, John Jost, and Tyus Williams.

About the Author

Betsy Gaines Quammen is a historian and writer who examines the intersections of extremism, public lands, wildlife, and western communities. Her work has appeared in the *New York Times*, *New York Daily News*, and the *History News Network*. She received a PhD in history from Montana State University and an MS in environmental studies from University of Montana. Betsy is the author of *American Zion: Cliven Bundy, God, and Public Lands in the West* and lives in Bozeman, Montana, with her husband, writer David Quammen.

Endnotes

Note to readers: Although I have trained as a historian, this is not an academic book. That said, I've used secondary sources very sparingly. I have met and talked with over a hundred people for this book, many quotes are from my own interviews, DMs, or emails. I've also attended rallies and recorded speeches myself.

Introduction

So let's look at how myths are understood, Don Snow was so very important to the way I now understand myth myself. After reading an early draft, he suggested these versions of myth that I tailored for the narrative.

You have to know the past, Sagan, 1980.

The act was later legalized; Johnson & Graham's Lessee v. McIntosh, 21 U.S. 543 (1823) https://supreme.justia.com/cases/federal/us/21/543/.

Some Chinese, Huang, February 10, 2019.

He advised members, Powell, 1878.

The year before, October 1893 Speech to Irrigation Congress, Los Angeles, California; Ross, September 10, 2018.

Chapter 1

The institution's breathless slogan, Creation Museum, creationmuseum.org.

As of late 2022, The statistics from October 2022 have shifted on Montana county vaccines rates. Dawson County still maintains a 38 percent vaccine rate, but when last checked in April, 2023, Prairie, as of April, 2023 is 42 percent and Powder River is 27 percent. Montana Geographic Information, MLS Geo Info Map, https://montana.maps.arcgis.com/apps/MapSeries/index.html?appid=7c34f3412536439491adcc2103421d4b.

Dawson County High School, Puckett, April 9, 2015.

Montana's current governor, Greg Gianforte, Healy, Oct 18, 2009.

On its website, Visit Creation, Glendive Dinosaur and Fossil Museum, https://visitcreation.org/item/glendive-dinosaur-fossil-museum-glendive-mt/.

For the record, the track, Meyers, July 28, 2008.

During an interview with the Billings Gazette, Healy, Oct 18, 2009.

Darwin begins the letter, Charles Darwin, June 2, 1859, Darwin Correspondence Project, University of Cambridge, https://www.darwinproject.ac.uk/letter/DCP-LETT-2466.xml.

Canen continues to minister, Cause IQ, Foundation Advancing Creation Truth, https://www.causeiq.com/organizations/foundation-advancing-creation-truth,300187495/. FACT's website has been redesigned since I first visited in 2021, and the comment about the "abyss of scientific deception," has been replaced with, "The mission of the Foundation Advancing Creation Truth (FACT) and its related ministries is to glorify God as Creator and Sustainer, emphasize man's accountability to Him, affirm God's revealed and inspired Word as the preeminent source of truth and authority, and to challenge mankind to think through the assumptions and consequences of the humanistic concept of evolution and its underlying premise that the earth is billions of years old" https://creationtruth.org. The older language referencing "abyss of scientific deception" can still be accessed on https://visitcreation.org/item/glendive-dinosaur-fossil-museum-glendive-mt/ as of April 2023.

CHAPTER 2

She currently is a representative, Nutrigenomics Test Provider at GeneticKey LLC, website no longer online when checked in April 2023.

Only 62% percent of Montana children receive the full slate, Newcomer, Freedman, Wehner, Anderson, Daley, July, 2021. According to the study, "Among 31,422 children, 38.0% received all vaccine doses on time; 24.3% received all doses, but some were received late; and 37.7% had not completed the combined 7-vaccine series. Approximately 18.7% had an undervaccination pattern suggestive of parental vaccine hesitancy, and 19.7% started all series but were missing doses needed for multidose series completion."

According to Karen Douglas, Haupt, Oct 19, 2020.

I later tracked the story down, Swenson, April 14, 2021.

A White House correspondent, Johnson, November 4, 2021.

The conspiracy theory of injecting microchips, Scherr, February 26, 2010; Kunkle and Helderman, February 10, 2010.

In 2000, when the FDA, Baard, June 6, 2006.

When Mather Fought the Smallpox, Diary of Cotton Mather, August 24, 1721; Microfilm Edition of the Cotton Mather papers, a Joint Publication of the Massachusetts Historical Society and the American Antiquity Society.

With zero medical training, Facebook and YouTube deplatformed Bigtree in 2020, but his program is still available on Rumble. https://rumble.com/search/all?q=highwire.

The word conspirituality, Ward and Voas, January 2011, p. 103.

Social historians, Lewis and Kahn, 2005, p. 70.

He told the audience that day, Derysh, July, 21, 2021.

In early 2023, US Dominion, Inc., Dominion Voting Systems, Inc and Dominion Voting Systems Corporation, v. Fox New Network, LCC, Filed March 8, 2023. *https://deadline.com/wp-content/uploads/2023/03/2023-03-08-PUBLIC-Dominion-SJ-Reply-Brief-Fox_Redacted.pdf.*

Willis introduces Mikovits, Willis, 2020.

The game is to prevent the therapies, ibid.

Though YouTube, Prasad, 2022.

"Contagion no longer exists," Anthony ***, Facebook, August 26, 2020. (screenshot)

As a former gun-company, Busse, p. 181.

One of the company's founders, ibid, p. 183.

In the last video, Sears, June, 7, 2022.

CHAPTER 3

Covered in blue paint, Sears, May 19, 2020.

Griffin has been ballyhooed, Jones, November 12, 2009.

He calls it an instrument, Griffin, p. 101, 103, 1998; Suebsaend, November 26, 2015.

On the first day of the conference, although Patrea Patrick's film is called "Titanic, a Perfect Crime," it was listed, at the time, on the 2020 Red Pill Expo schedule as "The Titanic Never Sank!"

After Trump's Loss, Levine, January 5, 2022.

Van Tatenhoven said, "Here's Every Word from the Seventh Jan. 6 Committee Hearing on its Investigation," Transcript House January 6th Committee Hearings, July 12, 2022, https://www.npr.org/2022/07/12/1111123258/jan-6-committee-hearing-transcript

That took place, Gaines Quammen, 2020, p. 227-229.

The West has now been won! Jones, April 13th, 2014.

He wrote, O'Sullivan,1845.

Some seventy years, Though I had read about this movie, I later saw it on Turner Classic Movies in March, 2023. Starring Debbie Reynolds and Gary Cooper, it's a schlocky musical, shot in three panel Cinerama, replete with wall-to-wall western myths.

According to, Murdoch, 2001, p. 17.

The initial indictment, "Leader of Oath Keepers and 10 Other Individuals Indicted in Federal Court for Seditious Conspiracy and Other Offenses Related to U.S. Capitol Breach," Department of Justice, January 13, 2022, https://www.justice.gov/opa/pr/leader-oath-keepers-and-10-other-individuals-indicted-federal-court-seditious-conspiracy-and.

Cliven Bundy posted, Bundy Ranch, Facebook, January 6, 2020, https://www.facebook.com/bundyranch.

At the Marble annual gathering, Capurso, July 22, 2017.

After his arrest, Tasha Adams, @That_Girl_Tasha, January 26, 2022, https://twitter.com/That_Girl_Tasha/status/1486500817339256834.

According to a 2022, According to a data leak, the ADL discovered "membership information for more than 38,000 individuals." *American Defamation League*, September 9, 2022. https://www.adl.org/resources/report/oath-keepers-data-leak-unmasking-extremism-public-life.

During a hearing, Jordan Fischer, WUSA9/ABCNews, December 22, 2022.

"He believes," Klasfeld, February 22, 2022.

This idea, Gaines Quammen, May 11, 2020.

He stockpiled weapons, Department of Justice, "Two Leaders of Oath Keepers Found Guilty of Seditious Conspiracy and Other Charges Related to U.S. Capitol Breach," U.S. Attorney's Office, November 29, 2022, https://www.justice.gov/usao-dc/pr/two-leaders-oath-keepers-found-guilty-seditious-conspiracy-and-other-charges-related-us; Invoking the 1807 Insurrection Act "allows the president to call out militias to put down rebellion against the United States." "Former Oath Keepers Spokesman: Invoking Insurrection Act Could Have Led to Civil War," House January 6th Committee Hearings, C-SPAN, July 12, 2022, https://www.c-span.org/video/?521495-1/seventh-hearing-investigation-capitol-attack

Yuval Noah Harari's, Harari, p. 31.

At play as well, Bateson, December, 1935.

When the cops commanded, Staff, *KATU.* April 5, 2016.

These enlistees, The Institute for Research and Education on Human Rights and the Montana Human Rights Network, 2021.

Please you're not allowed, Ashley Everly video of protest and arrest of Sarah Brady Walton, *Facebook,* April 21, 2020, https://www.facebook.com/ashleyeverlyvax/videos/2988430571178559/.

As she was taken away, Staff, Boise Guardian, April 22, 2020.

The night of the protest, Bustillo and Brown, April 21, 2020.

On the first occasion, Siegler, August 25, 2020.

Bundy was later, Brizee, February 21, 2023.

The protesters, 20220511 Redacted St Luke's Complaint and Demand for Jury Trial, Erik F. Stidham, HOLLAND and HART, May 11, 2022, https://www.documentcloud.org/documents/21992915-20220511-redacted-st-lukes-complaint-and-demand-for-jury-trial, p. 12.

St. Luke's suit states, ibid, p. 19, 13.

Just before year's end, Idaho Dispatch Facebook page, December 28, 2022, https://www.facebook.com/watch/live/?ref=watch_perma-link&v=958123531819046

Of his plea, Brizee, January 24, 2023.

"St. Luke's suffered," Brizee, February 21, 2023.

In neighboring, This account of the harassment of Matt Kelley and his family comes from interviews with neighbors, and my own observations. Story of the fart machine was conveyed by those who pulled the prank and watched the protestor's reaction—they asked to stay anonymous.

McGeachin made her views, Right Wing Watch, video clip of interview, *Twitter,* March 9, 2022.

"We have to make," Moseley-Morris, July 16, 2022.

Being right is, Richardson, p. 4, 53, 92.

According to a legal filing, "Amended answer, counterclaim, third-party complaint & jury demand filed 3/10/2022 Gregory Graf vs. Chad Christensen, Greg Pruett, Dustin Hurst, & EmmaLee Robinson," Jared W. Allen, Beard, St. Claire and Gaffney, Case No: CV10-21-1197, March 10, 2022, https://www.scribd.com/document/563879229/Gregory-Graf-AMENDED-ANSWER-COUNTERCLAIM-THIRD-PARTY-COMPLAINT-JURY-DEMAND#.

On May 22, 2023, Tasha Adams was granted a divorce from Stewart Rhodes. Three days later, he was sentenced to eighteen years in prison for seditious conspiracy.

CHAPTER 4

Let's face facts, Chewelah Independent, January 14, 2019.

The comma, Explanation of the comma comes by way of direct communications with by McAdam (email) and Neiwert (DM, Twitter).

According to, Cooper and Clarkson, May 25, 2021.

"I am a separatist," Rawles, March 28, 2011.

He has written, ibid.

The Byrds began, Capurso, July 22, 2017.

According to an investigation, Morlin, July 15, 2011.

It is said, "Louis Beam," American Defamation League, 2013. https://www.adl.org/sites/default/files/documents/assets/pdf/combating-hate/Louis-Beam.pdf

In 2018, Wiles, September 12, 2018.

Arthur explained, Eaton, March 15, 2022.

The Federal Reserve, Pounder, p. 9.

According to, Pogue, April, 2022.

As Pogue pointed out, Pogue, May, 2023.

Shea's plan, Shea, 2016, p. 2.

He now regrets, Baker, December 23, 2019.

When the news hit, Kathy and Paul Leodler, Rampart Group, December 1, 2019.

In his novel, Walter, p. 27.

According to journalist, Egan, August 20, 1991

One local said, ibid.

At last, Vestal, February 5, 2021,

Back in 2013, Spokesman-Review YouTube, February 25, 2020; Sokol, February 26, 2020.

In 2021, Vestral, Feb. 5, 2021.

Quoted in the Washington Post, Johnson, October 12, 1980.

In the same year, ibid.

Bob Pedersen, Crane-Murdoch, May 20, 2013.

Pedersen told reporter, ibid.

According to his Twitter, @BrentFRegan

Journalist Anne Helen, Petersen, October 22, 2017.

In 2022, Thornbrugh, March 10, 2022.

Months after, Story told to me in a conversation with Gregory Graf; Moseley-Morris, July 15, 2022 ,

Though the breakfast, "Idaho's Christian Taliban," Kootenai Dark Web, *YouTube*, https://www.youtube.com/watch?v=Xq2E7_sKayI.

Reporter Daniel, Walters, June 17, 2022.

Investigators, Fox 28, Spokane, June 14, 2022; Thornbrugh, June 15, 2022.

A patriot member, Daily Kos YouTube. April 28, 2022.

A twenty-four-year, Rosensaft, January 25, 2023.

Malkin is known, Carpenter, March 9, 2020.

During Malkin's talk, Kootenai County Republicans *YouTube*, March 2020.

A website, Idaho Action, https://www.actionidaho.org/about.

Liberty Boot Camp, A9 Collective, October 6, 2022.

During his unsuccessful, Bundy, 2022.

CHAPTER 5

Parker and another, Russell, January 22, 2018.

The Idaho Tri-Weekly, *The Idaho Tri-Weekly*, April 13, 1880; Spence, p. 9-10.

Historian Clark C. Spence, Spence, p. 103.

According to a post, The Doctors YouTube, 2021.

Crested Butte, Bowlin, January 1, 2021.

Friends heard him tell, Ames, April 3, 2020.

Idaho Mountain Express, Buitrago, March 20, 2020

Parker told, Kauffman, April 3, 2020.

Also known as consumption, According to said Dr. Shama Ahuja, director of TB Surveillance and Epidemiology at the New York City Department of Health and Mental Hygiene, "Tuberculosis spreads usually in hours, and for COVID, it's a virus with very short interaction, (which) results in the spread of the infection." Fauzia, August 30, 2020.

According to a statement, Colorado Springs Chamber of Commerce 1915, a display at "City of Sunshine, Colorado Springs Pioneers Museum," Curated by Leah Davis Witherow, http://www.cspm.org/wp-content/uploads/2014/10/City-of-Sunshine-Exhibit-Text.pdf .

In his 1885, Roosevelt, p. 14.

He writes of, Farmer, 2010, Kindle Location No. 2947.

On the morning, Hendrickson, p. 14.

CHAPTER 6

He later issued, McMillion, Sep 27, 2007.

Lang's ranch hand, Dixon is from Wellsville, Utah, according to his Facebook page. https://www.facebook.com/justin.dixon.5648/

He wrote, Sorenson, Winter, 1994, p. 27.

The campaign, ibid.

At a rally, Gaines Quammen, p. 236.

Earlier that year, ibid, p. 235.

It merely ran, Watson, 2013.

Of what consequence, ibid.

I'm tempted to construe, Andrews, 2014, Kindle, Location No. 2355.

In 1886, Williams, November 14, 2007.

The US Department of Agriculture, Gese, Hart, Terletzky, May 2021, p. 17

In a 2015, US Department of Agriculture, December 19, 2017.

A temporary restraining order, WildEarth Guardians, November 29, 2022.

Montana's efforts, ibid.

After evolutionary theory, Asma, p. 44.

Instead of, ibid.

But not all, Hornaday, p. 53.

According to, "Environmental Stewardship and Conservation Overview," The Church of Jesus Christ of Latter-day Saints, https://www.churchofjesuschrist.org/study/manual/gospel-topics/environmental-stewardship-and-conservation?lang=eng

CHAPTER 7

Sean worked, Sean Hawksford, *LinkedIn*, https://www.linkedin.com/in/sean-hawksford-a3a2091b8/.

In a 2021, McLaughlin, August 27, 2021.

Housing prices jumped, Lambert, December 23, 2021.

They're the picture, McLaughlin, August 27, 2021

Of course, @ChrisLaTray has since gone off Twitter, but I had him read the manuscript, because I deeply value his opinion, and I wanted to verify his comments sprinkled throughout the book. This tweet is no longer available.

That wasn't new either, "Come West and Be Cured," *American Experience*, February 10, 2015.

They sought, Turner, p. 2.

According to Turner, ibid, p. 22

Turner once wrote, ibid, p. 7, 9.

In a 2008, Cohan, February 6, 2008.

Blixseth couldn't, McMillion, April 12, 2008.

According to Celebrity, Lamare, March 2, 2018.

The website, Yellowstone Club, https://www.yellowstoneclub.com.

In 2004, McMillion, August 9, 2004.

The New York Times, Wallace, June 13, 2009.

Again in 2017, APNews, August 25, 2017.

Dave Hallac, Wilkinson, October 27, 2022.

Wilkinson wrote, ibid.

In early 2022, French, February, 6, 2022.

The average household, Zip Recruiter says $55,897, https://www.ziprecruiter. com/Salaries/--in-Montana#:~:text=Montana%20ranks%20number%20 20%20out,week%20or%20%244%2C658%20a%20month.

Another nearby property, One and Only Resort, https://www.oneandonlyre-sorts.com/moonlight-basin.

Currently, Johnson, October 15, 2021.

The story of Big Sky, Ring, March 31, 1997

CHAPTER 8

Her wild places, The Sun, November 4, 1906.

Later, in a 1910, Evelyn Cameron's letters, getting cards, clippings, poems, journals, and papers are housed at the Montana Historical Society Library and Archives, Helena Montana, Evelyn J. Cameron and Ewan S. Cameron papers, 1893-1920, Collection No. MS226; Milne, p. 101.

*****In a letter to Williams, ibid; p. 121.

In her diary, ibid; pg. 102, 106, 106, 107. Journal entries extolling affection towards Williams began as soon as they met in 1907 and continued, sprinkled throughout the entries, until Cameron's death. Unfortunately I was only able to spend a few hours in the collection, reading correspondence, journals, and cards while noting terms of affection. The Helena Historical Society archive is under renovation and closed to the public, preventing more thorough research.

On January, ibid, January 10, 1913.

I found tucked, ibid, undated.

After the legislator's actions, Constitution of Montana, Article X—Education and Public Lands, Section 9. Boards of education (2) (a).

CHAPTER 9

According to, Miller, Zhang, Azreal, February 2022.

Also alarming, Statista, Rates of suicide in the United States as of 2020, by state *(per 100,000 population),* https://www.statista.com/statistics/560297/highest-suicide-rates-in-us-states/.

Stewart Rhodes, Hsu, January 26, 2022.

"Let's face it, People's Rights, https://www.peoplesrights.org.

There were 647, Gal, Hall, and Ardrey. January 23, 2023.

Montana Territory, Lehman, June 26, 2021.

In Coeur D'Alene, Walters, July 16, 2020.

According to a: Schwartz June 24, 2020.

Researchers at Harvard and Radcliffe, Some serious issues did occur during BLM protests, but of the 7,305 BLM events across the country, according to a study by Erica Chenoweth (professor at the Harvard Kennedy School and Susan and Kenneth Wallach Professor at the Radcliffe Institute for Advanced Study) and Jeremy Pressman (associate professor of political science at the University of Connecticut), "96.3 percent of protests involved no property damage or police injuries, and in 97.7 percent of events, no injuries were reported among participants, bystanders or police." Chenowith and Pressman, October 16, 2020.

Although financial, Campbell, January 31, 2022.

According to Pew, Parker, Horowitz, and Anderson, June 12, 2020; Support dropped to 55% in 2021 according to a follow-up Pew study. Horowitz, September 27, 2021.

In 2022, Held, October 17, 2022.

In his book, Bender, p. 159.

He wanted to, Ibid, p. 164.

By blaming, Barron-Lopez and Thompson, August 10, 2020.

Using two, Goff and McCarthy, October 12, 2021.

Over the years, Woodson, p. 1

Mogelson reported, Mogelson, 2020.

Anti-government, "Homeland Threat Assessment, Department of Homeland Security, October 2020, https://www.dhs.gov/sites/default/files/publications/2020_10_06_homeland-threat-assessment.pdf.

CHAPTER 10

Still, despite, Travel Town museum Foundation, https://traveltown.org.

Of trains, Nelson, p. 173.

The trains, ibid, p. 187.

Between 2009, Lenzen, Sun, Faturay, *et al*, 2018.

Glacier National, Statista, https://www.statista.com/statistics/253875/number-of-visitors-to-us-glacier-national-park/.

That same year, National Park Service, Yellowstone, https://www.nps.gov/yell/learn/news/22003.htm.

In a piece, Randall, February 16, 2021.

In 2021, Lindquist, May 3, 2022.

A 2022 study, University of Montana Crown of the Continent and Greater Yellowstone Initiative, "Public Land Survey," 2022, https://crown-yellowstone.umt.edu/voter-surveys/2022/default.php.

Sarah Lundstrum, Lindquist, May 9, 2022.

A 2018, University of California – Berkeley, September 24, 2018.

On another trip, Grinnell, p. 150.

La Tray once, La Tray, July 24, 2020.

He has since, ibid, February 17, 2022.

Nick Estes, Estes, p. 10

In the documentary film, Jill Momaday, 2017.

He writes, M. Scott Momaday, 2020, p. 44.

CHAPTER 11

Researchers later, *History of the Church*, 2:79.; There is disagreement on the circumstances around Zelph and the story's role in Church geography theory, though I think it's fair to say that even if it was an embellished tale, it still had an impact on early Church culture. I do recommend reading Michael Ash, "Challenging Issues: Keeping the Faith: Account of Self Discovery Does Little to Advance Geography Theory, *Deseret News*, December 27, 2010. https://www.deseret.com/2010/12/27/20384804/challenging-issues-keeping-the-faith-account-of-zelph-discovery-does-little-to-advance-geography-the.

The unusual declaration, *AP*, February 18, 2017.

But two years, *Headwaters Economics*, Spring 2017.

It should be noted, from a private email correspondence with member of the Escalante Guard expressing frustrations of some community members over Headwaters Economics report.

Long-time resident, Maffly, August 17, 2015.

We have exceeded, ibid.

She explained, Insider, June 25, 2020.

Chapter 12

He thinks Blake, Jarmusch, 1995.

At one point, ibid.

According to journalist. Neiwart, August 3, 2022.

I later live-streamed, Idaho Listens, 2021.

We share, ibid.

I frequently learn, ibid.

I thought of, ibid.

I never knew, ibid.

She continued, ibid.

Haidt calls this, Haidt, p. 95.

When people know, ibid, p. 88.

"It's not enough," Petersen, October 22, 2017.

As Johnathon Haidt writes, Haidt, April 11, 2022.

Coda

In comments with, Theroux, 2004.

Selected Bibliography

A9 Collective. "The White Church Militant: The Black Robe Regiment Being Built by Right Wing Power." *Medium*, October 6, 2022. https://a9-collective.medium.com/the-white-church-militant-the-black-robe-regiment-being-built-by-right-wing-power-a75fc30f9251.

Abbott, E.C. "Teddy Blue." *We Pointed Them North: Recollections of a Cowpuncher*. Norman, Oklahoma: University of Oklahoma Press, 1955.

Abrams, Jeannie, "On the Road Again: Consumptives Traveling for Health in the American West, 1840-1925." *Great Plains Quarterly*, vol. 30, no. 4, Fall 2010, p. 271-285. https://digitalcommons.unl.edu/cgi/viewcontent.cgi?article=3602&context=greatplainsquarterly.

Administrator. "Keep Chewelah Weird: Why Our Town is Odd," *Chewelah Independent*, January 14, 2019, https://chewelahindependent.com/keep-chewelah-weird-why-our-town-is-odd/.

Aho, James A. *The Politics of Righteousness: Idaho Christian Patriotism*. Seattle, Washington: University of Washington press, 1990.

Ames, Michael. "Why an Idaho Ski Destinations has One of the Highest COVID-19 Infection Rates in the Nation," *The New Yorker*, April 3, 2020, https://www.newyorker.com/news/news-desk/why-an-idaho-ski-destination-has-one-of-the-highest-covid-19-rates-in-the-nation.

Andrews, Bryce. *Bad Luck Way: A Year on the Ragged Edge of the West*. New York, New York: Atria Books, 2014.

Anti-Defamation League. "The Oath Keepers Data Leak: Unmasking Extremism in Public Life," September 6, 2022, https://www.adl.org/resources/report/oath-keepers-data-leak-unmasking-extremism-public-life.

Anon. "A Woman's Big Game Hunting," *The Sun,* November 4, 1906, Chronicling America: Historic American Newspapers. Lib. of Congress. https://chroniclingamerica.loc.gov/lccn/sn83030272/1906-11-04/ed-1/seq-20/.

Anon. "Bulloch's Cows Released after Salina Auction is Called Off," *Garfield County News,* November 9, 2000, https://newspapers.lib.utah.edu/details?id=3466434&q=Bulloch+Cows+Released&page=1&rows=25&fd=title_t%2Cpaper_t%2Cdate_tdt%2Ctype_t&sort=date_tdt+asc&gallery= 0#t_3466434.

Anon. "Bunker Hill Mine Restart, Idaho, USA, *Mining Technology*, September 26, 2022, https://www.mining-technology.com/projects/bunker-hill-mine-restart-idaho-usa/.

Anon. "Escalante March in Support of Black Lives Matter Movement Celebrates Juneteenth, *The Insider: Serving Wayne and Garfield Counties*, Utah, June 25, 2020, https://issuu.com/snapshotmm/docs/062520insider_web.

Anon. *Glendive Dinosaur and Fossil Museum.* Self-published. 2020.

Anon. "Second Annual Escalante Wild Potato Days—a Celebration of the Four Corners Potato—to Be Held May 27th and 28th, *The Insider: Serving Wayne and Garfield Counties, Utah*, April 10, 2023, https://www.insiderutah.com/articles/second-annual-escalante-wild-potato-days-a-celebration-of-the-four-corners-potato-to-be-held-may-27-28/.

Anon. "Stewart Rhodes Poised to Play Villain in Second Oath Keepers Sedition Trial," *WUSA9/ABCNews*, December 22, 2022, https://www.wusa9.com/article/news/national/capitol-riots/stewart-rhodes-looms-over-trial-of-second-oath-keepers-group-roberto-minuta-edward-vallejo-joseph-hackett-david-moerschel/65-5590aedf-512c-4096-a3ca-a00f2e86d962.

Associated Press. "Gov. Herbert signs Resolution Urging Shrinkage of Monument," *Deseret News*, February 18, 2017, https://www.deseret.com/2017/2/18/20606516/gov-herbert-signs-resolution-urging-shrinkage-of-monument.

———."Haunted by the Sacred Past." *Deseret News*, Oct 4, 2009, https://www.deseret.com/2009/10/4/20344261/haunted-by-sacred-past.

———. "Ex-billionaire Tim Blixseth Reaches Deal with Creditors, Court Filing Shows," *Oregon Live/The Oregonian*, January 15, 2018, https://www.oregonlive.com/business/2018/01/ex-billionaire_tim_blixseth_re.html.

———. "Man Charged in New Mexico Oñate Protest Shooting; Militia Group's Presence 'Condemned.'" *KVIA/ABC News*, June 15, 2020, https://kvia.com/news/new-mexico/2020/06/15/man-shot-wounded-during-protest-to-remove-onate-statue-in-albuquerque/.

———. "St. Regis Sawmill Closing, 99 Workers to Lose Jobs," *Spokesman Review*, August 31st 2022, https://www.spokesman.com/stories/2021/aug/31/st-regis-sawmill-closing-99-workers-to-lose-jobs/.

———. "Western Montana Sawmill Closing this Fall, 99 to Lose Jobs." *APNews*, August 21, 2021. https://apnews.com/article/business-montana-9e4cd4e2afeacdfa57ecb1eb0a05d957.

———. "Yellowstone Club Fined by Montana DEQ for Wastewater Spill into Gallatin River," *Water World*, August 25, 2017, https://www.waterworld.com/drinking-water/potable-water-quality/article/16212722/yellowstone-club-fined-by-montana-deq-for-wastewater-spill-into-gallatin-river.

Baard, Mark. "RFID: Sign of the (End) Times?" *Wired*, June 6, 2006, https://www.wired.com/2006/06/rfid-sign-of-the-end-times/.

Baker, Mike. "GOP lawmaker had Visions of a Christian Alternative Government," *New York Times*, December 23, 2019, https://www.nytimes.com/2019/12/23/us/matt-shea-washington-extremism.html.

Barron-Lopez, Laura and Alex Thompson. "Facing Bleak November, Republicans Looked to Stoke BLM Backlash," *Politico*, August 10, 2020. https://www.politico.com/news/2020/08/10/elections-republicans-black-lives-matterbacklash-389906.

Bateson, Gregory. "Culture Contact and Schismogenesis," *Man*, vol. 35, December, 1935, p.178-183

Bender, Michael C. *Frankly We Did Win this Election*. New York, New York: Hachette Book Group, 2021.

Booker, R. Michael. *Images of America: Glendive*. Charleston, South Carolina: Arcadia Publishing, 2016.

Bossick, Karen. "The Giving Garden Gives to Seniors in More Ways Than One," Eye on Sun Valley, August 14, 2020, http://www.eyeonsunvalley.com/Story_Reader/7514/The-Giving-Farm-Feeds-Seniors-in-More-Ways-Than-One/.

Bowlin, Nick. "When COVID Hit, a Colorado County Kicked Out Second-Home Owners. They Hit Back." *High Country News*, January 1,

2021, https://www.hcn.org/issues/53.1/south-economy-when-covid-hit-a-colorado-county-kicked-out-second-home-owners-they-hit-back.

Brizee, Alex. "Ammon Bundy had yet Another Idaho Trespassing Case. This One Ended in a Plea Deal," *Idaho Statesman*, January 24, 2023, https://www.eastidahonews.com/2023/01/ammon-bundy-had-yet-another-idaho-trespassing-case-this-one-ended-in-a-plea-deal/.

———. "St. Luke's Suffered, St. Luke's Wants Ammon Bundy Held in Contempt of Court, at Least \$7.5M in Damages," *Idaho Statesman*, February 21, 2023, https://www.idahostatesman.com/article272563219.html.

Bugenstein, Michael. *Since the days of the Buffalo: a history of eastern Montana and the Kalfell Ranch.* Helena, Montana: Farcountry Press, 2013.

Buitrago, Alejandra. Outbreak Intensifies in Blaine," *Mountain Express*, March 20, 2020, https://www.mtexpress.com/news/blaine_county/outbreak-intensifies-in-blaine/article_64997bda-6a50-11ea-bb12-ff092b3d58e4.html.

Bulloch, Mary. "An Open Letter from Mary Bullock," *Garfield County News*, October 26, 2000, https://newspapers.lib.utah.edu/details?id=3469662&q=open+letter+mary+bulloch&page=1&rows=25&fd=title_t%2Cpaper_t%2Cdate_tdt%2Ctype_t&sort=date_tdt+asc&gallery=0#t_34696.

Bundy, Ammon. "Woke Cult," Ammon Bundy, *YouTube*, 2022, https://www.youtube.com/watch?app=desktop&v=F0CzTDp5CM8.

Burnett, John. "New Mexico Leaders to Militia: If You Want to Help Community, Stop Showing Up Armed," *All Things Considered, NPR*, June 7, 2020. https://www.npr.org/2020/07/06/886586653/new-mexico-leaders-to-militia-if-you-want-to-help-community-stop-showing-up-arme.

Busse, Ryan. *Gunfight: My Battle Against the Industry that Radicalized America.* New York, New York: PublicAffairs, 2021.

Bustillo, Ximena and Ruth Brown. "Anti-vaccination Idaho activist arrested after group gathers at closed playground" *East Idaho News,* April 21, 2020, https://www.eastidahonews.com/2020/04/update-anti-vaccination-idaho-activist-arrested-after-group-gathers-at-closed-playground/.

Campbell, Sean. "Where Did the Money Go?" *New York / Intelligencer*, January 31, 2020, https://nymag.com/intelligencer/2022/01/black-lives-matter-finances.html.

Campbell, William. "'Owning Eden': Ranch Land Comes with Social Obligations." *Billings Gazette*, March 26, 2005. https://billingsgazette.com/

news/state-and-regional/montana/owning-eden-ranch-land-comes-with-social-obligations/image_c3956279-fe9c-57c7-964a-897f6b2278ea.html.

Capurso, Donna. "Patriotism is Alive and Well in Marble Country," *RedoubtNews*, July 22, 2017, https://redoubtnews.com/2017/07/patriotism-alive-well-marble-country/.

Carpenter, Amanda. "Michelle Malkin: Mother of Groypers," *The Bulwark*, March 9, 2020, https://www.thebulwark.com/michelle-malkin-mother-of-groypers/.

Carrillo, Edmundo. "Witnesses Describe Chaos at Oñate Protest," *Albuquerque Journal*, August 13th 2020. https://www.abqjournal.com/1486240/witnesses-describe-chaos-at-ontildeate-protest-ex-steven-ray-baca-faces-battery-charges-in-preliminary-hearing.html.

Center for Disease Control and Prevention. "Suicide Mortality State by State." 2020 https://www.cdc.gov/nchs/pressroom/sosmap/suicide-mortality/suicide.htm.

Chenoweth, Erika and Jeremy Pressman. "This Summer's Black Lives Matter Protesters Were Overwhelmingly Peaceful, Our Research Finds," *Washington Post*, October 16th 2020, https://www.washingtonpost.com/politics/2020/10/16/this-summers-black-lives-matter-protesters-were-overwhelming-peaceful-our-research-finds/.

Clarke, Norm. *Tracing Terry's Trails: A Chronological History*. Compiled by Terry County Centennial Celebration, 1982.

Clarkson, Fredrick and André Gagné. "Christian Right Denialism is More Dangerous Than Ever: A Reporters Guide to the New Apostolic Reformation," *Religious Dispatches*, September 7, 2022, https://religiondispatches.org/christian-right-denialism-is-more-dangerous-than-ever-a-reporters-guide-to-the-new-apostolic-reformation/.

———. "Statement on NAR & Christian Nationalism Answers Few Questons but Exposes Growing Rifts in the Movement," *Religious Dispatches*, October 21, 2022, https://religiondispatches.org/statement-on-nar-christian-nationalism-answers-few-questions-but-exposes-growing-rifts-in-the-movement/.

Cohan, William. "Paradise Lost," *Forbes*, February 6, 2008, https://money.cnn.com/2008/02/04/lifestyle/paradise_lost.fortune/index.htm.

Condran, Ed. "Nicholas Sironka, Kenyan Artist who Worked on BLM Mural, Feels at Home in Spokane," *Spokesman Review*, January 21, 2021, https://www.spokesman.com/stories/2021/jan/21/nicholas-sironka-ken-yan-artist-behind-blm-mural-fe/.

Cooper, Chloe and Frederick Clarkson. "Convergence of Far Right, Anti-Democratic Factions in the Northwest Could Provide a Model for the Rest of the Nation," Chloe *Religious Dispatches*, May 25, 2021, https://religiondispatches.org/convergence-of-far-right-anti-democratic-factions-in-the-northwest-could-provide-a-model-for-the-rest-of-the-nation/.

Conover, Ted. *Cheap Land: Off Gridders at America's Edge.* New York, New York: Knopf, 2022.

Crane-Murdoch, Sierra. "How Right-Wing Emigrants Conquered North Idaho," *High Country News,* May 20, 2013, https://www.hcn.org/issues/45.8/how-right-wing-emigrants-conquered-north-idaho.

Daily Kos YouTube Channel. "'Panhandle Patriots' Announce Plans to Directly Confront Pride Event in Coeur d'Alene park 'Head to Head,'" *Daily Kos YouTube.* April 28, 2022. https://www.youtube.com/watch?v=9pbtUd-NAVYw.

Drake, Phil. "From Billionaire to Inmate, Tim Blixseth Remains Defiant." Great Falls Tribune, March 3, 2016. https://www.greatfallstribune.com/story/news/local/2016/03/03/billionaire-inmate-tim-blixseth-remains-defiant/81300642/.

Draper, Electra, "Rancher Draws Line in Grazing Fight," *Denver Post*, November 26, 2000, http://extrasdenverpost.com/news/news1126b.htm.

Du Mez, Kristin Kobes. *Jesus and John Wayne: How White Evangelicals Corrupted a Faith and Fractured a Nation.* New York, New York: Liveright, 2021.

Dunbar-Ortiz, Roxanne and Dina Gilio-Whitaker. *All the Real Indians Died Off: And 20 Other Myths About Native Americans.* Boston, Massachusetts: Beacon Press, 2016.

Eaton, Nate. "Pastor Linked to Mom and Toddler in Hiding Threatens Judge, Attorney, Reporter and Shows up in Idaho Falls," *East Idaho News*, March 15, 2022, https://www.eastidahonews.com/2022/03/pastor-threatening-attorney-judge-and-reporter-shows-up-in-idaho-falls-and-still-refuses-to-say-where-mom-and-toddler-are/.

Egan, Tim. "Gambling Raid Angers Mining Town, *New York Times*, August 20, 1991, https://www.nytimes.com/1991/08/20/us/gambling-raid-angers-mining-town.html.

————. *Worst Hard Time: The Untold Story of Those Who Survived the Dust Bowl.* Boston, Massachusetts: Mariner Books, 2006.

Editors, "How The West Was Won," *Life Magazine*, April 6, 1959 vol. 6, no.14, p. 78-104. (First in an ongoing series).

Elflein, John. "Number of COVID-19 Deaths in the United States as of February 27, 2023, by State." *Statista*, February 27, 2023. https://www.statista.com/statistics/1103688/coronavirus-covid19-deaths-us-by-state/.

Eliade, Mircea. *Myth and Reality,* London, UK: Harper and Row, 1975.

Estes, Nick. *Our History is the Future: Standing Rock Versus the Dakota Access Pipeline, and the Long Tradition of Indigenous Resistance.* New York, New York: Verso, 2019.

Evans, Tony Teraroniake. A History of Indians in the Sun Valley. Hailey, Idaho: Express Printing, 2017.

Evelyn, Kenya. "Man Shot as New Mexico Protesters Try to Remove Spanish Conquistadors Statue." *The Guardian*, June 16th 2020. https://www.theguardian.com/us-news/2020/jun/16/man-shot-as-new-mexico-protesters-try-to-remove-spanish-conquistador-statue-juan-de-onate.

Farmer, Jared. *On Zion's Mount: Mormons, Indians and the American Landscape.* Cambridge, England: Harvard University Press, 2008.

Farrell, Justin. *Billionaire Wilderness: The Ultra-Wealthy and the Remaking of the American West.* Princeton, New Jersey: Princeton University Press, 2020.

Fisher, Austin. "Prosecutors Clear Hurdle in Suit Against New Mexico Civil Guard." *NM Source*, September 28, 2021. https://sourcenm.com/2021/09/28/prosecutors-clear-hurdle-in-suit-against-new-mexico-civil-guard/.

French, Brett, "Montage Hotel Opens Taking Big Sky to a New Level," *Billings Gazette*, February 6, 2022, https://billingsgazette.com/news/state-and-regional/montage-big-sky-hotel-opens-taking-big-sky-to-a-new-level/article_09bb3f7d-1c75-556d-8c09-15346ba0424d.html.

Fauzia, Miriam, "Fact check: Tuberculosis is more dangerous than COVID-19, but context matters," *USAToday*, August 30, 2020. https://www.usatoday.com/story/news/factcheck/2020/08/30/fact-check-tb-more-dangerous-than-covid-19-but-context-matters/5435004002/.

Gaines Quammen, Betsy. *American Zion: Cliven Bundy, God, and Public Lands in the West.* Salt Lake City, Utah: Torrey House Press, 2020.

———. "COVID-19 and the White Horse Prophecy: The Theology of Ammon Bundy," *History News Network*, May 11, 2020, https://history-newsnetwork.org/article/175390.

———. "Way Beyond the Proud Boys: The Militias and Conspiracy Theorists to Worry About as the Election Approaches," *New York Daily News*, October 14, 2020, https://www.nydailynews.com/opinion/ny-oped-militias-conspiracy-theorists-trump-20201014-r7bm67szqvcwtnq2b5qnx-5n62u-story.html.

———. "Who Are the Self-Styled Liberators: Looking More Deeply at Those Protesting Covid Lockdowns," *New York Daily News*, April 20, 2020. https://www.nydailynews.com/opinion/ny-oped-who-are-the-self-styled-liberators-20200420-6tn4yn6ojresrnwj3fzgjm7ilu-story.html.

Gal, Shannon, Madison Hall and Taylor Ardrey. "The US had 647 mass shootings in 2022. Here's the full list," *The Insider*, January 23, 2023, https://www.insider.com/number-of-mass-shootingsin-america-this-year-2022-5.

Gale, William P. "Guide for Christian Posse Comitatus," *Identity* 6, no. 3, circa 1972.

———. "United States Christian Posse Association," *Identity* 6, no. 4, circa 1972.

Geddes, Linda. "Joe Rogan's COVID claims: What Does the Science Actually Say?" *The Guardian*, January 31, 2022. https://www.theguardian.com/culture/2022/jan/31/joe-rogan-covid-claims-what-does-the-science-actually-say.

Gese, Eric M., John P. Hart, Patricia A. Terletzky, "Wildlife Damage Management Technical Series: Gray Wolves," *U.S. Department of Agriculture, Animal and Plant Health Inspection Service, Wildlife Services*, May 2021, https://www.aphis.usda.gov/wildlife_damage/reports/Wildlife%20Damage%20Management%20Technical%20Series/gray-wolves.pdf.

Gilio-Whitaker, Dina. *As Long as Grass Grows: The Indigenous Fight for Environmental Justice, from Colonization to Standing Rock*. Boston, Massachusetts: Beacon Press, 2019.

Godfrey, Matthew C. "'We Believe the Hand of the Lord Is in It': Memories of Divine Intervention in the Zion's Camp Expedition." *BYU Studies Quarterly*, vol. 56, no. 4, 2017, p. 99–132. *JSTOR*, https://www.jstor.org/stable/26573493.

Goff, Kelly and McCarthy, John D. "Critics Claim BLM Protests Were More Violent Than 1960s Civil Rights Ones. That's Just Not True," *Washington Post*, October 12, 2021, https://www.washingtonpost.com/politics/2021/10/12/critics-claim-blm-was-more-violent-than-1960s-civil-rights-protests-thats-just-not-true/

Grandin, Greg. *The End of the Myth: From the Frontier to the Border Wall in the Mind of America.* New York, New York: Metropolitan Books, 2019.

Grinell, George Bird, *The Father of Glacier National Park: Discoveries and Exploration in His Own Words*, Charleston, South Carolina: The History Press, 2020.

Griffin, G. Edward, *The Creature from Jekyll Island*, Westlake, California: American Media, 1998.

Grove, Margaret, Julia. *Woman Inscribed: Ancient Memories, Found in Niches, Discovered in Fragments, Inscribed on Bodies, and Recreated from Archaeological Field Journals of the Past.* United States: Molten Lava Press, 2020.

Guilliford, Andy. "A Hard Look at History's Bitter Truths and Selective Memory." *High Country News*, October 11, 2017. https://www.hcn.org/articles/opinion-historys-bitter-truths-and-selective-memory-in-monuments

Gullotta, Daniel N. "QAnon and the Satanic Panics of Yesteryear." *The Bulwark*, February 25, 2021. https://www.thebulwark.com/qanon-and-the-satanic-panics-of-yesteryear/

Hagen, Lisa and Chris Haxel, "A One-Man Propaganda Band," No Compromise, NPR, October 20, 2020. https://www.npr.org/2020/10/19/925558235/a-one-man-propaganda-band

Hager, Kristi. *Evelyn Cameron: Montana's Frontier Photographer.* Helena, Montana: Farcountry Press, 2007.

Haidt, Jonathon. *The Righteous Mind: Why Good People are Divided by Politics and Religion.* New York, New York: Pantheon Books, 2012.

———. "Why the Past Ten Years of American Life Have Been Uniquely Stupid," *The Atlantic*, April 11, 2022 https://www.theatlantic.com/magazine/archive/2022/05/social-media-democracy-trust-babel/629369/

Harari, Yuval Noah. *Sapiens: A Brief History of Humankind.* New York NY, Harper perennial, 2018.

Hathaway, Henry, John Ford and George Marshall, "How the West was Won," Metro Golden Mayer and Cinerama, 1962.

Headwaters Economics. "Grand Staircase-Escalante National Monument: A Summary of Economic Performance in the Surrounding Communities," Spring 2017, https://headwaterseconomics.org/wp-content/uploads/Escalante.pdf

Held, Colleen. "Judge Restricts NM Civil Guard, *Albuquerque Journal*, October 17, 2022, https://www.abqjournal.com/2541198/judge-restricts-nm-civil-guard.html

Hendrickson, Paul. *Hemingway's Boat: Everything He Loved in Life and Lost.* New York, New York: Knopf, 2011

Hofstadter, Richard. *The Paranoid Style of American Politics and Other Essays*. New York, New York: Vintage Books, 2008.

Horowitz, Juliana, Menasce. "Support for Black Lives Matter Declined After George Floyd Protests, But Has Remained Unchanged Since,"*Pew Research Center*, September 27, 2021. https://www.pewresearch.org/fact-tank/2021/09/27/support-for-black-lives-matter-declined-after-george-floyd-protests-but-has-remained-unchanged-since/

Hornaday, William, Temple. *The American Natural History*. New York, New York: Charles Scribner's Sons, 1914.

Horowitz, Mitch. *Occult America: The Secret History of How Mysticism Shaped Our Nation.* New York, New York: Bantam Books, 2009.

Hsu, Spencer S. "Oath keepers Founder Stewart Rhodes to Remain Jailed Pending Trial on January 6 Seditious Conspiracy Charge," Washington Post, January 26, 2022. https://www.washingtonpost.com/dc-md-va/2022/01/26/stewart-rhodes-jailed-seditious-conspiracy/

Hyatt, Norman A. *A Hard Won Life: A Boy on His Own on the Montana Frontier.* Helena, Montana: Sweetgrass Books, 2014.

Idaho Listens: American Values, Boise State University, *YouTube*, 2022, https://www.youtube.com/watch?v=_gTyePCfzds

The Institute for Research and Education on Human Rights and the Montana Human Rights Network, "Ammon's Army: Inside the Far Right People's Right's Network," IREHR, 2021. https://www.irehr.org/reports/peoples-rights-report/

Israelson, Brent and Burr, Thomas "Sherriff's Defy Feds, Take Back Seized Cattle," *Salt Lake City Tribune,* November 9, 2000

Jahn JL. "Mapping Fatal Police Violence across U.S. Metropolitan Areas: Overall Rates and Racial/Ethnic Inequities, 2013-2017." June 24,

2020, PLoS ONE 15(6): e0229686. https://doi.org/10.1371/journal.pone.0229686

Jarmusch, Jim, Dead Man, Pandora Film Production, JVC Entertainment Networks, Newmarket Capital Group, 1996

Jarry, Johnathon, "Granola and Guns: The Rise of Conspirituality," McGill: Office for Science and Society, Oct 7, 2022, https://www.mcgill.ca/oss/article/granola-and-guns-rise-conspirituality

Johnson, Haynes. "The Flint and the Fire of Idaho's Sagebrush Rebellion," *The Washington Post*, October 12, 1980. https://www.washingtonpost.com/archive/lifestyle/1980/10/12/the-flint-and-the-fire-of-idahos-sagebrush-rebellion/7e5cc4f0-48eb-4cb6-9b74-cdbd46debfae/

Johnson, Quincey. "Gallatin River Goes Green for a Fourth Consecutive Year," *Upper Missouri Waterkeeper* press release, October 15, 2021, https://www.uppermissouriwaterkeeper.org/gallatin-river-goes-green-for-fourth-consecutive-year/

Jones, Alex. "Infowars quote historic! Feds forced to surrender to American citizens," Infowars, *YouTube*, April 13th, 2014, https://www.youtube.com/watch?v=bD61Y FxUga4.

———. The Alex Jones Show with G. Edward Griffin, *YouTube*, November, 12, 2009, https://www.youtube.com/watch?v=tVZ9R4QHDaMThe.

Kaplan, Elsie. "Man Arrested on Charges of Witness Intimidation," *Albuquerque Journal*, August 21, 2020. https://www.abqjournal.com/1488847/agents-arrest-man-suspected-of-intimidating-witness.html.

Kauffman, Gretel, "Real 3%ers of Idaho Leader Breaks with Bundy on COVID-19 Response, Mountain Express, April 8th 2020, https://www.mtexpress.com/news/hailey/real-3-ers-idaho-leader-breaks-with-bundy-on-covid-19-response/article_b5e4687a-7913-11ea-99a2-f3f3607c3651.html.

Ketcham, Christopher, "Grand Staircase-Escalante was Set up to Fail," *High Country News,* July 10 2017, https://www.hcn.org/articles/monuments-how-grand-staircase-escalante-was-set-up-to-fail.

Kimbel-Sannit, Arren. "ICYMI: 'We Need to Reclaim the Language of Liberty.'" The Daily Montanan, August 4, 2021. https://dailymontanan.com/2021/08/04/red-pill-fest-prepares-christian-conservatives-for-battle-at-the-ballot-box/

Kincanon, Matthew. Whistleblower Jay Pounder Receives Leadership of Conscience Medal, *SpokaneFAVS*, June 20, 2019. https://spokanefavs.com/whistleblower-jay-pounder-receives-leadership-of-conscience-medal/

Klasfeld, Adam. "Oath Keepers Founder's Estranged Wife Tells Why She Asked a Judge to Keep Ex in Jail, Fears He'll Take Their Kids and Become 'Brownshirt' for Trump," *Law and Crime*, February 22, 2022, https://lawandcrime.com/objections-podcast/oath-keepers-founders-estranged-wife-tells-why-she-asked-a-judge-to-keep-ex-in-jail-fears-hell-take-their-kids-and-become-brownshirt-for-trump/

Kootenai County Republicans YouTube Channel. "Michelle Malkin, KCRCC's Lincoln Say Dinner 2021, *YouTube*, March 28, 2021, *https://www.youtube.com/watch?v=-ZJHfe5Az8g*

Kuhn, Thomas. *The Structure of Scientific Revolution.* Chicago, Illinois: University of Chicago Press, 2012.

Lamare, Amy. "Inside the Ultra-Exclusive Celebrity Enclave of the Yellowstone Club," *Celebrity Net Worth*, March 2, 2018, https://www.celebritynetworth.com/articles/entertainment-articles/inside-ultra-exclusive-celebrity-enclave-yellowstone-club/

Lambert, Lance. "Homeowners Struck Gold during the Pandemic—here's the Breakdown in Every State, *Fortune*, December 23, 2021, https://fortune.com/2021/12/23/homeowners-real-estate-price-gains-breakdown-in-every-state/amp/

Larson, Seaborn. "Hard Pill to Swallow: Red Pill Festival Prepares Christian Conservatives for Battle at the Ballot Box." *The Montana Standard*, June 26, 2021. https://mtstandard.com/news/state-and-regional/govt-and-politics/hard-pill-to-swallow-red-pill-festival-prescribes-christian-conservatism-and-conspiracies/article_4823a23f-70c0-5f35-ba29-f0e2872b809d.html?mode=comments.

La Tray, "Land Acknowledgements: The Progressive Persons Versions of Thoughts and Prayers, *The Irritable Metis*, July 24, 2020, https://chrislatray.substack.com/p/land-acknowledgments?r=h5l6.

———. "Only Kitchi Manitou Can Do That: Mother Earth was Beautiful Beyond Words, for All Time," *The Irritable Metis*, February 17, 2022, https://chrislatray.substack.com/p/only-kitchi-manitou-can-do-that?s=w.

Lehman, Tim, "Montana's First Act as a Territory? Gun Control," *Daily Montanan*, June 26, 2021, https://dailymontanan.com/2021/06/26/montanas-first-act-as-a-territory-gun-control/.

Lenzen, M., Sun, YY., Faturay, F. *et al.* The carbon footprint of global tourism. *Nature Climate Change* 8, 522–528 (2018), https://www.nature.com/articles/s41558-018-0141-x.

Levine, Mike. "How a Standoff in Nevada Years Ago Set the Militia Movement on a Crash Course with the US Capitol," *ABC News*, January 5, 2022, https://abcnews.go.com/US/standoff-nevada-years-ago-set-militia-movement-crash/story?id=82051940.

Lewis, Tyson and Richard Kahn. 2005. "The Reptoid Hypothesis: Utopian and Dystopian Representational Motifs in David Icke's Alien Conspiracy Theory." *Utopian Studies* 16: 45–75.

Limerick, Patricia Nelson. *The Legacy of Conquest: The Unbroken Past of the American.* New York, New York: W.W. Norton, 1987.

Lindquist, Laura, "Poll: Montanans Want to Conserve Public Land, Worry about Growth, *Missoula Current*, May 3, 2022, https://missoulacurrent.com/poll-public-land/

———. "Tourism Promoters Now Searching for Solutions to Tourist Crowding, *Missoula Current*, May 9, 2022, https://missoulacurrent.com/tourist-crowding/

Leodler, Kathy and Paul. "Report of Investigation Regarding Representative, Matt Shea," *Rampart Group*, December 1, 2019, https://houserepublicans.wa.gov/wp-content/uploads/2019/12/RampartGroupReport.pdf

Lundin, John W. *Images of America: Sun Valley, Ketchum, and the Wood River Valley.* Charleston, South Carolina: Arcadia Publishing, 2020.

———. *Skiing Sun Valley: A History from Union Pacific to the Holdings.* Charleston, South Carolina, The History Press, 2020.

Lucey, Donna M. *Photographing Montana, 1894-1928.* New York, New York: Alfred A. Knopf, 1991.

Maffly, Brian, "Is Southern Utah Town Being Stifled by the Feds or by Residents Refusal to Roll with New Industries, *Salt Lake Tribune*, August 17, 2015, https://www.sltrib.com/news/2015/08/17/is-southern-utah-town-being-stifled-by-the-feds-or-by-residents-refusal-to-roll-with-new-industries/

Mathias, Christopher. "The Far-Right's Assault on an Idaho Pride Event was Meticulously Planned." *Huffington Post*, June 18, 2022. https://www.huffpost.com/entry/groomer-panic-idaho-white-supremacists-lgbtq_n_62acc960e4b06594c1d6348b

McBride, Deborah L. "American Sanatoriums: Landscaping for Health, 1885-1945." *Landscape Journal*, vol. 17, no. 1, 1998, p. 26–41. *JSTOR*, http://www.jstor.org/stable/43324287.

McLaughlin, Kathleen, "Who Can Afford to Live in the West When Locals Can't?" The Guardian, August 27th 2021, https://www.theguardian.com/society/2021/aug/26/american-west-income-inequality

McMillion, Scott. "Here's How Blixseth Did It," *Bozeman Chronicle*, April 12, 2008, https://www.bozemandailychronicle.com/news/here-s-how-blixseth-did-it/article_9996b63d-d08b-5451-9a62-c99505f51b9c.html

———. "Sun Ranch Issued Citation for Wolf Killing," *Bozeman Chronicle*, Sep 27, 2007. https://www.bozemandailychronicle.com/news/sun-ranch-issued-citation-for-wolf-killing/article_9467381b-d88a-5bfa-833b-02176c3340f3.html

———. "Yellowstone Club Agrees to Record Fines," *Bozeman Daily Chronicle*, August 9, 2004, https://www.bozemandailychronicle.com/news/yellowstone-club-agrees-to-record-fines/article_c4592fab-2365-55e0-a62c-32c21912e53a.html

Meyers, PZ. "Transparent Fakery," *pharyngula*, July 28, 2008, https://scienceblogs.com/pharyngula/2008/07/28/transparent-fakery

Miller, Carlin, "Garfield, Escalante on the Verge of Devastation, State of Emergency is Imminent," *St. George News Archives*, June 17, 2015. https://archives.stgeorgeutah.com/news/archive/2015/06/17/cmm-garfield-escalante-on-verge-of-devastation-state-of-emergency-imminent/#.ZDV62y-B3BA

Miller, Matt, Wilson Zhang and Deborah Azreal, "Firearm Purchasing During the COVID-19 Pandemic: Results from the 2021 National Firearms Survey, *Annals of Internal Medicine*, February 2022, https://www.acpjournals.org/doi/full/10.7326/M21-3423

Miller, Robert J. *Native America, Discovered and Conquered: Thomas Jefferson, Lewis and Clark, and Manifest Destiny.* Westport, Connecticut: Praeger Publishers, 2006.

Milne, Lorna. *Evelyn Cameron: Photographer on the Western Prairie.* Missoula, Montana: Mountain Press Publishing Company, 2017.

Mikovits, Judy. *Plague of Corruption: Restoring Faith in the Promise of Science,* narrated by Muriel Hemingway, Oasis Audio. July 2020.

Mogelson, Luke. "In the Streets with Antifa," *The New Yorker*, October 25, 2020. https://www.newyorker.com/magazine/2020/11/02/trump-antifa-movement-portland

Momaday, Jill. *Return to Rainy Mountain*, Vision Maker Media, 2017.

Momaday, Scott M. *Earthkeeper: Reflections on American Land*. New York, New York: Harper, 2020.

Morlin, Bill. "Influential Christian Identity Pastor Dies," *Southern Poverty Law Center*, July 15, 2011, https://www.splcenter.org/hatewatch/2011/07/15/influential-christian-identity-pastor-dies

Morris, Larry E. *Ernest Hemingway and Gary Cooper in Idaho: An Enduring Friendship*. Charleston South Carolina: The History Press, 2017.

Moseley-Morris, Kelcie. "Pizza for the hungry GOP Flyers cause confusion for people facing homelessness in Twin Falls," *Idaho Capital Sun*, July 15, 2022. https://idahocapitalsun.com/2022/07/15/pizza-for-the-hungry-gop-flyers-cause-confusion-for-people-facing-homelessness-in-twin-falls/

———. "Rep. Dorothy Moon becomes new chairwoman of Idaho Republican Party," *Idaho Capital Sun*, July 16, 2022, https://idahocapitalsun.com/2022/07/16/rep-dorothy-moon-becomes-new-chairwoman-of-idaho-republican-party/

Moutsos, Eric. "American Moutsos: The Cost For Liberty, Ammon Bundy and Eric Moutsos," YouTube, May 2023, https://www.youtube.com/watch?v=wooAwsU2o3

Munson, Karen M. *In the Aisles: Of a Rural Utah Hardware Store*. Provo, Utah: BYU Printing Services, 2019.

Murdoch, David Hamilton. *The American West: The Invention of Myth*. Wales, Great Britain: Welsh Academic Press, 2001.

Nelson, Maggie. *On Freedom: Four Songs of Care and Constraint*. Minneapolis, Minnesota: Graywolf Press, 2021.

Neiwart, David. "Idaho Nears the Fulfillment of Aryan Nations Leader's Vision for Creating a White-Nationalist Haven," *Daily Kos*, Aug 3, 2022, https://www.dailykos.com/stories/2022/8/3/2114308/-Tide-of-far-right-newcomers-is-realizing-Richard-Butler-s-vision-of-a-white-homeland-in-Idaho

———. "Montana 'Red Pill Festival' Manifests How Far-Right Conspiracism is Mainstreamed in Rural U.S.," Daily Kos, July 26, 2021, https://www.dailykos.com/stories/2021/7/26/2042148/-Montana-Red-Pill-Festival-manifests-how-far-right-conspiracism-is-mainstreamed-in-rural-U-S

————. *Red Pill, Blue Pill: How to Counteract the Conspiracy Theories that are Killing Us*. Lanham Maryland: Prometheus books, 2020.

Newcomer, Sophia R., Rain E. Freedman, Bekki W. Wehner, Stacey Anderson, and Matthew F. Daley. "Timeliness of Early Childhood Vaccines and Undervaccination Patterns in Montana," *American Journal of Preventative Medicine*, July, 2021, Vo. 6, 1, https://www.ajpmonline.org/article/S0749-3797(21)00140-9/fulltext#seccesectitle0014

Okoren, Nicole. "The Birth of a Militia: How an Armed Group Polices Black Lives Matter Protests." The Guardian, July 27, 2020, https://www.theguardian.com/us-news/2020/jul/27/utah-militia-armed-group-police-black-lives-matter-protests

Onibada, Abe. "A Black Lives Matter Protester was Shot at a Demonstration in Albuquerque," *BuzzFeed News*, June 16, 2020, https://www.buzzfeednews.com/article/adeonibada/black-lives-matter-protester-shot-albuquerque

Oregonian Staff. "Oregon Standoff Timeline: 41 Days of the Malheur Refuge Occupation and the Aftermath," *The Oregonian/Oregon Live*, February 14, 2017, https://www.oregonlive.com/portland/2017/02/oregon_standoff_timeline_41_da.html

O'Sullivan, John. "Annexation," *The United States Magazine and Democratic Review*, vol. 17, 1845, p. 2.

Parker, Kim, Juliana Menasce Horowitz, and Monica Anderson, "Amid Protests, Majorities Across Racial and Ethnic Groups Expressed Support for the Black Lives Matter Movement," *Pew Research Center*, June 12, 2020, https://www.pewresearch.org/social-trends/2020/06/12/amid-protests-majorities-across-racial-and-ethnic-groups-express-support-for-the-black-lives-matter-movement/.

PBS, "Come and Be Cured," American Experience, *February 10*, 2015, S27, E5.

Pendley, William Perry. *Sagebrush Rebel: Reagan's Battle with Environmental Extremists and Why It Matters Today*. Washington DC: Regency Publishing, 2013.

Penny, Daniel. "An Intimate History of Antifa," *The New Yorker*, August 22, 2017, https://www.newyorker.com/books/page-turner/an-intimate-history-of-antifa

Petersen, Annie Helen. "The Fight to Bear Arms," *BuzzFeed News*, November

22, 2019. https://www.buzzfeednews.com/article/annehelenpetersen/ida-ho-redoubt-gun-control-rights-second-amendment

———. "Welcome to Idaho, Now Go Home: Here's What Happens when Republicans Have No One to Fight." *BuzzFeed News*, October 22, 2017. https://www.buzzfeednews.com/article/annehelenpetersen/wackadoo-dles-north-idaho

———. "Why the Small Protests in Small Towns across America Matter." *BuzzFeed News*, June 3, 2020. https://www.buzzfeednews.com/article/annehelenpetersen/black-lives-matter-protests-near-me-small-towns

Pilgeram, Ryanne. *Pushed Out: Contested Development and Rural Gentrification in the US West.* Seattle, Washington: University of Washington Press, 2021.

Pogue, James. "Notes on the State of Jefferson." Harper's Magazine, April, 2022. https://harpers.org/archive/2022/04/notes-on-the-state-of-jeffer-son-secession-northern-california/

———. "Inside the New Right, Where Peter Thiel is Placing his Biggest Bets." *Vanity Fair*, May, 2022. https://www.vanityfair.com/news/2022/04/inside-the-new-right-where-peter-thiel-is-placing-his-biggest-bets

Pounder, Jay. *The Red Pill.* Spokane, Washington: Self-published. 2012.

Powell, John Wesley. "Untitled Remarks," Official Report of the International Irrigation Congress, October, 1893, p. 112.

———. "Report on the Arid Region of the United States," Washington, DC: Government Printing Office, 1878.

Puvec, Holly, R. and Douglas Geivett. *Counterfeit Kingdom: The Dangers of the New Revelation, New Prophets, and New Age Practices in the Church* Nashville, Tennessee: B&H Books, 2022.

Randall, Brianna, "Welcome to Polebridge: One of the US' Last Frontiers," BBC, February 16, 2021, https://www.bbc.com/travel/article/20210215-welcome-to-polebridge-one-of-the-us-last-frontiers

Randall, Cassidy. "For Wolves, the Culture War is Extremely Deadly." *Rolling Stone*, April 5, 2022. https://www.rollingstone.com/politics/poli-tics-features/monata-wolf-hunt-conservation-republicans-greg-gian-forte-1321126/

Rawles, John Wesley. "The American Redoubt: Move to the Mountain States," *Survival Blog*, March 28, 2011, https://survivalblog.com/redoubt/

Rea, Tom. *The Bone Wars: The Excavation and Celebrity of Andrew Carnegie's Dinosaur*. Pittsburgh, Pennsylvania: University of Pittsburgh Press, 2021.

Reality Check team. "Joe Rogan: Four Claims from his Spotify Podcast Fact-checked." *BBC News*, January 31, 2022. https://www.bbc.com/news/60199614

Redniss, Lauren. *Oak Flat: A Fight for Sacred Land in the American West*. New York, New York: Random House, 2020.

Rein, Lisa. "Montanans Used to Live and Let Live. Today Bitter Confrontations Dim Big Sky Country." *Washington Post*, October 25, 2021. https://www.washingtonpost.com/politics/montana-extreme-trump/2021/10/22/0f82afbc-0037-11ec-a664-4f6de3e17ff0_story.html

Richardson, Heather Cox. *How the South Won the Civil War: Oligarchy, Democracy and the Continuing Fight for the Soul of America*. Oxford, UK: University of Oxford Press, 2020.

Richardson, Hubert Leon. *Confrontational Politics*. Ventura California: Nordskog Publishing, 2002.

Ring, Ray, "Big Mess in Big Sky," High Country News, March 31, 1997, https://www.hcn.org/issues/101/3127

Rogers, Paul. "Betting the Ranch." Stanford Magazine, November/December, 2004. https://stanfordmag.org/contents/betting-the-ranch

Roosevelt Theodore. *The Winning of the West: From the Alleghenies to the Mississippi*. New York, New York: First Skyhorse Publishing, 2015.

Rosensaft, Menachem Z. "Coming Soon to a Fascist Get-Together Near You," *Just Security*, January 25, 2023. https://www.justsecurity.org/84884/coming-soon-to-a-fascist-get-together-near-you/

Ross, John F. "How the West was Lost," *The Atlantic*, September 2018, https://www.theatlantic.com/ideas/archive/2018/09/how-the-west-was-lost/569365/

Russell, Betsy. "Man Involved in Bundy Standoff Greeted by Idaho House," Spokesman-Review, January 22, 2018. https://www.spokesman.com/blogs/boise/2018/jan/22/man-involved-bundy-standoff-greeted-idaho-house/

Sagan, Carl. "One Voice in the Cosmic Fugue," *PBS*, Ep. 2, 1980, https://vimeo.com/284643737.

Sears, JP. "Blue pill people," *YouTube*, May 19, 2020, https://www.youtube.com/watch?v=dC_lZLzCrOI

———. "I Was WRONG About Abortion! - Why I Changed My Mind," *YouTube*, June 7, 2022. https://www.youtube.com/watch?v=RLZgPjrXU54

Semler, Dean. *The Patriot,* Touchstone Studios, 1998, https://www.youtube.com/watch?v=5nKLzD2QZS4

Shea, Matt. "The Biblical Basis for War," 2016, https://s3.documentcloud.org/documents/5026577/Biblical-Basis-for-War.pdf

Siegler, Kirk, "Ammon Bundy is Arrested and Wheeled Out of The Idaho Statehouse – Again" *NPR*. August 25, 2020, https://www.npr.org/2020/08/25/906046911/ammon-bundy-is-arrested-and-wheeled-out-of-the-idaho-statehouse

Silverman, Kenneth. *The Like and Times of Cotton Mather*, New York, New York: Welcome Rain Publishers, 2002.

Sokol, Chad. "'Blood is Required of Every Generation': Video Surfaces of Matt Shea Speaking in 2013," *Spokesman-Review*, February 26, 2020, https://www.spokesman.com/stories/2020/feb/26/blood-is-required-of-every-generation-video-surfac/.

———. "Washington state lawmaker Matt Shea defends advocacy for 'Holy Army' as Spokane sheriff refers his writings to FBI." *Seattle Times*, November 1, 2018 https://www.seattletimes.com/seattle-news/politics/state-lawmaker-matt-shea-defends-advocacy-for-holy-army-as-spokane-sheriff-refers-his-writings-to-fbi/.

Sorenson, Victor. "The Wasters and Destroyers: Community Sponsored Predator Control in Early Utah Territory." *Utah Historical Quarterly*, vol. 62, no. 1. Winter 1994, p. 26-41. https://issuu.com/utah10/docs/uhq_volume62_1994_number1.

Sottile, Leah. "Who is Oregon?" *Sotille: The Truth Does Not Change According to Our Ability to Stomach It, Substack*, February 8, 2022. https://leahsottile.substack.com/p/19-who-is-oregon.

———. "Bundyville, Season Two: The Remnant," *Oregon Public Broadcasting*, July 15, 2019, https://www.opb.org/news/article/bundyville-occupation-podcast/.

———. *When the Moon Turns to Blood, Lori Vallow, Chad Daybell, and a Story of Murder, Wild Faith, and End Times,* New York, New York: Twelve, June 21, 2022.

Spence, Clark C. *For Wood River or Bust: Idaho's Silver Boom of the 1880s.* Moscow, Idaho: University of Idaho Press, 1990.

Spokesman Review YouTube Channel. "Rep. Matt Shea speaks at 2013 event in Marble, Washington (1 of 2), *YouTube,* February 25, 2020, *https://www.youtube.com/watch?v=wBnd3M7mNsY&t=4s.*

Staff, "Ryan Bundy's cell phone video of moments before and after Finicum shooting released" *KATU*, Portland, Oregon. April 5, 2016. https://katu.com/news/local/ryan-bundys-cell-phone-video-of-moments-before-and-after-finicum-shooting-released.

Staff, "Tension Rises Over Virus Lock Down," *Boise Guardian*, April 22, 2020, https://boiseguardian.com/2020/04/22/tension-rises-over-virus-lock-down/.

Stanfel, Rebecca, "Reclaiming Montana's First Synagogue," *Independent Record*, August 12, 2022, https://helenair.com/opinion/columnists/rebecca-stanfel-reclaiming-montana-s-first-synagogue/article_a1a752de-eda5-59a4-8d69-b386feb05fda.html.

Strong-Leek, Linda. "Bell Hooks, Carter G. Woodson, and African American Education." *Journal of Black Studies*, vol. 38, no. 6, 2008, pp. 850–61. *JSTOR*, http://www.jstor.org/stable/40035027.

Sun Ranch Group, "Montana Rancher's Gift Establishes Conservation Fund: Sun Ranch Owner Donates $3.9 Million to Protect Madison Valley, *CSRwire*, August 12, 2008. https://www.csrwire.com/press_releases/13948-montana-rancher-s-gift-establishes-conservation-fund-sun-ranch-owner-donates-3-9-million-to-protect-madison-valley

Sutton, Michael, Avery. *American Apocalypse: A History of Modern Evangelicalism.* Cambridge, Massachusetts: Belnap Press, 2017.

The Doctors YouTube Channel. "Mariel Hemingway and Bobby Williams on Why 60 Is the New 30," *The Doctors YouTube*, 2021, https://www.youtube.com/watch?v=AsUVv0HhYZg.

Thompson, A.C., Ali Winston and Darwin Bond Graham, "Racist, Violent, Unpunished: A White Hate Group's Campaign of Menace," *ProPublica*, Oct. 19, 2017, https://www.propublica.org/article/white-hate-group-campaign-of-menace-rise-above-movement.

Thompson, Johnathon P. "Data Dump: The Alfalfa Question," *The Land Desk*, February 10, 2021. https://www.landdesk.org/p/data-dump-the-alfalfa-question.

Thornbrugh, Kaye. "'If they want to have a war, let it begin here': New documents Detail Patriot Front's Plan, June 15, 2022, https://www.idahostatesman.com/news/local/community/boise/article262546257.html#storylink=cpy.

———. "Recording Allegedly Reveals Kootenai County GOP Plan to Take Over Kootenai Democratic Party," *Idaho Capital Sun*, March 10th 2022, https://idahocapitalsun.com/2022/03/10/recording-allegedly-reveals-kootenai-county-gop-plan-to-take-over-kootenai-democratic-party/".

Theroux, Louis. Lewis and the Nazis, BBC, 2004.

Tlapoyawa, Kurly. "Juan de Oñate and the Legacy of White Supremacy in New Mexico." *Medium*, June 13, 2020, https://kurlytlapoyawa.medium.com/juan-de-oñate-and-the-legacy-of-white-supremacy-in-new-mexico-da4a526f9037.

Vincentelli, Elizabeth. "Big Sky is Sprawling, Luxurious and Pricey. And Maybe, the Future of Skiing." *New York Times*, March 15th 2022, https://www.nytimes.com/2022/03/15/travel/big-sky-montana-skiing.html.

Turner, Fredrick Jackson, "The Significance of the Frontier in American History," *Annual Report of the American Historical Association, 1893, p. 197-227.*

University of California - Berkeley. "National parks bear the brunt of climate change: Temperatures in national parks are increasing at twice the rate of the US as a whole." ScienceDaily. ScienceDaily, September 24, 2018, www.sciencedaily.com/releases/2018/09/180924091654.htm.

US Department of Agriculture, "USDA NAHMS Report on Cattle and Calves Death Loss in the U.S.," Animal and Plant Health Inspection Services, December 19, 2017, https://content.govdelivery.com/accounts/USDAAPHIS/bulletins/1cd6c28.

Wallace, Amy. "Checkmate at the Yellowstone Club," *New York Times, June 13, 2009,* https://www.nytimes.com/2009/06/14/business/14yellow.html.

Walter, Jess. *The Cold Millions*. New York, New York: Harper Publishing, 2020.

Walters, Daniel. "Antifa is Anonymous, Militant and Ill-defined—But There's Still Little Evidence They're to Blame for Riots in Spokane, *Inlander*, July 9, 2020. https://www.inlander.com/spokane/antifa-is-anonymous-militant-and-ill-defined-but-theres-still-little-evidence-theyre-to-blame-for-riots-in-spokane/Content?oid=19897896.

———. "Idaho Voters Stand Up to McGeachin, Giddings… and a Whole Bunch of Moderates." *Inlander*, May 18, 2022. https://www.inlander.

com/spokane/idaho-voters-stand-up-to-mcgeachin-giddings-and-a-whole-bunch-of-moderates/Content?oid=23843102.

———. "The Man in the Antifa Mask: Who he is and why he regrets showing up at a Coeur d'Alene protest with a crowbar." *Inlander*, July 16, 2020. https://www.inlander.com/spokane/the-man-in-the-antifa-mask-who-he-is-and-why-he-regrets-showing-up-at-a-coeur-dalene-protest-with-a-crowbar/Content?oid=19899065.

———. "Why Coeur d'Alene's 'Pride in the Park' became the target for white supremacist groups like Patriot Front." *Inlander*, June 17, 2022.https://www.inlander.com/spokane/why-coeur-dalenes-pride-in-the-park-be-came-the-target-for-white-supremacist-groups-like-patriot-front/Content?oid=24009613.

Ward, Charlotte and David Voas. "The Emergence of Conspirituality," *Journal of Contemporary Religion*, 2011, vol. 26 no. 1 p.103–121. http://dx.doi.org/10.1080/13537903.2011.539846.

Watson, Jarren, "The Fox," *Origami Journal*, Winter 2013, https://origami-journal.com/jarenwatson/.

Weill, Kelly. *Off the Edge: Flat Earthers, Conspiracy Culture, and Why People Will Believe Anything*. Chapel Hill North Carolina: Algonquin Books of Chapel Hill, 2022.

West, Elliott. "Selling the Myth: Western Images in Advertising," *Montana the Magazine of Western History*, vol. 46, no. 2, Summer 1996, p. 36-49. https://www.jstor.org/stable/i405755.

WildEarth Guardians, "Court refuses to limit Montana's unscientific wolf hunting and trapping season," Press release, November 29, 2022, https://wildearthguardians.org/press-releases/court-refuses-to-limit-mon-tanas-unscientific-wolf-hunting-and-trapping-season/.

Wiles, Tay. "Militia, MAGA Activists and One Border Town's Complicated Resistance," *High Country News*, March 13, 2019. https://www.hcn.org/issues/51.9/us-mexican-border-militias-maga-activists-and-one-bor-der-towns-complicated-resistance.

Wilkinson, Todd, "'Unbroken Wilderness:' Some Call The Porcupine And Buffalo Horn 'Holy Land.'" *Mountain Journal*, May 14, 2020. https://mountainjournal.org/is-yellowstone-wildlife-and-montana-wilder-ness-threatened-by-outdoor-recreation.

———. "Why 'Yellowstone' Rancher John Dutton Says 'Progress' Is Destroy-ing The Wild Rural West." *Mountain Journal*, October 27, 2022. https://

mountainjournal.org/famous-wildlife-migrations-in-yellowstone-region-being-lost-to-private-land-development.

Williams, Paige. "Killing the Wolves to Own the Libs?" *The New Yorker*, April 4, 2022. https://www.newyorker.com/magazine/2022/04/04/killing-wolves-to-own-the-libs-idaho.

Williams, Terry Tempest. *The Hour of the Land: A Personal Topography of America's National Parks*. New York, New York: Farrar, Strauss and Giroux, 2016.

Williams, Walt. "Mystery Monster Returns Home After 121 Years, *Bozeman Daily Chronicle*, November 14, 2007, https://www.bozemandailychronicle.com/news/mystery-monster-returns-home-after-121-years/article_461c6958-ea1e-5f57-bee9-a3c11b0a18a6.html.

Willis, Mikki. "Plandemic: The Hidden Agenda Behind Covid-19," Elevate Films, 2020.

Wilson, Jason. "Idaho Republican Club Host Speech by Antisemite, January 6th Attendee," *Southern Poverty Law Center*, January 17, 2023, https://www.splcenter.org/hatewatch/2023/01/17/idaho-republican-club-hosts-speech-antisemite-jan-6-attendee.

Woodson, C. G. *The Mis-education of the Negro*. Trenton, NJ: Africa World Press, 1933.

Worster, Donald. "Landscape with Hero: John Wesley Powell and the Colorado Plateau," *Southern California Quarterly* April 1, 1997, vol. 79 no. 1, p. 29–46. https://doi.org/10.2307/41171839.

INDEX

D

G

J

K

L

N

Q

R

TORREY HOUSE PRESS

Torrey House Press exists at the intersection of the literary arts and environmental advocacy. THP publishes books that elevate diverse perspectives, explore relationships with place, and deepen our connections to the natural world and to each other. THP inspires ideas, conversation, and action on issues that link the American West to the past, present, and future of the ever-changing Earth.

Visit www.torreyhouse.org for reading group discussion guides, author interviews, and more.

As a 501(c)(3) nonprofit publisher, our work is made possible by generous donations from readers like you.

Join the Torrey House Press family and give today at
www.torreyhouse.org/give.

Torrey House Press is supported by the King's English Bookshop, Maria's Bookshop, the Jeffrey S. & Helen H. Cardon Foundation, the Sam & Diane Stewart Family Foundation, the Barker Foundation, the George S. and Dolores Doré Eccles Foundation, Diana Allison, Klaus Bielefeldt, Joe Breddan, Karen Edgley, Laurie Hilyer, Susan Markley, Marion S. Robinson, Kitty Swenson, Shelby Tisdale, Kirtly Parker Jones, Robert Aagard & Camille Bailey Aagard, Kif Augustine Adams & Stirling Adams, Rose Chilcoat & Mark Franklin, Jerome Cooney & Laura Storjohann, Linc Cornell & Lois Cornell, Susan Cushman & Charlie Quimby, Kathleen Metcalf & Peter Metcalf, Betsy Gaines Quammen & David Quammen, the Utah Division of Arts & Museums, Utah Humanities, the National Endowment for the Humanities, the National Endowment for the Arts, the Salt Lake City Arts Council, the Utah Governor's Office of Economic Development, and Salt Lake County Zoo, Arts & Parks. Our thanks to our readers, donors, members, and the Torrey House Press Board of Directors for their valued support.